How to Select & Care for
Shrubs & Hedges

Created and designed by
the editorial staff of ORTHO BOOKS

Written by
A. Cort Sinnes

Plant Selection Guide written by
Michael McKinley

Art Direction and Design by
Craig Bergquist

Illustrations by
Raul del Rio

Front Cover Photography by
John Neubauer

Photo Coordination by
Laura Ferguson

Special Consultant
Dr. Joseph E. Howland,
Professor of Horticulture,
University of Nevada

Ortho Books

Publisher
Robert L. Iacopi

Editorial Director
Min S. Yee

Managing Editors
Anne Coolman
Michael D. Smith
Sally W. Smith

Production Manager
Ernie S. Tasaki

Editors
Jim Beley
Susan Lammers
Deni Stein

Design Coordinator
Darcie S. Furlan

System Managers
Christopher Banks
Mark Zielinski

Photographic Director
Alan Copeland

Photographers
Laurie A. Black
Richard A. Christman

Production Editors
Linda Bouchard
Alice Mace
Kate O'Keeffe

Asst. System Manager
William F. Yusavage

Chief Copy Editor
Rebecca Pepper

Photo Editors
Anne Dickson-Pederson
Pam Peirce

National Sales Manager
Garry P. Wellman

Sales Associate
Susan B. Boyle

Operations Director
William T. Pletcher

Operations Assistant
Gail L. Davis

Administrative Assistant
Georgiann Wright

Address all inquiries to
Ortho Books
Chevron Chemical Company
Consumer Products Division
575 Market Street
San Francisco, CA 94105

7 8 9
84 85 86 87 88 89

ISBN 0-917102-88-6
Library of Congress Catalog Card
Number 80-66346

Chevron Chemical Company
575 Market Street, San Francisco, CA 94105

Acknowledgements

Horticultural Consultants:
Fred Galle, Curator,
  Callaway Gardens,
  Pine Mountain, GA
Richard Hildreth, Director,
  State Arboretum of Utah,
  Salt Lake City, UT
Paul W. Meyer, Curator,
  Morris Arboretum,
  Chestnut Hill, PA

Typography by:
Terry Robinson & Co.
San Francisco, CA

Color Separations by:
Color Tech Corp.
Redwood City, CA

Burlingame Garden Center,
  Burlingame, CA
Jane Gates, Helen Crocker
  Library, Strybing Arboretum,
  San Francsico, CA
Orchard Nursery, Lafayette, CA
Jane Wilson

Photography by:
(Names of photographers in
alphabetical order are followed
by page numbers on which their
work appears. R = right, C =
center, L = left, T = top, and B =
bottom.)

John Bryan: 7TL; 9CR; 15C;
  41BR; 49; 63CR; 71BR
Josephine Coatsworth: 6TR; 12
David Fischer: 53
Fred Galle: 86TR
Pamela Harper: 7BR; '10B;
  57BL; 59TR; BL; 61BL;
  62(all); 63TR; 64; 65C; 66BL;
  67TL, BC, BR; 68BC; 69BL,
  C; 70R; 71BC, BL; 72TC; 73C,
  BR; 74(all); 75C, TR, BR;
  76(all); 77L; 78TC, BC; 79BL;
  80(all); 81L; 82TC; 84TC, R;
  85R; 86R; 87TL, BL, TC, TR;
  88CL, BL, C; 89TL, CL; BL;
  90L, TC; 91L; 92TL, C; 93C.
Horticultural Photography/
Pictures Library: 9B; 43; 73L;
  75C; 79TR
Elvin McDonald: 6C; 33TR

Michael McKinley: 1; 6TL;
  13BL, BR, TR; 15B; 16B; 18;
  19; 21; 22; 23(all); 25; 32T;
  33L; 38; 41L; 45T; 46; 47; 50L;
  51BR; 53TR; 54; 58BL; 60BL;
  61TR; 65R; 67TC; 69TL, BR;
  62BC, R; 81BC; 82L; 83C,
  BR; 87BR; 89C; 91C; 93R
James McNair: 4; 13BC;
  63B; 90
Paul Meyer: 10T; 92BR
John Neubauer: Cover;
  7TR; 16T
Ray Rogers: 86BC; 88TL
Martin Schweitzer: 26; 34;
  40; 55
Michael D. Smith: 44; 45BR;
  50R; 51L; 52(all); 53L
George Taloumis: 65L; 66TL;
  71TL; 84BC; 90
Ron Taven: 57R; 58R; 62T; 66R;
  67TR; 68T; 69TR; 70L; 71TC;
  78R; 81TC; 82BC; 83TR; 85L;
  87BC; 93L
Tom Tracy: 6B; 9
University of California: 51TC
Wolf Von dem Bussche: 35

How to Select & Care for
Shrubs & Hedges

Designing with Shrubs and Hedges

Shrubs and hedges are the workhorses of garden design. They can provide color and beauty, a quiet backdrop, traffic control and security, private places for quiet contemplation, or protection from the wind and sun.

As a group, shrubs contain some of the most beautiful and dramatic plants available to the gardener. But because shrubs are so familiar, many of their special traits are frequently overlooked.

People tend to think of shrubs as obscure masses of green plants that don't have the flair or distinction of annuals, perennials, or bulbs. But the fact of the matter is, there are thousands of varieties of shrubs, all with their own unique features.

Shrubs come in every form and size imaginable, with an array of leaf shapes and textures that seems almost infinite. Some burst into seasonal bloom with exquisite, colorful flowers, and others remain a steady, stately green all year long.

While shrubs are commonly used as backgrounds for other plants, they often deserve to be featured as garden highlights, with all their elegance on full display.

Shrubs can shape and define spaces, create privacy, accentuate doorways and entrances, and hide unsightly views. They can muffle noise, improve the climate of your yard, and even help to protect against burglary. And they can do all these things with natural grace and beauty and a minimum of maintenance. It is no wonder that landscape architects call shrubs the "workhorses" of the garden.

As for hedges, they have been a part of gardening for as long as there have been gardens. In spite of their upkeep demands, they are not only considered an integral part of the most beautiful gardens, but they also provide many versatile ways to define, limit, or protect areas of your garden.

◀

These azaleas define a strong curve and provide color in this garden.

In this book we try to give you the information you will need for every gardening situation: whether you are landscaping your entire yard from scratch, are looking for a single shrub for a special place, or simply want to know more about caring for the shrubs you already have. How to design with shrubs and hedges, how to buy them, how to plant and transplant them, how to water and fertilize, prune and spray—all these subjects, and more, are covered in the chapters that follow. And the "Plant Selection Guide" will equip you with everything you will need to know about specific shrubs to make the best possible selections for your garden.

The photographs on the next four pages illustrate some of the lovely as well as practical ways in which shrubs can be used, which we hope will suggest some new possibilities for your own garden. Since shrubs represent such a superb value to the gardener on all counts, the time, expense, and effort required to purchase, plant, and maintain them is minimal compared to the returns they so willingly give you. The purpose of this book is to help you maximize those returns.

What Is a Shrub?

While there is no hard and fast definition of what constitutes a shrub, this one is commonly accepted: *a woody plant with multiple stems or trunks that grows less than 15 feet high when mature.*

A *woody* plant has stems and branches that survive from one year to the next, which do not die back to the ground after each growing season. Their woody nature distinguishes shrubs from herbaceous plants, which are subject to winter damage and which die back to the ground each year.

The fact that shrubs have *multiple stems or trunks* sets them apart from trees, which usually have only a single stem or trunk. There are exceptions: Many shrubs can be deliberately trained to have only a single trunk. Shrubs trained in this way are called *standards*; basically, they are miniature trees, often used for a formal effect. Some trees also have multiple trunks, but they usually grow higher than 15 feet.

The loosest part of our definition is that a shrub must be *less than 15 feet tall when mature.* Certainly, a shrub that grows taller than 15 feet isn't automatically thought of as a tree. In fact, in different regions of the country, the same plants reach widely varying mature heights. Common sense is the best guide for distinguishing between shrubs and trees. Most trees are capable of reaching impressive heights, while shrubs remain comparatively small—somewhere in the vicinity of 15 feet.

What Is a Hedge?

Hedges are simply shrubs or other plants that have been put to special use: They have been planted closely together so that they form an unbroken line and in most cases are carefully trimmed. Formal hedges are similar to fences in their solid, even appearance. A hedge is a way of delineating space, forming a garden border, acting as a boundary, or creating a screen for privacy. You can use just about any shrub to make a hedge, but some shrubs, more than others, lend themselves to regular trimming and uniform growth. A list of shrubs that are particularly good for hedges appears on page 63.

Hedge shrubs come in 3 basic heights: *low*—12 inches or less—for bordering flower beds and walks; *medium*—up to 6 feet—for property borders and as backdrops for other plants; *tall*—over 6 feet—for controlling wind and sun and screening out objectionable views.

Establishing and maintaining a good-looking hedge may require some effort, but for many people it is effort well spent. We will give you specific information about planting, trimming, and maintaining hedges in the following chapters. In our general discussions of shrubs, however, we are referring to *all* shrubs, including those that are commonly used for hedge plantings.

Above: Fuchsias in a container grace a patio. Left: The versatility of shrubs is dramatically revealed in topiary.

Below: Juniper and Irish moss mix in this informal ground cover.

Above: The hedges enclosing this garden provide much of its intimate charm.
Left: Shrubs provide privacy for this secret garden corner.

Above: Azaleas are famous for their brilliant spring displays.

Below: Shrubs provide interest and beauty in every season.

Above: Shrubs provide sculptural interest in this colorful garden.
Right: Daphne can fill a garden with its delightful fragrance.

Above: Vines, too, can be used as shrubs! This climbing hydrangea makes a delightful, informal hedge.
Right: A garden path sparkles with the spring bloom of azaleas.

Above: Flowering hedges must be pruned at the appropriate time in order to flower.
Right: Foundation shrubs make a visual link between the house and the pavement.

Location and Form

The form a shrub takes depends on its species and on the way it is pruned, but its form also depends on the location in the garden. If you want a shrub to be dense and full, plant it in full sun. If you wish to have a lacy, open look, plant your shrub in the shade. While this generalization is true, the extent to which the shape of a shrub is changed by the amount of light it receives depends on the shrub. The shapes of some shrubs are almost independent of the light levels they receive. Others will look like two different species if their sun and shade shapes are compared. Japanese maple, for instance, are open, spreading, and graceful when grown in a shady location. The same variety is compact and globular when grown in the sun.

Above: A variety of foliage color emphasizes this formal design.
Left: Autumn leaves, as on this winged euonymous, are often as brilliant as flowers.

In nature, shrubs form much of the *understory* of forests: the plants that grow under the tree canopy. These understory plants spread their branches to better catch the little light that penetrates the trees above. Leaves are arranged in horizontal planes, with no leaf under another. Their habit is open, delicate, and graceful.

On the other hand, shrubs that grow in full sun, in meadows or brushland, grow smaller and are more closely knit. There is no shortage of light here. Rather, their problem is one of exposure: to sun, wind, rain, and snow. A compact form, with smaller leaves that are packed tightly together and stems that are short and thick, gives better protection against the elements.

Deciduous and Evergreen Shrubs

Shrubs may be deciduous or evergreen. Simply put, *deciduous* plants lose their leaves in the fall and grow new leaves in the spring. Deciduous shrubs, that are best known for their spring flowers, such as lilacs, need sufficient winter chilling to put on an optimum spring display. These same plants can be successfully grown in mild winter areas, but their performances may be somewhat diminished.

In comparison, *evergreen* plants are ever green: They keep their leaves the year around. Evergreens break down into two other major categories: broad-leafed evergreens and coniferous (cone-bearing) evergreens.

Generally speaking, the *broad-leafed evergreens* tend to be more tender than deciduous shrubs, and find their widest adaptability in areas with reasonably mild winters. *Coniferous evergreens* grow satisfactorily in most climates—you will see them in almost every part of the United States.

Keep in mind, though, that any of these broad generalizations about growing deciduous and evergreen shrubs can be proven false by determined gardeners. If you want to have certain plants in your garden, even though your winter temperatures say "No," see page 39 for ideas about winter protection and pages 32 and 33 for growing shrubs in containers.

The surest way to grow shrubs successfully is to choose varieties that you know are hardy for your climate—check the "Plant Selection Guide" on page 55.

Basic Forms

To pick the right shrub for each garden area, you should get some idea of what form a shrub will mature into. Often a shrub will look one way in a 5-gallon can and quite another after it has been planted in the garden for a few years. Most shrubs have a naturally occurring form. When you plant new shrubs, you will succeed best by knowing what forms to expect and by letting each plant develop in its own way rather than trying to make it into something it is not.

Deciduous shrubs and trees lose their leaves in the winter. This Japanese maple adds strength and contrast to the winter landscape.

Broad-leafed evergreens retain their leaves all year. The hedge in this photograph is a boxwood. Behind it are pruned Japanese privets.

Coniferous evergreens do not have conspicuous flowers, but come in a wide variety of foliage colors. Many are hardy in the North.

Commercial shrub growers have divided shrubs into eight forms:

- pyramidal
- lowbranching
- roundheaded
- prostrate or spreading
- columnar
- dense or compact
- open
- weeping

These basic forms are indicated in the shrub descriptions in "The Plant Selection Guide." The accompanying drawings will give you an idea of what these categories look like. One plant may combine several of these characteristics, but most often, one form dominates.

Any plant can be pruned and trained into almost any shape the owner desires. But remember, when you direct a plant's growth into a shape or form that is different from its natural inclination, you create more work for yourself. So, the best advice is to select shrubs that naturally grow into forms that please you.

Choose Shrub Height To Match Situation.

1 foot

Use for low ground cover or as an edging for planting bed or path.

1½ feet

A hedge this height is difficult to step across. Use to direct traffic.

3 feet

Use as a barrier, as a hedge, or as a deep ground cover.

6 feet

A hedge this height gives privacy without a sense of being walled in.

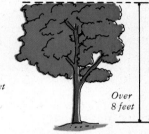

8 feet

Use as a background planting, a windbreak, or as a screen for privacy and security.

Over 8 feet

Use as a background for a large garden, a wind or sound screen, or as a small tree.

Forms of Shrubs

Pyramidal—*a neat shape, common to many conifers. Use it in the formal garden without frequent pruning.*

Lowbranching—*the lowest branches reach, or nearly reach, the ground. Use as a filler for low maintenance areas.*

Roundheaded—*gives a casual, natural look in the landscape. Use as a specimen.*

Prostrate—*the branches either grow horizontally, or are weak and lie on the ground. Use as a ground cover.*

Columnar—*the branches angle upward sharply, keeping the outline narrow. Use for dramatic emphasis in the landscape.*

Compact—*the leaves grow close together, making it dense and opaque. Typical of shrubs grown in full sun. Use as a screen.*

Open—*the shrub can be seen through, making its framework visible. Typical of shrubs grown in the shade. Use as a specimen.*

Weeping—*the stems and branches are strong, but new twigs are weak and bend toward the ground. Use for a solemn, graceful touch.*

Designing with Shrubs

The design basics discussed here will help you to make most general design decisions. If you are creating an entirely new landscape or are considering making a major change in your existing garden, you may also want to refer to Ortho's book, *All About Landscaping*, which details processes of design and construction from beginning to end.

There are two extremes in landscape style—formal and informal—and there's a tendency to think that the choice of plants is largely responsible for creating those styles. But that's not so: The same plants can appear in either setting and the formal or informal feeling will remain intact. It is *how* plants are used that makes the difference. A garden's overall style is established by lines, shapes, spaces, and enclosures. Plants, materials, and structures are chosen to complement and enhance the desired effect.

Formal Design

The earliest recorded garden designs —in Egypt in 2200 BC—were laid out along formal lines. The ancient Greeks, and the Romans after them, also fashioned gardens in the formal style. Much later, during the Renaissance, the classical formal garden was revived in Europe, and as a type of garden design the formal garden has been with us ever since.

Formal designs have survived for thousands of years because they are basically simple and pleasing to the eye. With such a venerable history, the guidelines for establishing a formal garden have become highly refined, although not necessarily complex. In many ways, a formal garden is the easiest kind of garden to lay out.

The key to a formal garden is symmetry. Take a look at the photograph below. A symmetrical garden is usually laid out on straight lines, and what appears on the left side of the garden is repeated on the right. The outermost dimension of the garden is frequently rectangular, and this shape is repeated in other parts of the plan—pools, patios, flower beds. Often a single object—a statue, pool, sundial, or outstanding specimen plant—is chosen as the center of interest; for optimum effect, it is usually placed to the rear of the garden.

Traditionally, a formal garden relies on compact evergreen plants, but other kinds of plants are possible. Evergreens are often pruned and kept trimmed to various well-defined shapes. This method of pruning, in its extreme form, is called topiary and is covered on page 43. And the neatly trimmed rows of privet or coniferous evergreen plants, the most common type of formal hedge planting, is a descendent of time-honored design concepts.

While a formal garden may be easy to design, it's not always so easy to maintain. The precise, tailored look favored in most formal gardens requires frequent visits with the pruning shears. Because order reigns supreme in the formal garden, any clutter will stand out in sharp contrast.

Informal Design

The straight lines and symmetry that represent the formal garden are replaced by curved lines and a disregard for symmetry in the informal garden. Informal gardens are frequently considered more "natural" than formal gardens, and in a sense they are. The curved lines give a relaxed feeling, and plants are allowed to develop their shapes along their own natural lines.

Most of the common flowering shrubs, such as lilac, viburnum, abelia, or hibiscus, make very attractive hedges for informal gardens. They produce the most flowers and require less frequent and less drastic pruning than is required by the privet, for example. The result is that most flowering hedges have a less even appearance, but serve as hedges nonetheless.

There are also broad-leafed plants— both evergreen and deciduous—that are not as compact or finely textured as the traditional hedge plants, but that still make good hedges. These less uniform, more sprawling hedges are often referred to as "informal" hedges. It is debatable, though, whether any hedge can be considered strictly an informal planting: Plants of a single variety in a straight line will give a structured, formalized feeling to the garden, no matter how they are pruned. If a truly informal effect is what you desire, you are better off planting a variety of plants in a curved line, similar to what might occur in nature. The result will be more like a barrier than a traditional hedge, but it will be more in keeping with an informal, naturalistic garden.

If you prefer the informal look, don't make the mistake of skipping the design step: You will still need clear ideas about planting patterns and the particular ambience you want to convey. The best informal gardens are laid out every bit as carefully as their formal counterparts.

Both deciduous and evergreen plants live together well in informal settings, with as many different combinations as there are gardens. Because no precise rules govern the informal garden, more design freedom, and hence, more choices, are possible at every step of the way.

With less emphasis on order, maintenance chores are somewhat reduced. Plants will need less pruning, leaves can be left where they fall, and a tricycle or hammock will be viewed as part of the whole.

Balanced Plantings

Good design in either a formal or informal garden requires *balance*. In a formal garden the balance seems obvious, although there may be more to it than immediately meets the eye. The balance in an informal garden is not as obvious, but is every bit as important. Balance leads to a sense of continuity between different kinds of plants. No matter what the garden style, balance can be achieved in these time-honored ways:

■ First, *plant taller-growing varieties behind shorter-growing ones.* While rules were made to be broken, they should not be broken carelessly. There's no sense in planting short plants behind tall ones unless you intend to keep the tall ones severely pruned.

■ Second, *place plants with lighter-colored foliage in front of those with darker foliage.* Dark-foliaged plants can certainly be placed in front of light ones, but the effect is not always as dramatic. Gardeners

Formal gardens delight us with their balance and order, but require constant care and attention to detail.

usually find the arrangement of light leaves in front of dark leaves more pleasing. When the sun shines down on lighter green leaves against a dark backdrop, the color is particularly intense and striking.

■ Third, *select background plants for their dark foliage, their base-branching form, and their leaf texture.* Background plants are just that—backgrounds for more showy plants in front. They often perform the same function as hedges, but are not pruned as regularly and are allowed to reach greater heights. To minimize confusion, it is usually wise to make a background out of the same variety or two similar varieties in an alternating pattern.

■ Four, *limit the number of plant varieties,* not just in the background, but everywhere in the garden, as well. There are sound reasons for this contemporary trend. Grouping one plant variety makes a stronger design statement than planting individual specimens of assorted, unrelated varieties. Spindly plants with an "open" growing habit will look more substantial when several of them are planted in a group. Also, gardens composed of a few select varieties have an organized, purposeful look and tend to be easier to take care of than gardens that are a potpourri of plants.

Granted, a landscape with only a few kinds of plants may not be your idea of what a garden should look like at all. If you like a lot of variety, as in the deliberate and charming confusion of an English cottage garden, don't feel constrained to follow present trends. The question of style is, after all, a personal one; your garden should reflect your taste, and no one else's.

The casual elegance of this informal garden masks a sophisticated design that integrates many different plants into a unified landscape.

Shrub masses provide structure and visual containment to the garden.

Light, splashy azaleas provide a spectacular show against a background of dark foliage.

A tall, finely textured hedge serves as a backdrop for the drama of roses about to bloom.

Color

Most people only think of flowers when they think of color in the garden. But while flowers, including flowering shrubs, may present the most obvious color, don't overlook the truly amazing variations of leaf color. For example, green has many modifiers: grey-green, blue-green, yellow-green, brownish-green, bright green, dull green. There are so many different shades of green that it would be difficult to go to a nursery and pick out five different shrubs of an identical color.

Besides the many hues of green, shrubs have grey, red, purple, yellow, and variegated foliage. Put any of these beside a green shrub and judge the effect for yourself. And don't overlook the colors the seasons bring—the bare bark and branches of winter, the bright new growth and flowering of spring, the more muted tones of summer, and the fruits and changing foliage of fall.

Some gardeners like the understatement of an all-green garden, while others want more variety. Before you select a shrub, consider your preferences for a seasonal show—do you want a display of green, or other colors, as well? Consider that in those parts of the country that have extended winters, shrubs with colorful bark and twigs, persistent fruit, and interesting leaf texture may actually be present in the garden as long as those with flowers and green leaves. When choosing flowering shrubs, find out what colors the flowers are and when they bloom. Then plot their locations so that the colors will complement each other rather than clash. This formula applies to foliage, too. Try to imagine—in advance—whether a new shrub with grey-green leaves will look attractive with an existing shrub with yellow leaves, and so forth.

Texture

In the process of selecting shrubs, notice the different kinds of texture produced by a shrub's leaf size and pattern. And don't forget the texture produced by the pattern of the bare branches, twigs, and bark during the dormant season. Are the leaves small and compact, giving a neat, clipped appearance? Or are the leaves large and uneven, creating a bold, informal feeling? Do the leaves have a coarse or fine pattern to them? What does the shrub look like in winter?

Judge the texture of a plant close up, then look at it again from 40 feet away. Does the texture still look the same? Some shrubs lose their pleasing effect when they are planted too far away. Similarly, the texture of a large-leafed shrub may be out of scale when it is planted in a confined space or where viewing it up close is the only option.

The general rule is to plant more finely textured plants in front of more coarsely textured varieties. The combined pattern of graduated textures is a pleasing one that follows tried-and-true theories of

The brilliant display of this specimen azalea is framed by the border of dark green foliage.

The purple of Japanese barberry 'Atropurpurea', the dark green of bird's nest spruce, the silver touch of Japanese pieris 'Variegata', and the yellow of fullmoon Maple produce a symphony of color.

The fine texture of juniper foliage contrasts with evergreen euonymus.

Camellias can grace any mild-winter garden from fall to spring. See page 67.

proportion and scale. If a dramatic effect is what you are after, favor coarsely textured, large-leafed shrubs. If you like a more tailored, formal landscape, look for compact shrubs with comparatively small leaves. Many of the conifers can also contribute to the formal effect, depending on how they are used.

Special Effects

Special effects can easily be achieved using unique shrubs known as *specimen plants* or just *specimens*. Specimen plants draw attention to themselves. They usually have some feature or combination of features that sets them apart from other shrubs.

The uniqueness of a specimen shrub may be its form, flowers, berries, shape, color, texture, or rarity, as well as its personal significance. The number of specimens used in a single landscape is usually limited to one or two—any more than that and the special quality would be diminished.

Specimen plants depend a great deal for their specialness on the locations they are given in the garden. They should be carefully placed in spots where they can command center stage. For example, if a specimen's unique features need close viewing, place the plant by the front door or walkway so that it receives the attention it deserves.

Plan As You Buy

It requires care to achieve a pleasing, balanced planting of shrubs. When you are at the nursery or garden center, take your time. Remember that once you get the shrubs in the ground they are going to be there a long time (although they can be moved with relative ease the first year or two, if necessary).

If you plan to buy more than one shrub, arrange your candidates together in one place at the nursery in much the same way as you want them to appear in your garden. How do they look together? Do their textures, forms, and colors complement each other? A certain amount of diversity is necessary to create interest. For example, a dark green, needled evergreen shrub may look attractive with a finely textured, light green, broad-leafed shrub. Or a plant with spiky, swordlike foliage may combine well with a compact, leafy shrub.

If you are adding new shrubs to established plantings, take samples of the existing plants with you to the nursery. As you pick out new plants, mentally reconstruct your garden as it is now. Will the additions fit into the picture, creating an interesting, balanced scene?

Taking the time to consider these elements of design will not only increase your appreciation of the unique qualities of shrubs, but also will ultimately result in a landscape filled with the natural beauty most pleasing to you.

Differences in leaf texture (the sizes and shapes of foliage) enhance the differences in color between this Japanese barberry 'Atropurpurea' and Japanese pieris 'Variegata'.

Spring-blooming shrubs like this forsythia complement bulbs and perennials.

The stems of red-osier dogwood provide interesting winter color.

Practical Considerations

As you design your ideal garden, keep in mind that shrubs can be practical as well as attractive. By shielding your yard from the wind, cutting down on noise, hiding an ugly ground area, or camouflaging part of an oddly shaped building, you can vastly improve the environment in your garden in general. Here are some of the ways in which shrubs and hedges can do double duty.

Wind Protection

A windbreak should be placed on the side of the yard from which the wind usually blows. Sometimes you will need to plant windbreaks on more than one side. A single hedgerow of shrubs is effective, but a double row, planted on staggered centers, is even better at stopping the wind.

Experiments using anemometers have shown that maximum wind reduction occurs within a space of from four to seven times the height of the windbreak. Using this calculation, a hedge that will eventually grow 6 feet high should be planted, at the most, 24 to 42 feet away from the area you want to protect from the wind.

Dust Reduction

A solid row of shrubs can reduce the amount of dust considerably. A test in one large city revealed that the dust count on the leeward side of a planted area was reduced by 75 percent. Larger pieces of debris are also trapped by shrubs, keeping them from spoiling your yard. If you live in a dusty, sooty area, select pollution-resistant species and give the leaves of barrier plantings a good shower now and then to keep them healthy. A list of pollution-tolerant shrubs is included in the "Plant Selection Guide" on page 59.

The thorny twigs of a flowering quince espalier will stop even the most determined burglar— or at least make his job most painful!

Noise Reduction

In addition to absorbing dust and debris, shrubs also absorb noise. For the best noise reduction, shrubs should be planted as densely and as tall as possible. Plants with compact, leafy foliage act more as noise deterrents than more open varieties. University tests have shown that thick shrub plantings can reduce noise up to 20 percent, compared with unplanted areas. If noise is a year-round problem, choose an evergreen variety.

Barriers

Landscape designers are well aware of another practical property of shrubs, namely, their ability to act as barriers.

Homeowners often overlook this important attribute of shrubs. Barrier plantings can keep people out of areas where you don't want them and guide them to areas where you do.

When you want to use shrubs as guides or barriers, it is helpful to think of them as architectural forms rather than as plants. When you select barrier plants, do so with an eye for their density and sturdiness. If you are serious about keeping people out of certain areas, look for thorny or prickly plants. See the list of thorny barrier plants on page 61.

These types of shrubs also work well under windows to deter prowlers; there isn't much defense against a thorny shrub that blocks the entrance to a window. Make sure, though, that the shrub grows tightly against the house. If there is access space between the house and the shrub, the shrub will actually aid the prowler by acting as a screen while he jimmies the window open.

Structural Aids

If your house has some architectural features that you wish it hadn't, sensitively placed shrubs can help to disguise the problem. Houses with uneven proportions, oddly shaped windows, or tall foundation walls are all candidates for shrub rehabilitation. These kinds of custom corrections can make a big difference for a relatively small investment of time and money.

Once again, when selecting shrubs for this purpose, it's best to view them as architectural forms. What form is needed to correct a proportion problem or to balance out a poorly placed window? You can even go so far as to take a picture of your house, then use a pen to draw in the shape that is needed. Take the picture to your local garden center and see what suggestions the staff there has to offer.

These two boxwood globes break the monotony of a long flight of stairs, bringing the stairs into balance with the house.

Noise Control

An unbroken, dense row of shrubs can significantly reduce noise levels from traffic, a playground, or a neighboring commercial district. Not only does the hedge help to cut down on the noise, but it also acts as a baffle for dirt and debris, keeping your yard cleaner and more pleasant.

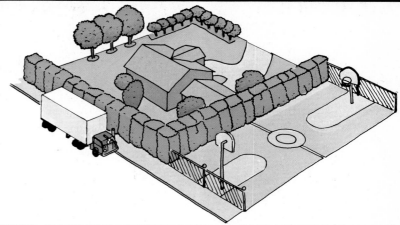

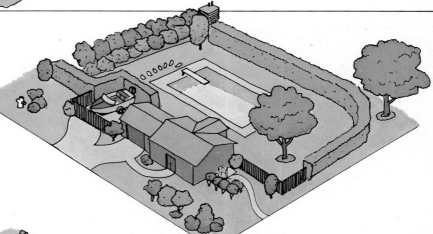

Wind Control

The wind control properties of hedges and rows of trees have been known by gardeners and farmers for centuries. When the force of the wind is broken and diffused, the microclimate of your yard is improved. If you live in an area where afternoon winds are a common occurrence, a hedge can do a great deal to increase the enjoyment of your garden.

Privacy

There are many ways to achieve privacy in a garden, but none is as attractive as a wall of leafy green, with occasional splashes of color, if desired. Besides formal, trimmed hedges, you can have less formal plantings of shrubs, left to grow in their own way. In localities where there are height limitations on fences between neighboring yards, a hedge is a good way to achieve the maximum in privacy.

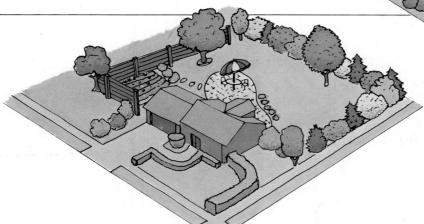

Traffic Control

Shrubs can do a great deal to direct pedestrian traffic. Shrubs can also act as barriers, keeping people, bicycles, and cars from entering areas where they are not intended. Delicate plants should not be used; for maximum results, favor plants with thorns or prickly foliage. If you live on a street with heavy automobile traffic, you will probably want to choose dense shrubs to help deflect light from streetlights and headlights.

Before You Buy...

Careful planning before you buy a shrub helps avoid mistakes. Assess your soil and the microclimate where the shrub will be planted. Choose a nursery that will give you the best value, then select a healthy plant with a strong root system.

No matter what style you choose for your garden, the most attractive landscape is one filled with plants that are vigorous and healthy. Vigorous, healthy plants get that way by receiving proper care and by being planted in an environment they find suitable. The importance of matching a plant's needs with the conditions of a particular spot in your yard cannot be overemphasized.

Admiring a shrub in a catalog, nursery, or friend's garden is not sufficient reason to plant it in your own garden, unless you have a particularly strong desire or conviction about one you would like to try. Before you plant anything, you should know what its requirements are: Does it need full sun, filtered shade, or morning sun only until 11 o'clock? In what kind of soil does it grow best—an acid peat soil, deep garden loam, or quick-draining, sandy soil? Will this shrub tolerate "wet feet," being content to grow next to a leaking hose bib, or will regular applications of water from a nearby sprinkler system cause it to curl up and die?

It's easy to get carried away at the nursery or garden center and make purchases on the basis of looks alone; but don't cause yourself needless aggravation by purchasing plants that won't grow in the locations you have in mind. Talk to the clerks about plant requirements, or take helpful descriptions along, such as the ones found in the "Plant Selection Guide." Then match those requirements to the sites you have available in your own yard. Don't think, though, that all shrubs

have strict cultural and climatic requirements. Except for the fussiest varieties, shrubs will tolerate a considerable range of environments and conditions. Just make sure that your yard is in the proper climate zone for the particular shrub, and don't ask it to grow in conditions that are alien to its needs.

Even if just the right spot doesn't naturally occur in your garden, you can make

many modifications that will change the site. The information on the following pages will give you the specifics on how to change the growing conditions, including the climate, to suit your particular plants' needs. This chapter also contains information on the various ways plants can be purchased, advice on mail-order firms, and how to find the best plants at nurseries and garden centers.

Seeing a plant before you buy it is one advantage of buying from your local nursery.

Carefully selecting the healthiest shrubs will give your garden its best possible start, paying big dividends later.

Assessing Your Soil

In general, shrubs are very adaptable plants. They will grow well in most soils, given the proper care. However, you will be far ahead of the game if you know what type of soil you have. In most cases, you will simply be reassured that your soil falls into a large middle range that provides a healthy environment for your plants. But if your soil happens to fall into an extreme at either end of that range, you will be able to select plants that are particularly adaptable to that type of soil or determine what can be done to improve the soil. Be aware that there are many exceptions to every statement about soils, but some general comments will help you to organize the vast amount of information available on this important gardening subject.

Every soil has these elements: depth, fertility, texture, and structure. An ideal garden soil has a topsoil that is several feet deep, is reasonably fertile, has a good balance of sand, silt, and clay particles (texture), and has just the right amount of air space between those particles to promote both good drainage and water retention (structure). In addition, it has an acceptable acid/alkaline balance conducive to the healthy growth of most plants.

Very few soils are absolutely ideal. In most cases, however, there are relatively simple solutions to problems. And because of the complex nature of soil, when you do something to improve one aspect of it, you usually eliminate several other problems, as well.

Finding Soil Texture

Shake a sample of your soil in water with a little Calgon. The larger particles (sand) will settle out in the first minute, the silt will settle out in the next 2 hours, and the clay over the next several weeks.

Soil Testing

The most accurate way to find out what kind of soil you have is to take samples from the areas in which you intend to plant and have them tested in a soil laboratory. Instructions for doing this are detailed in Ortho's book *Fertilizers, Soils & Water*, which also shows you how to interpret the test results. For more information on soil testing, call your local county extension agent and find out whether or not your state offers a soil testing program.

While we recommend that you have your soil professionally tested, you can do some relatively simple tests yourself that will provide you with rudimentary but helpful information.

First, you can ask your neighbors, local nursery, garden center, or county extension agent what the general soil type is in your area. Then you can test your own soil in this way:

To test for texture (the relative proportions of sand, silt, and clay particles): In the general area where you expect to plant new shrubs or hedges, dig several holes 6 to 8 inches deep. If you are planning to plant many shrubs in different parts of the yard, conduct the same experiment for each area.

Fill a quart jar about ⅔ full of water. Add soil until the jar is almost full. To achieve the clearest stratification, also add about 1 tablespoon of Calgon per quart of water. Screw on the jar lid and shake vigorously. Then let the soil settle. In a short time the heaviest sand particles will sink to the bottom, making the sand layer visible. The next layer to form will be the silt layer, and finally the extremely small clay particles will settle on the top. The clay particles are so small that the molecular action of the water alone may keep the particles in suspension indefinitely. The experiment should be ready to read in two to three hours.

Carry out this same test using soil from different places in your garden. Then chart each of them by marking off the layers on a piece of paper held up to the jar. Compare the proportions of the elements with the information in the charts below.

✓ Your soil is sandy if there is less than 5 percent clay.
✓ Your soil is sandy loam if there is 5 to 10 percent clay.
✓ You have a medium loam if there is 10 to 20 percent clay.
✓ Your soil is clay if there is 25 to 30 percent clay.
✓ You have a heavy clay soil if there is 35 to 50 percent clay.

The loam soils are the best garden soils, but both sandy and clay soils can be dramatically improved with the addition of organic matter. The organic matter may be compost, rotted manure, nitrogen-stabilized bark or sawdust, ground corn cobs, or other locally available material. You can add the organic matter to the entire yard or concentrate its addition to the areas about to receive new shrubs. The one rule to follow with organic matter is to be sure to add enough. From ⅓ to ½ of the final mixed soil should be organic matter. This means that if you cultivate to a depth of 8 inches, add 3 to 4 inches of organic matter over the top of the soil before you mix it in.

To test for drainage (how fast or slow water moves through the soil): Remove both ends from a coffee can. In the area you want to test, push the can into the soil to a depth of 4 inches. Fill the can with water and allow it to drain through. Fill the can again, and time how long it takes for the water level to drop 1 inch. If it takes longer than two hours, you can probably expect to have problems with plants "drowning," especially those plants intolerant of "wet feet."

The way in which a soil drains relates to its structure, which is the way the various soil particles are held together. The same methods for improving the texture of the soil also work to improve the structure, which in turn helps drainage. Whether there is too much air space, as in sandy soils, or too little, as in clay soils, the addition of organic matter will help to correct the problem.

If areas of your property have standing water, the problem is more serious, and you may want to install drainage tiles. The process for doing this is outlined in

Clay
40-100% clay
0-40% silt
0-45% sand

Sandy Clay
35-55% clay
0-20% silt
45-65% sand

Sandy Clay Loam
20-35% clay
0-28% silt
45-80% sand

Clay Loam
27-40% clay
15-43% silt
20-45% sand

Silty Clay Loam
27-40% clay
40-73% silt
0-20% sand

Silty Clay
40-60% clay
40-60% silt
0-20% sand

Sand
0-10% clay
0-15% silt
85-100% sand

Loamy Sand
0-15% clay
15-30% silt
70-90% sand

Sandy Loam
0-20% clay
15-50% silt
45-80% sand

Loam
7-27% clay
28-50% silt
23-52% sand

Silty Loam
0-27% clay
50-80% silt
0-28% sand

Silt
0-12% clay
80-100% silt
0-15% sand

Ortho's book *All About Landscaping.*

To test for fertility: Even professional soil laboratories have difficulties testing soil fertility accurately. Because levels of specific nutrients are so difficult to determine, most gardeners simply add a complete fertilizer to the soil, at prescribed intervals during the growing season, to make up for any deficiencies. Whatever product you use, be sure to read and follow all label instructions.

To test for hardpan: Hardpan is a cementlike layer of soil, a few inches thick, that is sometimes found a foot or two under the surface of porous soil. Hardpan stops the downward movement of water. To find out if you are going to have drainage problems because of hardpan, dig a test hole about 2 feet deep. You may use a post hole digger. If you hit hardpan, the simplest way to provide drainage is to break up the hardpan with a pick or crowbar under each plant. You do not have to remove or replace hardpan—just provide a way for the water to pass through it.

To test for pH: Testing the pH of a soil is easy when you use an inexpensive kit, available at most nurseries and scientific supply houses. If you have a soil test made, the pH reading will automatically be included in your report. See the other information about pH on this page. There's also a meter that will check the pH of your soil. When you insert the electronic probe into the soil, the meter reports the level of acidity or alkalinity.

The pH Scale

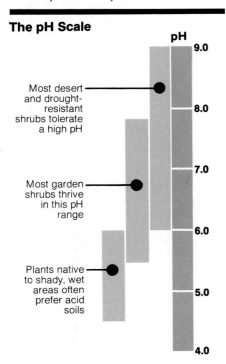

Most desert and drought-resistant shrubs tolerate a high pH

Most garden shrubs thrive in this pH range

Plants native to shady, wet areas often prefer acid soils

pH
9.0
8.0
7.0
6.0
5.0
4.0

Soil pH—How Important Is It?

You may have heard about soil pH and wondered whether it is really important.

The canopy of an evergreen oak shelters these azaleas from sun and wind, providing a microclimate in which they thrive.

Assessing Your Microclimates

The positions of your house, fences, and slopes all contribute to modifying the climate in your yard. The most successful gardeners are those who know all the different climates available in their yards. Ideally, when you see a plant that you admire and find that it likes cool soil and diffused sunlight, and will tolerate excessive moisture, you will know your garden so well that you can say, "I've got just the spot for that."

So, before you buy any new shrubs, take an inventory of the microclimates in various parts of your yard. Each plant has its optimum climatic requirement; those shrubs able to grow on the north side of the house will probably find conditions on the south side intolerable.

Your house is a constant climate regulator, with almost perpetual shade on the north side, full sun and the most radiation to the south, half shade and hot sun to the west, and half shade and milder sun on the east side. The walls themselves radiate heat to varying degrees, and roof overhangs conserve outgoing radiation, making

The pH of soil *is* important, but if a problem does exist, it is easily correctable.

The pH (potential Hydrogen) is a chemical term that is a measure of acidity or alkalinity. The pH scale indicates relative acidity or alkalinity. The scale runs from 0—extremely acid—to 14—extremely alkaline. The middle of the scale—7—is the neutral point. Most shrubs do best in a slightly to very slightly acid soil, down to a pH of about 6.

Among the popular plants that thrive in acid soil are rhododendrons, azaleas, daphne, pieris, blueberries, gardenias, camellias, and nandina. To make the soil more acidic, most gardeners simply add considerable quantities of sphagnum peat moss to the soil. However, if your

it warmer under the eaves on frosty nights. With those basics alone, you can assess areas in your yard and match them with plant requirements.

Tips for Climate Modification

Once you know what microclimates exist in your garden, you may find a need to change them. Here are some pointers for increasing or decreasing certain climate characteristics:

To Make It Warmer:

■ Plan for maximum flat surfaces—paved areas, patios, untilled ground, rock or masonry areas. These surfaces absorb large amounts of the sun's radiation and, in turn, give off heat to surrounding areas.

■ Plan for a "ceiling" in your yard, such as a patio cover or an overhead lath, which traps the warm air that reradiates from other surfaces at night.

■ Plant or build windbreaks and cold-air diverters. Cold air sinks to the lowest part of the yard. If you can divert its path with a hedge or fence, you can keep the shielded area warmer.

soil is overly acidic for the shrubs you want to plant, a condition common in areas of the country where there is heavy rainfall, the most reliable cure is to add ground limestone to the soil. Check with your nursery or county agent for application rates and times.

If alkalinity is the problem, common in some of the arid soils of the West and in the limestone soils of the East and Midwest, garden sulfur or ferrous sulphate (both available at your nursery) will help to correct the condition. For specific rates of sulfur to add, ask your nursery or county agent. Tell your informant the present pH of your soil, the type of soil you have, and what pH level you are trying to achieve.

- Plan sun pockets that trap the sun on cool spring mornings. A two-sided fence or screen can create a warm climate that is radically different from the rest of your yard.

To Make It Cooler:
- Grow vines on overhead structures and plant shade trees.
- Plant bare soil with ground covers, lawns, or other plant material. This deflects summer heat, which can affect the temperature of adjoining areas.
- Prune the lower growth of trees and large shrubs for increased air circulation.

To Make It Less Windy:
- Plant or build windbreaks, baffles, or diverters. For the best placement of hedges and fences, see the information on pages 16 and 17.
- Make semienclosed outdoor living areas with fences and solid overhead coverings.

To Make It Less Humid:
- Provide maximum ventilation by pruning trees and shrubs in an open manner.
- Make sure the drainage of the entire yard is good, so that there is no standing water in any spot.
- Make maximum use of paved or decked areas, since flat areas encourage drying winds.

To Make It More Humid:
- Plan for thick overhead vegetation, which slows evaporation and adds water through transpiration.
- Use plenty of ground covers.
- The addition of a pool or fountain can have both a real and an imagined effect in making a yard seem less arid.

Nurseries and Garden Centers

Nurseries and garden centers are usually delightful places to shop. There's something about being surrounded by living, growing plants that makes a trip to the nursery different than a trip to the grocery store or furniture store. Most people who go to a nursery have a little extra time to spend "just looking around."

While you're strolling, keep your eyes open for clues that will tell you something about the nursery and the plants that are growing there. Are the growing beds well ordered and easy to walk through? Do the plants look as if they have been well watered? How about the signs and plant labels? Are they informative and legible, giving both common and botanical names? Most importantly, how about the sales staff? Are they helpful and knowledgeable? A short talk with a good nursery professional can result in your finding out a considerable amount of information that would be difficult to get otherwise. If a clerk doesn't know the answer to a specific question, he or she should be able to find someone who does, or find the information in a reference book. Aside from

Attractive displays and informative signs are indications that a nursery has dependable merchandise.

carrying good-quality plants, a highly trained staff is what makes one nursery or garden center better than another. The information that you receive from your nursery is localized and the result of many years of individual experiences. The staff of your local garden center can be a continuing source of trustworthy information.

It's enjoyable to stroll through the nursery to see what's new, but if you're an impulsive shopper, perhaps you should forego the temptation. It's a good idea to stick to the list you made out at home—the list of plants you have room for and are ready to plant *now*. If you follow the design considerations on pages 12 to 17, you'll know what sizes, shapes, colors, and textures you're interested in, so spend your time picking out the best plants, variety by variety, that you've decided on before arriving at the shop.

Mail-order Nurseries

For those who don't have the convenience of a local nursery or garden center, mail-order nurseries offer a good alternative. Their colorful catalogs, sent during the cold days of winter, offer an enticement to garden-hungry readers. Mail-order nurseries often have a limited shipping season and limited supplies of certain plants. On the other hand, mail-order houses are often good sources for rare or unusual plants that are unavailable at your local nursery.

Many of these mail-order nurseries have been in business for generations, and

offer the highest quality of plant material. The fact that it may be sent from some distance away should not be considered a detriment; most local nurseries receive their plants from outside the area, also. Nonetheless, plants that have been shipped through the mails will have undergone a degree of stress, and should be "babied" as soon as you receive them. Take them out of the shipping containers and get them planted as soon as you can. Follow the planting instructions on pages 28 to 30 carefully.

If you're ordering plants from a particular mail-order firm for the first time, it's a good idea to limit your order to a reasonable size. Find out how you like their plants, whether they arrive in good condition, and whether they perform well in your yard before ordering more. Most reputable mail-order nurseries will stand behind their stock with a reasonable guarantee.

How Shrubs Are Sold

Containers
Shrubs are most commonly sold in containers. The containers may be metal, plastic, fiber, or wood, and are available in many sizes. Most shrubs are planted in 1- or 5-gallon containers. Specimen shrubs are sometimes sold in 15-gallon containers. The decision of whether to buy the same variety of shrub in these different gallon sizes can be a difficult one. The key here is patience: It may be hard to buy a smaller size, knowing you will have to wait longer for the shrub to grow

to ideal proportions. For that reason alone, many people will choose the 5-gallon-sized shrub, even though the cost is considerably higher.

Keep this formula in mind when it comes time to make your choices: It takes approximately 1½ to 2 years for a 1-gallon-sized shrub to reach 5-gallon size. But in 2½ to 3 years, shrubs starting out in both 1-gallon and 5-gallon containers will have reached about the same size.

Shrubs in plastic cans can be slipped out easily, without doing any damage to the root system, with the added bonus that the plastic container can be reused. Metal cans, except for those with sloping, crimped sides, will have to be cut in order to get the plant out. You can cut it yourself or have it done when you're at the nursery. Large specimen shrubs in wooden containers will require the container to be dismantled before planting.

Make sure the container, no matter what it is made from, is in good shape when you purchase the shrub. Rusted metal cans, split plastic, or disintegrated wood usually means that the roots of the plant have grown into the ground soil at the nursery. By taking the plant away from its accustomed site, it's likely that it will suffer severe shock.

Checking the root system: The shrub should be well anchored in the container, but not to the point of being rootbound. Try gently lifting the plant by the trunk: If the soil moves at all, the plant has not had time to develop roots throughout the rootball.

But if the plant has been in the container too long, growth will have stopped and will be difficult to start again. Check for thick masses of roots on the soil surface or around the sides of the soil ball. Without pruning and straightening, the roots will go on growing in the same circle and never expand into the garden soil. In the event of heavy winds, the plant may topple over because it is so poorly

anchored in the soil. Even if it remains upright, the plant will just struggle along with a small ball of soil the size of the original container, despite the good garden soil surrounding it.

Roots that are tightly wrapped around the stem are called *girdling* roots, and will restrict growth as they slowly choke the shrub. Avoid this shrub or cut the girdling root when you plant.

Wrong-sized Container: A small plant in a 5-gallon can is as poor a buy as a large plant in a 1-gallon can, but for different reasons. More than likely, the small plant in the 5-gallon container was recently moved from a 1-gallon can. In effect, you are paying a 5-gallon price for a 1-gallon plant. There's nothing wrong with nurseries transplanting 1-gallon stock into 5-gallon containers, but the plants should be held in a growing area until the plant reaches 5-gallon size before they are offered for sale. Tell-tale signs that plants have recently been potted into larger-sized containers include: the relatively small size of the plant; a small rootball, disclosed by probing a little; and the soil in the container being unusually soft and loose, because it has not yet been packed down by repeated waterings.

An over-sized plant in a small can is sure to be rootbound, or has possibly sent its roots past the can, down into the soil below. In either case, the plant should be avoided.

Balled and Burlapped Shrubs
Balled and burlapped (B&B) shrubs can be bought and planted any time, but spring is the preferred season. To pick a balled and burlapped plant, untie the tip of the burlap and look carefully at the rootball. It should have a well-developed network of small, fibrous roots. Don't choose a shrub with a ball of soil that is loose, cracked, broken, or bone dry.

In addition, check for roots circling back around the trunk—they can girdle the trunk

These 1- and 5-gallon India hawthorns are in good proportion to their containers.

after the shrub has been planted in the soil. To check for girdling roots, brush away the soil on top of the rootball or stick your finger in the top 2 or 3 inches near the trunk. You can usually see or feel them in the top of the rootball.

After you select the shrub that you want, retie the burlap and carry it from the bottom of the rootball—don't use the trunk as a handle. Balled and burlapped plants are top heavy and not very stable. To keep them from falling over, tie or lean them against a wall or fence. Until planting, store the shrub in the shade, and keep the rootball moist by watering slowly from the top. In warm weather, it's a good idea to wet the foliage occasionally, as well.

Burlap is the traditional wrap, but many other materials are used. The advantage of burlap is that it rots readily, and can

From a Mexican orange in a 1-gallon container, to a balled-and-burlapped azalea, to a bareroot rose, shrubs are produced and sold in a number of ways.

Buying Container Plants

A container plant should be moved to a larger container before its roots are too crowded, and then offered for sale only when its roots are established in the new soil.

If the roots are thick and exposed, it has been in the container too long.

Tug gently to see if it is well rooted in the container.

Buying Balled and Burlapped Plants

Balled and burlapped plants are raised in the field then dug up with a ball of soil around their roots. The twine and burlap hold the rootball together. Open the top of the wrapping and lay it back so you can inspect the root ball.

If the rootball is broken, many roots are damaged.

Roots that circle tightly around the trunk can eventually strangle the shrub, restricting its growth or even killing it.

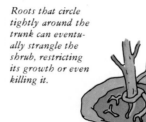

Buying Bare-root Plants

Bare-root plants are also grown in the field, but they are deciduous plants that are dug up in the winter, when they are out of leaf and dormant. They can remain out of the ground until they begin to grow again in the spring. Bare-root plants are usually less expensive than container or balled and burlapped plants, but are only available in the winter or early spring.

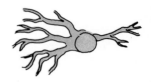

The root system should be symmetrical and evenly balanced. A lopsided root system will form a lopsided top.

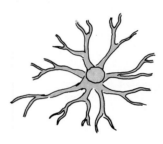

Inspecting the Shrub

The following list contains some sound advice that will help you make the best selections.

Branches

The shrub branches should be evenly spaced, indicating that the plant has had continuous growth under good growing conditions. New shoot growth should be uniform all the way around the plant. This indicates that the plant has a fully developed, balanced root system.

Pruning Cuts

When you inspect a plant before buying it, make sure there are no signs of recent severe cutting back. All pruning cuts should be to outside buds so that the plant will keep its natural shape and not grow crisscrossed branches. There shouldn't be any short stubs left from pruning: They invite disease and insect attacks as they die back.

Check the Label

Make sure that you are buying the variety you set out to buy. Plants within a species usually look similar, while species within a genus can be widely dissimilar and yet look surprisingly alike when they are small plants at the nursery. Caution: After planting your shrubs, remove the labels attached by wires to prevent later girdling of a branch or the trunk.

be left under the shrub when you plant it. See page 30. Synthetic material must be removed before planting, since it does not rot.

Bare-root Shrubs

Bare-root plants are a good value if you know what to look for, and if you are in the mood to garden when others are still shaking off the winter doldrums. Bare-root plants are not only less expensive, but also they do not have to make the transition from nursery container soil to your garden soil, thus tending to establish themselves more rapidly.

Bare-root plants are only available during the dormant season, and they should always be planted before growth begins. For the best selection, shop at the beginning of the bare-root season—late winter or early spring. Many varieties of deciduous shrubs are available bare root, particularly roses and shrubs commonly used as hedge plants.

At one time, when bare-root trees and shrubs would arrive at the nursery, they would be "heeled in," or temporarily held, in raised beds of bark or sawdust. Customers would pick out the plants they wanted, pull them out of the beds, and have them pruned. Today, bare-root plants often go directly from the delivery truck into individual cans. However, customers can still consider that they're buying plants bare root as long as the new, little, white roots have not started to grow when plants are taken out of their containers. When roots and leaves have already sprouted, plants are sold as containerized plants at increased prices.

Before you buy a bare-root shrub, you should carefully examine its root system. Look for several good-sized, brown-colored roots going in different directions at different levels from the main root. In most cases, the upper portion of the plant should be pruned before it leaves the nursery. If you cannot plant it right away, cover the roots with sawdust or damp earth to keep them from drying out. Dried roots quickly lose their ability to continue growing. Store the plants in a cool place to keep the buds from opening too early.

Selecting Hedge Plants

The deciduous plants commonly used for hedges are often available as bare-root plants. One of the most popular and best-looking hedge shrubs is the privet, botanically known as *Ligustrum*. There are many varieties of *Ligustrum*, but the one offered bare root at your garden center will most likely be the one best adapted to your climate. Good-quality bare-root privets are usually from 12 to 24 inches tall, and should have sturdy stems and well-developed root systems.

If no bare-root plants are available at the time you want to start your hedge, the best bet is to buy 1-gallon-sized plants. The largest plant is not always the best buy, considering that you will immediately want to prune the plant heavily to force as many new shoots as possible from the base. Look for vigorous plants that are well branched.

Slow-growing evergreen shrubs, such as *Taxus* (yew), *Ilex* (holly), and the various varieties of *Buxus* (boxwood) are among the most preferred varieties for hedges. Their slow growth may be a drawback to the gardener who wants quick privacy, but in the long run, slower-growing plants make a denser hedge that needs less pruning maintenance than some of the faster-growing choices, such as privet.

If you want a neatly trimmed hedge, plants with large leaves will demand more specialized care than smaller-leafed varieties. The English laurel (*Prunus laurocerasus*) is a good-looking, broad-leafed, evergreen shrub sometimes used for hedges. The large size of its leaves, however, demands that a hedge be pruned selectively rather than sheared. See the top photograph on page 45. Shearing plants with oversized leaves will cause an abundance of imperfect, cut-up leaves.

Bringing Your Plants Home

When you purchase new shrubs, be sure to follow these next two bits of advice:

■ Because cut metal cans are almost impossible to water correctly, don't have a can cut unless you are going to plant the shrub that same day.

■ Don't attempt to bring a shrub home in a car in which the plant does not comfortably fit. Any plant, but especially a leafy one, can become rapidly windburned if left exposed in a speeding automibile. If you must take your new shrub home with you, protect it by wrapping it securely in cloth or some other protective material. Most nurseries and garden centers will deliver purchases free of charge. Take advantage of this service, and both you and your new plant will benefit.

These slow-growing boxwoods were planted a year ago, but are already filling in nicely. Note the appropriate spacing between plants.

Planting, Transplanting and Containers

Step-by-step instructions simplify planting, either for shrubs brought home from the nursery, or for shrubs that are moved from one location in your garden to another. Or plant your shrubs in containers for mobility and garden versatility.

Planting a seed, bulb, shrub, or tree in the ground is an important event. It's significant for the plant or plant-to-be, and special for the gardener, as well. It has been said that you cannot plant a garden without being an optimist. Many positive thoughts are affirmed on planting day: the desire for a more beautiful environment, the anticipation of flowers, shade, fruit, or privacy, and the recognition that you will enjoy the future rewards, season after season. In this chapter, each of the basic planting steps is made clear to ensure that this gardening optimism is well founded.

By shaping and developing a garden, this gardener is participating in the creative process of nature.

The best ways to plant shrubs and other plants have remained essentially the same for centuries. However, some recent changes in nursery methods have resulted in a few modifications of these techniques. Also, continuing research adds to our information about planting.

Transition Soil
As we discussed in the section on soils (pages 20 and 21), most shrubs will adapt well to the large middle range of native soils available to most gardeners. But because nursery shrubs are grown in a lightweight, porous growing medium formulated to keep the plants healthy while they are in their containers, shrubs go through a period of *transition* in which they become used to the garden soil, usually quite different from the container soil. Some plant experts feel that the plant's transition

is eased by the use of *transition soil* when it is planted. This simply means that before you replace the soil from the planting hole, you mix in amendments to approximate the container soil.

However, recent research indicates that while plants started out in transition soil do better than other plants at first, after five years they are not as healthy as ones planted with unamended backfill soil. If you have a real problem soil, chances are that your best gardening success will come from selecting plants that are particularly adapted to that soil. Otherwise, your plants will probably do well using either method of planting. Plants in transition soil may grow a bit faster at first, but eventually the roots must penetrate the native soil, and the research indicates that doing so sooner rather than later may actually help establish a stronger root system.

Planting Tools

Shovel
The main differences in shovels are the shape of the blade and the angle at which it is attached to the handle. Square-bladed shovels are made for moving loose material; round-bladed shovels are for digging or for moving compact material.
Choose a shovel that has the blade nearly in line with the handle for turning over soil, and one with an angled blade for moving loose material.

Trowel
A trowel is a general-purpose garden tool. It cultivates, plants, digs, weeds, and performs a multitude of other gardening chores. Pick one with a strong shank.

Crowbar
For digging holes, grubbing out stumps, or moving heavy rocks nothing beats a crowbar. Buy one that is about 5 feet long, with a chisel on one end and a point on the other.

Spade
A spade is a cutting tool. Its edge should be kept filed to a 45-degree angle. Besides being useful for digging holes, it is one of the best tools for dividing large perennial plants. Most gardeners prefer a spade with a D-handle, like the one shown here, but they are also available with long handles.

The Planting Steps

If you carefully follow the eleven planting steps outlined here, success is practically guaranteed. The steps are described for shrubs bought in containers. The procedures for planting bare-root and balled and burlapped plants are essentially the same; the few other things you should know about planting them are discussed in the sections that immediately follow the basic steps (page 30).

1. Plant at the Right Time

In the past, early spring and early fall have been recommended as the ideal times for planting shrubs. Recent information suggests that this traditional advice may be a bit limiting. Actually, it is satisfactory to plant at any time, with these exceptions:

Don't plant before the soil is workable. If you can't use a spade or cultivator easily, wait until the soil dries out somewhat.

Don't plant immediately preceding a period that will cause the shrub climate-related stress. Late spring and late fall are usually times when the approaching heat or cold will place newly established plants under stress.

2. Dig the Hole

Dig the planting hole approximately twice as wide and to the same depth as the rootball, or 1 inch shallower. Plants have a tendency to sink after they have been planted, so if the hole is dug deeper than the original rootball, the plant may suffer from crown and root rot in the future. The rootball should be sitting on firm, undisturbed soil.

3. Amend the Backfill Soil (Optional)

If you are going to make a transition soil, this is the time to do it. The soil that you take from the hole is called backfill soil. *Keep the backfill in one pile, and make a rough estimate of its volume. Next, add an organic soil amendment to the pile, one that decomposes slowly. The proportion of soil conditioner to backfill soil is flexible, but approximately 25 percent of the final mix should be conditioner.*

4. Add Nutrients

If you are planting your new shrub in early spring or when you expect leaf growth to begin, now is a good time to add a complete fertilizer. To add a dry type, throw in a small amount of fertilizer, according to the manufacturer's recommended ratios. As a rule of thumb, 1 to 2 tablespoons is adequate if you are planting a shrub from a 1-gallon container, and ¼ cup is all you need for plants in 5-gallon containers. Stir it into the soil so that the rootball does not come into direct contact with straight fertilizer.

5. Take the Shrub Out of the Container

If the plant has been grown in a plastic container, it will slip out easily, especially if the rootball is damp. Whatever you do, don't break the rootball trying to get it out—you may permanently damage the root system. If the container is a straight-sided metal can and you are going to plant the shrub the same day you buy it, have the can cut at the nursery. If you are going to wait, even for a day or two, leave the can intact, and you can cut it at home with a large pair of tin snips or a can cutter like the type used at the nursery.

6. Place the Shrub in the Hole

Before placing the shrub in the hole, check the rootball. Cut or pull away any circled, matted, or tangled roots so that they radiate out from the rootball. Shorten the roots to the width of the planting hole so they will not be bent when planting. Shrubs planted with matted roots often stay that way, not venturing into the surrounding soil. To compensate for damaged or cut roots, lightly trim the top of the shrub. Now check the rootball depth in relation to the planting hole depth, and in it goes.

7. Fill the Hole

Fill the hole with backfill soil to the level of the surrounding soil.

8. Build a Basin

Build a shallow basin around the shrub so that irrigation water will be concentrated in the area where it is needed most. Be sure to build it so that the water drains away from the stem of the plant. Thoroughly water the soil around the root zone. Apply water until the soil is loose and muddy. Gently jiggle the plant until it is positioned exactly how you want it. This action will eliminate any remaining air pockets. Check again to be sure water drains away from the stem of the plant. Use the basin for primary watering until some roots have had a chance to expand into the surrounding soil—usually around six weeks later. If dry weather conditions require continued irrigation, enlarge the basin at this time. However, if you live in an area with sufficient summer rain or if you have installed another irrigation system, you can break down the basin.

9. Stake, If Necessary

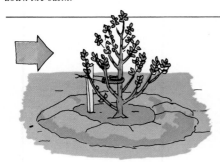

Recent tests have shown that some back-and-forth movement of the tops of plants actually results in faster and better-quality growth. The only reasons to stake a newly planted shrub are if the plant is extremely top heavy or if it is planted in an area of high winds. If a stake is necessary, place it on the side of prevailing winds, or use two stakes on either side of the shrub and tie them loosely for support with something that will not damage the surface of the stem, such as an old bicycle inner tube. Your nursery will have a supply of other suitable materials.

Check ties frequently to make sure that they are not cutting into the growing plant. Remove the stake after the plant is securely rooted in its new location, usually after the first year.

10. Prune, If Necessary

Shrubs planted from containers will rarely require any pruning immediately after planting, except for cosmetic purposes. See the chapter on pruning for the methods appropriate for your particular kind of shrub, beginning on page 41.

11. Water

Keep a watch on the plant to see how much water it requires. If a newly planted shrub wilts during the hottest part of the day, the rootball is not getting enough water, even though the surrounding soil may appear wet. Even if it rains or if the plant is in the path of a sprinkler, you may need to water it by hand two to three times a week for the first few weeks, if the soil seems dry. But, do not overwater. *Too much water is as bad as too little.*

Planting Balled and Burlapped

Shrubs

Along with the steps described for planting containerized plants, balled and burlapped shrubs require a couple of extra procedures.

Handle the ball carefully, and set it in the hole with the burlap still on. Adjust the height of the rootball, as you would with a shrub from a container. If the burlap has been treated to retard rotting (ask at the nursery), it will have to be removed or have large holes cut in it.

In the hole, untie the burlap from the trunk of the plant and pull it away from the top of the rootball. If the strings pull away easily, discard them; if not, leave them to rot in the soil. (Remove synthetic twine, since it does not rot.)

Cut or fold the burlap back so that it will be below the surface of the soil. Because any exposed burlap acts like a wick, drawing water out of the soil, be sure all edges are buried. If the plant is wrapped in synthetic material instead of burlap, you must remove it completely.

You may want to do a little pruning to compensate for the roots that were lost when the shrub was dug up by the grower. Sometimes a little extra fertilizer and water will compensate for any roots that were pruned away earlier.

Planting Bare-root Shrubs

The nursery will usually prune a bare-root shrub for you after it has been pulled from the holding bed. Sometimes ⅓ or more of the growth is cut back, but this results in a stronger, better-looking shrub.

Unless they are planted immediately after their purchase, bare-root shrubs should be stored in a cool spot with their roots in moist soil, sawdust, or bark to prevent them from drying out.

Dig a hole large enough to accommodate the span of the roots without bending them. Also, prune off any broken or very long roots, and place the plant in the hole with the top root 1 inch under the soil level. Work the backfill soil between the roots with your hands, getting rid of any air pockets.

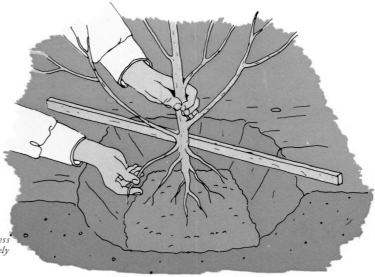

Since bare-root shrubs are always planted while they are dormant, adding fertilizer is a wasted step. And, unlike other plants, a bare-root shrub will probably not need watering again until the spring. Nor do bare-root shrubs need staking, unless you have extremely high winds.

Planting Hedges

There are two basic ways to plant a hedge—you can dig a trench the length of the hedge or you can dig individual holes. Although the methods are interchangeable, the trench method generally works best for bare-root plantings, and the individual hole method works best for plants from containers. With either method, the eleven basic steps of planting apply. Generally speaking, the width of the trench should be two times the width of the rootball.

A double, staggered row of shrubs results in the more rapid growth of a thicker, denser, and wider hedge, but involves twice the initial expense and effort. If you plant a double row, stagger the plants so that no two plants are directly opposite from each other.

The width of the spacing between individual plants will depend partly on the potential branch spread of the shrub variety and partly on how fast you want the hedge to fill in. Spacing can be from 18 inches to 30 inches apart. Most gardeners recommend a spacing of 18 to 20 inches within the row to avoid root crowding. Some dwarf varieties are planted 12 inches apart. Ask at your nursery for advice on your particular plant variety.

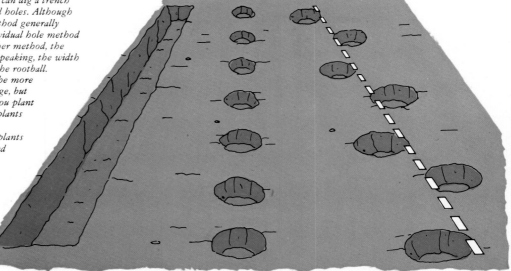

Transplanting

Transplanting means moving an established shrub from one spot in the garden to a new one. Transplanting any shrub, whether large or small, represents some danger to the plant. The worst problems are caused by root loss, either because some of the roots are mechanically broken off while the shrub is being dug out of the ground or because the rootball is allowed to dry out before the shrub is safely placed in its new location.

Here are a few tips for transplanting:
■ Try to transplant during cool, moist weather; roots will dry out quickly on warm, windy days. Just before transplanting, you may want to spray both broad-leafed and coniferous evergreens with an antitranspirant, a chemical that prevents leaves from losing water through transpiration.
■ Move a shrub when it is dormant or as inactive as possible.
■ Dig as large a rootball as you can handle to minimize root loss, and be careful not to break it. For best results, the soil should be fairly moist but not muddy. If you lose roots during the digging process, compensate by pruning the top of the shrub by the same proportion that is lost from the root system. It is usually advisable to prune by thinning out rather than by cutting back tips. See page 42.

Small Shrubs

For the purpose of transplanting, the definition of a small shrub is one that can be carried on a shovel or spade after it has been dug.

The first step is to dig the hole in the new location, as in planting step 1 on page 31. Then, with a sharp spade, cut around the entire shrub you want to transplant. On the last downward cut, tip the spade back and lift the shrub out. Carry the shrub gently on the spade to the new location and lower it into the hole. Next, follow planting steps 7 through 11, on page 29, for filling the hole, building a basin, and watering the shrub.

Transplanting Large Shrubs

The first step in transplanting a large shrub is to dig the new hole and have it ready to receive the plant. Next, prune away or tie up the low branches of the shrub you're going to move to permit easy access to its base. Dig a ditch around the plant, as shown in the accompanying illustration. Using a sharp shovel, undercut the rootball from one side until the shrub is about to topple over. Have a piece of burlap ready—a gunny sack cut so that it spreads open is fine—and push it down evenly on the undercut side. Continue digging on the opposite side until it is possible to topple the shrub onto the burlap. Wrap the burlap around the rootball and tie with twine to keep the rootball together. Lift the shrub onto a piece of heavy plastic so that you can slide the shrub to its new location, or put it on a wheelbarrow or handtruck. Plant according to the instructions for balled and burlapped shrubs on preceding page.

Transplanting Small Shrubs

Moving a small shrub is a simple process, normally done in moments. First, cut the roots on all sides of the shrub with a sharp spade. On the last cut, push the spade as far under the shrub as you can and pick it up.

Carry the shrub on the spade to the hole you have previously dug and gently lower it into place. Fill the hole with soil, then build a basin and puddle the plant in with a thorough irrigation. Prune to compensate for the roots you have cut.

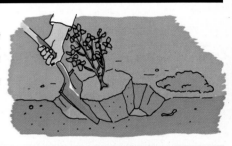

Transplanting Large Shrubs

This is a more complex process than the one described above. Give yourself room to work by pruning away the lower branches or tying them out of the way.

Dig a ditch all the way around the shrub, as deep as you wish the rootball to be. A mattock and shovel or spade are best for this job. Be careful not to break the rootball with the mattock.

Undercut the ditch on one side with the spade. Cut gently, by chopping with the spade until the rootball begins to loosen. You will probably cut more than half-way through, leaving a narrow neck of soil and roots.

Tuck burlap into the cut you have made under the rootball. Try to wad as much material into the cut as you will need to wrap the other side of the rootball. Spread the rest of the burlap on the ground.

Cut the neck of soil from the other side of the shrub, lowering it gently onto the burlap. Reach under and pull the wad of burlap toward yourself. Wrap the rootball in burlap and tie it tightly with twine before lifting it from the hole.

The easiest way to move a heavy shrub is to slide it on a piece of plastic or cardboard. Plant it in the new hole according to the directions on the opposite page.

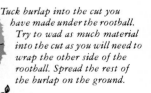

Compare the compact habit of Pittosporum tobira *'Wheeler's Dwarf' (upper left) with the nondwarf species (lower right).*

Growing Shrubs in Containers

The minute you plant a shrub in a container you give it a singular importance that can turn it into a prized specimen. Although it may be easy to walk past a row of shrubs in the garden without giving it a second glance, most gardeners find it difficult to resist regularly poking around a potted shrub, just to see how it's getting along. Shrubs in containers often turn out to be the pets of the garden, and the extra attention they receive often results in spectacular plants. See the list of shrubs that do well in containers on page 60.

Mobility
Besides the specimen qualities they achieve, shrubs planted in containers also have practical benefits:
■ If you move frequently, you can take your shrubs with you.
■ You can grow shrubs that you wouldn't be able to grow in your native soil.
■ You can grow shrubs that would not survive a cold winter out of doors, because you can roll the containers to protected areas before cold weather begins.
■ It's easy to make your patio or entranceway attractive with the right container shrubs, and it's possible to change their positions.
■ Shrubs in full bloom can be brought to center stage for a few days, then returned to their normal locations after the show.
■ You can shift your shrubs around as the seasons dictate, growing species that don't normally do well in your climate by providing the right protection at the right time.

Choosing Appropriate Shrubs
Size. The intermediate size of most shrubs makes them good candidates for container culture. To people who are only familiar with shrubs grown in the open ground, the thought of growing a wisteria, boxwood, or lilac in a container may seem impractical. But remember that many plants you see at your local nursery are growing very well in containers.

Growth. Although any shrub can be grown in a container, the best choices are those that are somewhat slow growing and have a compact plant habit. Fast-growing shrubs will need to be repotted more often and will require more pruning. Because of their naturally small size, dwarf shrubs are ideal subjects for container culture. See page 64 for information on dwarfs, and make a point of admiring these unusual plants on your next trip to the nursery.

Hardiness. Container plants are particularly prone to winter damage. Use species that are hardy to at least one zone (10°) colder than your area, or affix movable bases to the containers so that you can move the plants to a protected location, such as under the eaves of the house.

Maintenance Procedures
Growing shrubs in containers is very similar to other forms of gardening, except that a few of the plants' requirements are more critical. For the complete story on growing shrubs and other plants in containers, see another Ortho book, *Container and Hanging Gardens.*

Soil requirements. The soil used to fill containers is important. If your containers are not overly large or if there aren't too many of them, consider using one of the lightweight packaged soil mixes. Proper drainage is vital with container-grown plants, and these mixes provide nearly perfect drainage.

If you decide to use soil from the garden to fill your containers, be sure to mix in large quantities of soil amendments, such as compost, peat moss, nitrogen-stabilized sawdust, leaf mold, ground fir bark, or pine bark. Blend; do not layer. The addition of perlite will lighten the mix and improve drainage. At least ½ of the final mix should be made up of amendments. Common proportions are: 1 part garden soil, 1 part perlite or sand, 1 part organic material.

When you fill a container with soil, be sure to leave 2 or 3 inches between the top of the soil and the top of the pot. This space holds the water while it soaks through the soil to the bottom of the container. It means one watering rather than several.

Watering and feeding. Any plant in a container depends almost totally on the gardener for the water and nutrients necessary for growth. Unlike plants in the garden, the roots of a container shrub are very restricted. They do not have the free run of a good garden soil from which to draw moisture and nutrients. Sensitive gardeners compensate for this restricted root space by never allowing their plants to wilt from lack of moisture. Water must be

Even as unlikely a subject as this wisteria, usually a large vine, can make an excellent container plant when properly trained.

applied on a regular basis; it's common for nurseries to water plants in containers every day during the summer. To make sure that the soil from the top to the bottom of the pot is evenly wet, apply enough water so that it runs out of the drainage hole.

The increased amount of water flushes nutrients through the soil much more rapidly than with plants growing in the ground. So the gardener must compensate by lightly feeding plants in containers with a complete fertilizer, as frequently as every two weeks during the active growing season of spring and summer. Or you may use a slow-release fertilizer. Many gardeners prefer to feed container plants with liquid fertilizer because it is so easy to apply. See page 38 for information about fertilizers.

Caring for roots. Over a period of years, the roots may fill the container to the point of being rootbound. When this condition occurs, you can do one of two things: transplant the plant into a larger container, or shave off a portion of the roots, and add some new soil to the container. When you shave off the roots, you should compensate for root loss by lightly pruning the top of the plant. This process of revitalization should be repeated every few years, or when the shrub seems to have diminished in vigor, despite regular waterings and feedings.

Changing locations. If you decide to move shrubs in containers from one spot

Container shrubs need frequent watering.

Rhododendrons are favorite container subjects.

to another, do so gradually. A radical change in environment can injure plants if it is made too abruptly. Be especially careful about moving a plant grown in the shade into a sunnier location; leaves used to the shade can be rapidly burned by the hot sun. Likewise, a plant acclimated to a sunny location will produce unusually long branches and large leaves when moved suddenly to a shady spot. The key to success is to make the change

in a succession of moves, allowing the shrub a few days to adjust to each stage.

Many flowering shrubs can be moved inside the house for a few days of special attention during the blooming period. However, with any outdoor shrub, a stay indoors of more than five days is not recommended. While outdoor shrubs are inside, they should be kept in as cool a location as possible, and especially kept away from direct blasts of dry furnace heat.

Planting in Containers

1. *Check Drainage Holes*
Drainage holes should be large (a minimum of ¾ inches) and plentiful (a maximum of 1 foot apart). If necessary, make more holes. There should be enough room between the container and the ground surface it sits on for water to escape from the holes in its bottom. If necessary, nail 1-inch cleats to the bottom or improvise some sort of stand.

2. *Cover Drainage Holes*
Place a piece of broken crockery over each hole or spread a piece of window screen across the bottom of the container to keep the soil from washing out.
3. *Place Soil in Container*
Put enough planting mix into the container so that the top of the shrub's rootball will be 2 to 3 inches below the rim of the container.
4. *Remove Shrub from Can*
See Step 5 of Planting Steps on page 28.

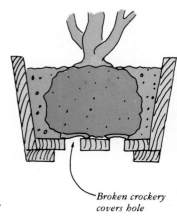
Broken crockery covers hole

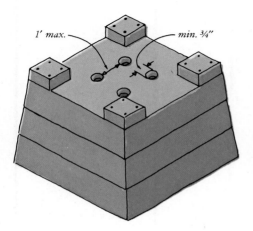
1' max.　min. ¾"

5. *Place Shrub in Container*
Orient the shrub so that the stem is at the center of the container and is not leaning, even if you have to tilt the rootball to accomplish this.

6. *Add Soil*
Pour soil around the rootball until it is level with the top of the rootball. Do not plant the shrub deeper than it was in the nursery container. The soil level should be 2 inches to 3 inches below the edge of container.
7. *Water*
Water the shrub a number of times. This will help to leach out excess salts in the soil as well as ensure that the soil is thoroughly wet and settled around the rootball.

The Basics of Care

Shrubs are among the easiest of plants to care for. Still, the right fertilizer at the right time, effective methods for watering, and ways to protect your shrubs from heat, cold, wind and snow, help them to thrive and perform as you wish them to.

One of the primary advantages of most shrubs is that they require so little maintenance. Give a little extra attention to newly planted shrubs to assure their establishment, then after the first year you can simply sit back and enjoy them.

Once a shrub is established in a location, its roots spread out through many cubic feet of soil. They may extend far beyond the limits of the branches and many feet down into deep layers of the soil. The large volume of soil that they "mine" for water and nutrients gives them more flexibility in their maintenance needs than flowers or vegetables.

Often, shrubs need no extra water or fertilizer at all, because their roots extend under the vegetable garden or the lawn, which you water and feed regularly, or just because their roots cover such a wide area that they are able to find enough naturally occurring food and water.

Slow-growing shrubs are particularly independent of fertilizers. Camellias often do well on the nutrients that are released as a mulch decomposes, and need no extra fertilizers.

Proper maintenance is nevertheless important for most shrubs and will result in beautiful plants year after year. Here are the main things to remember:
■ When you water, water thoroughly.
■ To keep roots and soil healthy and to help retain moisture around root zones, add a layer of mulch.
■ For spectacular and healthy shrubs, give them the added nutrients they need at the right times.
■ Protect your shrubs from severe weather conditions.

In addition to these points, the only other requirement is occasional pruning; the next chapter is devoted to this aspect of shrub gardening. This chapter focuses on the watering, fertilizing, and protection of shrubs. If you give your shrubs the care outlined on these pages, they will continue the healthy growth they started when you planted them.

◀

While this garden requires little maintenance, its healthy bloom is due to regular, light attention.

The secret of easy gardening is staying alert to potential problems on a daily basis. Act to prevent them at once and avoid letting little problems become big.

Watering

Getting Shrubs Established

A shrub that's selected to suit its site will be easy to care for, only making demands for special care during the first few months after it has been planted. During this period of initial establishment, a shrub's roots will only grow about an inch into dry soil. Contrary to popular belief, roots do not "search" for water. It is possible for a plant to die of thirst, even though plenty of water is available just a couple of inches away from the root tips. The message is: If you want a shrub to develop a healthy, extensive root system, the area in which the roots are to grow must be kept moist.

If you do not have an irrigation system set up, the most efficient way to ensure that a newly planted shrub gets sufficient water is to create a basin around it for filling with water. See page 29 for details about how to make basins.

Filling a basin only once with water is rarely sufficient, especially in hot weather. And few people have the patience required to water a shrub properly with a hand-held hose turned on to a moderate trickle. The best bet is to fill a basin twice, allowing the water to drain into the soil between waterings. If you have a number of shrubs to water, fill each basin, then start at the beginning again, repeating the process. Or, if you would rather be doing something else while you water, put the hose in the basin and turn the water on to a trickle. Set a kitchen timer for however long it takes to wet the soil thoroughly.

Your new shrub will be settled in its new place in the garden after about six weeks, but you should watch its development carefully for the first year. Make sure it gets sufficient amounts of water during that crucial first summer.

After Shrubs Are Established

Once a shrub is well developed, your watering worries are virtually over. Except in arid parts of the country, you will seldom need to water your shrubs at all! If you have a prolonged drought, you should still water infrequently but thoroughly. The reason established shrubs need little or no water from the ground surface is that their root systems are extensive. As a shrub's roots grow, they penetrate deeper into the soil and draw on deeper reservoirs of moisture held in the soil.

When you do water, remember to water slowly over a long period of time to allow the water to soak deeply into the soil. Avoid frequent light watering, since this leads to a shallow root system.

Testing for Wetness

To find out how wet your soil is, you can cut into the soil with a shovel or trowel and check below the top 4 inches of soil. Or you may want to use a soil moisture tester—see the illustration on this page. If you are watering a newly planted shrub, you want to be sure the rootball is moist. It is possible for the surrounding soil to be wet when the rootball is not. Check it by poking your finger into the rootball area.

It is best to do this every day until you know how much watering your new shrubs need to maintain the proper moisture level. For established plantings, make sure the deeper levels of soil are providing enough moisture.

Watering Problems

It doesn't take long to discover that when you talk about watering problems, you are really talking about soil problems. See the soil section on pages 20 and 21. *Clay* soils absorb water slowly and drainage is very slow. Air in the soil, so necessary for healthy root growth, is minimal in clay soils, especially after watering. If water fills too many of the air spaces for too long, roots may die, causing top growth to die, as well. *Sandy* soils, on the other hand, allow water to drain through rapidly—leaving plenty of air, but little water. The middle range of soils, *loam*, has good water retention and drainage.

If you don't have loam, you can still improve your soil—the secret is *organic matter*, and lots of it. The best and most immediate results occur when you amend

---

Tools for Watering

Garden hose: *Choosing a good hose is like buying tires for your car—the more your hose is reinforced, the less likely it will be to have a "blowout" or any other defect. Look for nylon (tire cord) reinforcement in both vinyl and rubber hoses; some have a radial design for added strength.*

The best hose to buy is a vinyl one that is treated to stay flexible in cold weather. Check the inside diameter measurement (ID) when selecting the water volume necessary for your gardening needs. A hose with a ⅝-inch diameter, or one with a ¾-inch diameter for long distances, is fine for average gardening use.

Hose nozzles: *In addition to a good hose, special nozzle attachments will help you to water your shrubs properly. The nozzles illustrated here are examples of bubblers— nozzles that will supply maximum amounts of water without disturbing the soil or gouging roots.*

Water timer: *Many types of water timers are available, from the simple to the sophisticated. Pictured here is a simple model that will turn on a hose or sprinkler for a preset length of time and then turn the water off. Other, more elaborate models can be programmed to water on a permanent schedule or to turn on automatically whenever the soil needs water. Check at your local garden center for more details.*

Soil moisture tester: *A soil moisture tester lets you know if your shrubs need water. The amount of moisture in the soil activates an electrical charge: the more moisture in the soil, the higher the electrical response. A combination light and moisture meter reads the amount of light that is reaching your plants, along with testing for moisture.*

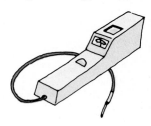

Soaker hose: *A soaker hose oozes water along its entire length. Older types were made of canvas and lasted only one season, but newer ones are of plastic, and last for two or more watering seasons.*

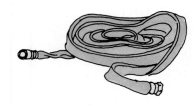

all the soil in the area you intend to plant. But if you are planting in an area that has established plantings, you can mulch with organic matter and improve the soil gradually. However, unless your soil is extraordinarily bad, which is rare, you can compensate for drainage difficulties by watering clay soils a little less frequently and sandy soils a little more often.

Irrigation Systems

Although shrubs aren't at all demanding in terms of regular watering, if you install an irrigation system for your other plants and trees, you will probably want to include watering devices for your shrubs. Step-by-step instructions for installing your own irrigation system are included in Ortho's book, *All About Landscaping.* Many kinds of systems are available, from the conventional sprinkler systems to the more sophisticated drip systems (see below). Any system will save you work; the one you choose will depend on the type of gardening you do and the terrain of your garden.

If you have a shrub border around the outside of a lawn area, plan to have a separate system for each, with a different type of sprinkler head for each. If the two systems are hooked together, every time you water the lawn the shrubs will also receive water, which is too frequent for the shrubs. Ask about the sprinkler heads that are best for shrubs at your nursery or garden center. (Even with an automated sprinkler system, remember that infrequent but deep irrigation is better than frequent light watering, and less wasteful of water.)

Drip Irrigation: Drip irrigation is a system of watering that basically consists of small plastic irrigation tubes installed directly next to the plants to be watered. Outlets (emitters) located at appropriate points along the tubes deliver water to the plants slowly, a drop at a time. The amount of water needed by a plant is supplied almost on a constant basis. This method differs radically from conventional irrigation methods, which provide quantities of water followed by periods of drought. Drip systems cost about as much as conventional sprinkler systems.

Here's how drip irrigation works. Emitters control the amount of water that reaches the soil. Emitter models vary; some have porous walls, others are more complex mechanical units that deliver water to a specific point. These are the ones most often used for shrub plantings (see illustration). Emitters reduce the flow of water so that it is released drop by drop. The flow rate, which is fixed, ranges from ½ to 2 gallons per hour.

The emitters are connected to lateral lines. Usually made of plastic, they have relatively small diameters—⅜ to ¾ inch or less. Lateral lines can cover long distances without losing pressure—a problem with conventional watering systems—because the flow rates are so low. Even so, they should be installed as level as possible, particularly for systems using less than 10 pounds of pressure.

The main lines are also plastic, and can be installed above or below ground.

The size of the main lines depends on the number of lateral lines and the flow of water needed. One cautionary note: These main lines and laterals are frequently gnawed by gophers and ground squirrels, even when buried.

The "head" is the control station where the water flow is measured and filtered, and the pressure regulated. If an automatic time clock is included in the system, it is installed as part of the main control.

Because foreign matter may plug the emitters, water used for drip irrigation must be free of sand and other small particles. To ensure water cleanliness, various types of sand or cartridge filters are used.

Most systems also require some kind of pressure reduction using a pressure regulator valve. The manufacturer will indicate the pressure needed by the particular emitter you choose. Some emitters require only 2 to 3 pounds of pressure, while others may need as much as 30 to 40 pounds.

Drip systems can be customized with the addition of a variety of equipment. Some of the most popular extras are: fertilizer injectors, time clocks, and moisture sensors. Check at your local nursery or garden center for details on specific drip systems and accessories.

Drip Irrigation

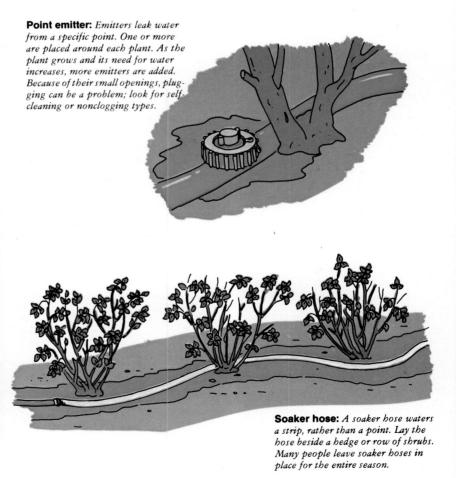

Point emitter: *Emitters leak water from a specific point. One or more are placed around each plant. As the plant grows and its need for water increases, more emitters are added. Because of their small openings, plugging can be a problem; look for self-cleaning or nonclogging types.*

Soaker hose: *A soaker hose waters a strip, rather than a point. Lay the hose beside a hedge or row of shrubs. Many people leave soaker hoses in place for the entire season.*

Use your fingers to tell if your shrubs need water.

Fertilizing

Most soils contain most of the nutrients shrubs need. Fertilizers are added to supplement this natural reservoir of nutrients and to make up for any possible deficiencies. Experienced neighbors, nurserypeople, or your county extension agent can tell you which nutrients are generally needed in your area. One nutrient, nitrogen, is needed in almost all areas, and is usually added routinely.

Shrubs demand little fertilizer compared to the amount required by lawns or vegetables. Light applications at regular intervals greatly increase growth and stimulate optimum flower production.

Nutrients

Among other substances, commercial fertilizers contain three primary nutrients: nitrogen, phosphate, and potash (NPK). Fertilizers are labeled by percentages of these three nutrients. The percentages differ, but this order is always the same. The percentage variations reveal two important things. First, they tell how much of a nutrient is in the fertilizer, by weight. In a 5-pound box of 5-10-10 fertilizer, 5 percent of that 5 pounds is nitrogen, 10 percent is phosphate, and 10 percent is potash. Furthermore, 5 pounds of 5-10-10 contains only ½ as much nitrogen as 5 pounds of 10-12-16.

Second, the numbers tell the relative proportions of the three major nutrients. Ratios of 2-1-1 (like 10-5-5 or 20-10-10) indicate that there is twice as much nitrogen as phosphate and potash, and 1-2-2 ratios (like 5-10-10) indicate the opposite.

While plants need all of these nutrients, each nutrient tends to stimulate different types of growth. Plants respond to a fertilizer according to the proportionate amounts of nutrients in it. Nitrogen tends to stimulate leafy growth, while phosphate and potash tend to further flowering and fruiting and other kinds of growth. Ratios of 2-1-1 are normally used to promote leafing when plants are growing actively. Ratios of 1-1-1 or 1-2-2 are best used when plants are forming flower buds or growing new roots (in late summer).

When To Fertilize

Shrubs need nitrogen the most when they are growing rapidly. For this reason, the heaviest application should be made just before or during rapid spring growth. In areas where the ground freezes in winter, nitrogen is sometimes applied in the fall as well, after top growth has stopped. Root growth, which continues into the winter and resumes in early spring, is stimulated by this practice. Heavy applications of nitrogen should not be made in late summer, or new growth will start that will not have time to harden off by winter.

Since nitrogen stimulates leaf growth, it should be used in moderation on any shrub that you must prune regularly. Extra nitrogen on a hedge will only mean more frequent shearing for you.

If you want to promote flower or fruit production on shrubs that bloom in early spring, fertilize before the buds set in late summer. The fertilizer should have a low proportion of nitrogen (such as the 1-1-1 or 1-2-2 ratios), since too much nitrogen can keep some shrubs from setting flower buds and making fruit by diverting energy to leaf production.

Shrubs need phosphate and potash all the time they are growing, but these nutrients persist in the soil for long periods, so timing their application is only important if you specifically want to stimulate flowers or fruit.

Types of Fertilizers

There are three basic types of fertilizers: dry, liquid, and organic.

Dry Fertilizers are available in powders, granules, and pellets. In most cases, dry fertilizer is the most convenient kind to use. It can be scattered on the ground and watered in, cultivated into the soil, or buried deep in the root zone.

Some dry fertilizers are soluble in water and become instantly available to plants.

This type usually leaches from the soil in a few weeks and must be reapplied regularly.

Other dry fertilizers are insoluble in water, but become available to plants over a period of time. These are known as slow-release fertilizers. In the most common form, urea formaldehyde, bacterial action in the soil slowly releases the nitrogen into a soluble form available to plants. Other slow-release fertilizers use different methods of releasing nitrogen. These fertilizers remain effective in the soil for six weeks to two years, depending on the type. They can be applied less often, but are more expensive than the soluble forms.

The amount of slow-release nitrogen in the fertilizer is shown on the label as part of the nitrogen analysis. It is called *water-insoluble nitrogen* and is shown as a percentage of the total fertilizer. A fertilizer with 10 percent nitrogen might contain 8 percent water-soluble nitrogen and 2 percent water-insoluble nitrogen.

Liquid Fertilizers may be bought as a liquid or a powder, but both must be dissolved in water before use. You can mix either kind in water in a watering can and apply it directly to the root zone, or meter it into a hose and spray it on with irrigation equipment.

Liquid fertilizers are often preferred for container plants, where light, frequent feeding is desirable. They are also useful with drip irrigation systems, where they can be metered into the system and fed to the plants with regular irrigations.

Liquid fertilizers are also used for foliar feeding, a method in which a dilute fertilizer solution is sprayed directly onto the leaves. Foliar feeding is useful when very quick results are desired, or when a soil problem inhibits the uptake of nutrients by the roots. Because it is time consuming and its effects are temporary, this method is only used on a curative basis and not as a regular fertilizing method.

Compare the nitrogen deficient leaves (top) with the healthy leaves (bottom).

Nutrient Content of Fertilizers

Percentages of nitrogen, phosphate, and potash, in that order.

Ammoniacal nitrogen is derived from ammonia.

Derived from urea, a synthetic organic nitrogen source.

Water insoluble nitrogen is slow release and will last for about six weeks.

10-5-5
GUARANTEED FERTILIZER ANALYSIS
Total Nitrogen (N)........ 10%
   2% Ammoniacal Nitrogen
  4.2% Urea Nitrogen
  3.8% Water Insoluble Nitrogen
Available Phosphoric Acid
(P_2O_5)........................ 5%
Soluble Potash (K_2O) 5%
Primary Nutrients from Urea, Ureaform, Ammonium Sulfate, Ammonium Phosphate, and Muriate of Potash

Organic Fertilizers are derived from plant or animal sources. Manure, compost, seed meals, blood meal, and fish meal are all organic. Fish emulsion is a liquid organic fertilizer; most of the rest are sold in a dry form. Most of them are expensive, but they last for a long time in the soil, and the nonnutrient part of the fertilizer improves soil structure.

When you need to purchase a fertilizer, take the time to read the labels. By knowing what you are fertilizing for and when to do so, you can purchase just the right fertilizer at the right time. And the directions on the package will help you to determine how much fertilizer to apply.

Mulches

Any of the organic materials used as soil amendments can also be used as a mulch. The difference is in the way you apply it to the soil. A mulch is intended to stay on top of the soil, usually in a layer about 3 inches thick, whereas a soil amendment is incorporated into the soil.

A layer of mulch covering the root zone of a shrub has many beneficial effects. Tests have shown that mulches:
- keep the soil temperature cooler, which is helpful for root growth
- keep the soil moisture at a more even level, thus reducing the amount of watering needed
- keep weeds from taking hold
- aid in the long-term development of good soil structure

An organic mulch is the most effective when it is renewed once or twice a year. We especially recommend a layer of mulch around newly planted shrubs. Since organic matter floats in water, the best time to add it is after you break down the water basin—usually about six weeks after planting. Spread the mulch evenly around the root zone area of a shrub, but keep it a couple of inches away from the stem. Moist mulch against shrub stems encourages crown rot, the growth of various fungi, the breeding of insects, and the burrowing of mice and other rodents.

While any organic material can serve as a mulch, certain kinds do better than others. Recommended are finely ground fir or pine bark, pine straw, compost, well-rotted manure, and, where available, redwood soil conditioner. Peat moss, however, makes a poor mulch, because it forms a crust on top and becomes difficult to water. Check with your nursery or garden center for good mulching material that is readily available in your area.

Climate Protection

If the shrubs in your garden are climatically adapted to your area, you will rarely need to supply them with protection from weather extremes. Only an occasional cold snap or heat spell will demand that you take protective measures for sensitive

plants. However, if you grow shrubs outside their natural boundaries—trying a frost-tender plant in the northern states or a shade-loving plant in the sun—the need to modify the microclimate surrounding these plants will be a more common occurrence. In most gardens, wind, heat, and cold are the most likely sources of plant damage.

Wind

If you are bothered by high winds in your area, one of the best actions you can take is to plant a windbreak (see page 17). A living windbreak will make the climate of your garden more pleasant for both people and plants. High, hot winds accelerate water evaporation and transpiration. But the worst damage from high winds can be done to the roots of newly planted shrubs; plants that have not had the chance to become established can be easily toppled, harming tender new roots. If high winds are a problem, see page 29 for information on staking new plants.

Heat

During periods of unusual heat, the most important protection you can give your shrubs is to keep them well watered. Do not let the soil around the plants dry out. Mulch to keep the soil cool and moist. For plants with particularly tender foliage, erect a simple, temporary structure of four stakes to support a burlap shade. As emergency relief for larger shrubs, sprinkling the leaves with water *will* help, despite what you may have heard to the contrary. There are a few plants whose foliage might be damaged by such action, but, by and large, the benefits of a quick sprinkling during a hot spell far outweigh the drawbacks.

One simple way to protect shrubs from excessive heat is to plant them suitably in the first place. For example, most shade-loving shrubs will tolerate morning sun until 11 o'clock or so and afternoon sun during the winter. But don't expect a shade plant to thrive in a location where it receives afternoon sun in the summer, especially if the heat reflects off of a wall or where searing winds prevail.

Cold

If you garden in an area where occasional hard frosts damage sensitive plants, the best advice is to pay attention to the weather reports. If you know in advance that the early morning temperatures are going to be unusually cold, you can take protective measures the night before. If the shrubs are in movable containers, move them close to the house where they will receive protection from the eaves. If the shrubs are stationary, cover them with burlap, cardboard, or plastic; be sure to remove this protection the following morning.

To protect tender plants in an area that has regular frosts, it's best to build a lightweight structure that can be used from year to year. Cover the structure tightly with fabric so that warm air rising from both the ground and the plant will be trapped during the night.

Tender deciduous shrubs grown in areas of extreme cold need special protection to make it through the winter. A coarse mulch, such as leaves or straw, should be packed around the crown of a plant, or, if necessary, around the entire plant. Hold the mulch in place with a wire cylinder.

Winter damage to broad-leafed evergreens is frequently the result of leaf transpiration, which occurs when the soil is solidly frozen so that water is unavailable to the plants. To prevent this kind of damage:
- Water thoroughly if the soil is dry. Water holds heat and a moist soil freezes more slowly than a dry soil.
- Mulch heavily.
- Spray an antitranspirant, available at garden centers and nurseries, on the leaves to retard drying.

Snow can damage shrubs, particularly needled evergreens, by packing on the branches and breaking or flattening them from the accumulated weight. You can provide protection against snow damage by tying up plants of this kind with cord before the first snow (see illustration above). Applying an antitranspirant to coniferous shrubs will also give them some measure of winter protection.

Pruning

To prune properly, you should know how the shrub is going to grow in response to various types of pruning cuts. Using different cuts, you can achieve a natural look, make a hedge, or create a topiary sculpture. Special pruning techniques for roses, rhododendrons and azaleas are included.

Pruning can direct the growth of shrubs, improve their health, and increase the production of flowers and fruit. With pruning, you can direct growth to balance a shrub that is lopsided, keep a shrub small and compact, make one grow tall, or open another up.

The basics of pruning are really quite simple. You need to know *what* and *how* to prune, and *when* to do it. The information and drawings in this chapter are intended to remove any mystery that may surround the subject of pruning shrubs. For more detailed information on pruning all types of plants, refer to Ortho's book, *All About Pruning.*

Pruning Styles

There are two basic styles of pruning: a *natural style,* which responds to the natural pattern of a shrub's growth, and a *formal style,* which includes espaliers, topiaries, hedges, and other severely shaped specimens.

The natural look is achieved by exploiting the natural growth habit of the shrub. Take a look at the "Plant Selection Guide" beginning on page 55; the naturally occurring form is included in each shrub description. The type of pruning that results in a natural shape is called *thinning.* See page 42.

A formal effect is possible either with the ambitious use of pruning shears or by planting varieties of shrubs that are naturally neat and compact. If the shrubs in your garden are not naturally inclined to compactness, occasional *heading back*

(see page 42) or frequent shearing will be necessary to create that tailored, formal look. If you shear plants, you should do it frequently so that only a little bit of growth is taken off each time. This situation is similar to getting your hair cut: If you have frequent haircuts, it's difficult to tell you've had one, but if you only get one every six months, the effect will be very noticeable.

When To Prune

The appropriate time of year in which to prune a particular shrub depends on what type of shrub it is. Shrubs that are grown primarily for their flowers require greater attention to timing than evergreen shrubs, both coniferous and broad leafed.

Flowering shrubs divide into two groups: those that flower on old wood and those that flower on new wood. On this basis alone, you can determine when to prune your flowering shrubs.

How can you tell whether a shrub

blooms on new or old wood? First, you need to know how to distinguish between the two types of growth. *New wood* is new stem growth that is produced during the current growing season. It is usually light green or pinkish in color. *Old wood* has been grown during a previous season. It is usually much darker in color than new wood, and is much more brittle. While a plant blooms, take a close look to see where the flowers form: on new wood or old?

If you've just bought a shrub and it's not yet in bloom, or you've moved into a house with an established but dormant garden, the best advice is not to prune any shrub until you know whether it blooms or not, and if it does, on what type of wood.

Once you know what type of wood a shrub flowers on, knowing when to prune is easy. Shrubs (and trees, for that matter) that bloom in early spring bloom on old

Clipping foliage results in tight, dense shapes.

Selective thinning creates a picturesque, open form.

◀

Shearing a hedge is especially satisfying to the gardener who loves neatness and order.

Types of Pruning

Heading

Pruning the end of a branch causes the dormant buds closest to the cut to begin growing. A shrub that has been pruned by heading is denser, has more growing points, and is smaller than an unpruned shrub.

Thinning

Thinning removes an entire branch. Since there are no dormant buds left under the cut, the energy that would have gone into that branch is spread throughout the shrub. The entire shrub will be larger and more open than an unthinned shrub.

Pinching

Shearing

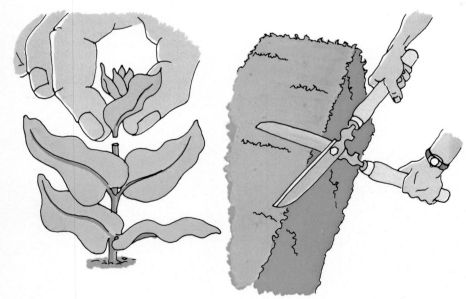

A pinch removes only the growing point. This causes buds below the pinch to break dormancy and begin to grow, resulting in a thicker plant. Since the pinch also delays growth for a couple of weeks as the buds break, it is used to retard growth in one part of a plant.

Shearing removes many growing points at once. With each shearing more buds are released from dormancy, resulting in a dense mass of growing points at the surface of the shrub. Sheared shrubs have a sculptured look.

wood, and should be pruned a week or two after the flowers drop. If you prune them during the dormant season, you will remove the blossom buds. Pruned at the correct time, in the spring or early summer, the plants have the rest of the season to produce more blossom buds for next year's display.

Shrubs that blossom in late spring or in the summer produce flowers on wood that was grown during the same growing season. The time to prune these shrubs is during the dormant season, or just before growth starts in very early spring. By so doing, you encourage more new stem growth, and hence, more blossoms.

Types of Pruning

When you remove any part of a plant, you are pruning. The two basic pruning methods are thinning and heading. *Thinning*, or *thinning out*, removes entire branches back to a main trunk, or major branches to the ground. *Heading*, or *heading back*, removes only part of a branch.

The important difference between thinning and heading is their effect on plants. When you thin, the shrub's energy is diverted to the remaining branches, which, in turn, grow more. The long-term result of thinning a shrub is that it will have an open, natural look. Shrubs that are only thinned also become larger than shrubs that are headed back.

When you head back a branch, the plant will grow multiple branches where there was previously only one. Heading forces the dormant buds closest to a pruning cut to grow. Over the long term, heading results in a more dense shrub that has more branches, but is smaller than a shrub that has been thinned. This type of pruning is most often associated with formal shapes.

Two special forms of heading are *pinching* and *shearing*. They have the same effect as other heading cuts, but are accomplished in special ways.

Pinching is done with the finger tips. A pinch removes only the growing point of a branch, allowing the lateral buds near the end of the branch to grow. This usually results in two, three, or four growing points where there had been only one. Pinching is used to make a small plant bushy and thick or to redirect energy within the plant, guiding its growth as it develops.

Shearing, or clipping, is like pinching in that only the growing points are removed. The difference is that shearing removes growing points *en masse* with hedge shears or power trimmers. The effect is the same —the plant responds by increasing the number of its growing points. Shearing is used to make hedges or topiary. Its use as a pruning method is associated with formal styles; just as thinning produces a natural, open shape, so does shearing produce a dense, sculptured shape.

Hedge trimmers

Hedge shears

Pruning loppers

Pruning Shears

There are several models to choose from, but favor the ones with a scissors action rather than those with a blade and anvil construction; they tend to crush the stems being cut. Keep your shears sharp, clean, dry, and well oiled, and they will last a lifetime.

Electric hedge trimmers have taken most of the work out of the trimming process.

If electricity is beyond reach, look for cordless electric trimmers that can be recharged—some models can be used for 35 minutes without stopping.

Some hedge shears have a notch at the base for cutting through thicker branches, but they are really designed to shear light new growth. Heavier pruning should be done with loppers.

Heavy-duty loppers may be necessary to prune mature shrubs with sturdy branches. They can lop off limbs up to 1½ inches in diameter with little effort, leaving a cleaner cut than a saw would.

Pruning Saw: If you have large shrubs that need pruning, you may want to own a pruning saw. The teeth are designed to cut green wood without binding. Pruning saws cut with a pulling motion, which makes them very efficient for movable branches.

Pruning Cuts

Before leaves and new stems appear, *growth buds* form in small swellings on the stems and branches. Inside these buds await tiny, undeveloped leaves, branches, and flowers.

There are two types of buds: terminal buds and lateral buds. A *terminal bud* grows at the *tip* of a shoot, and a *lateral bud* appears at the *side* of a shoot. These buds are the keys to making good pruning cuts.

When you prune, always cut *above* a bud. To place your cut near a lateral bud, select one that is pointing outward so that the new branch will grow away from the main trunk rather than crisscrossing with interior branches. Cutting above an outward-pointing lateral bud will also open up the plant to light, air, and orderly growth—important goals in pruning.

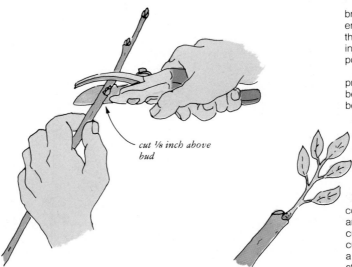

cut ⅛ inch above bud

If you cut off lateral buds or side branches, you will force the shrub's energy to go to the terminal buds, thus pushing the branches to grow in the directions they are already pointing.

When you get ready to make a pruning cut, hold the branch just below where you want the cut to be. Put the cutting blade of your hand pruners under the branch. Cut at an upward angle. The slant of the cut should be in the direction you want the new branch to grow. Never leave a budless stub of wood behind on the shrub. Unsightly stubs usually die and become an entry point for insects and diseases. *Think* about each cut before you make it. No pruning cut should ever be made without a good reason and a clear understanding of what the results are likely to be.

This "poodle" shape is a simple and popular topiary form.

Topiaries

Topiaries are living garden sculptures; plants can be shaped into geometrical and animal forms. The ideal plant choice for topiary work is a finely textured and hardy evergreen. The two varieties most often used in creating topiaries are boxwood and yew. Start with a young, 1-gallon plant with plenty of low branches that will fill out close to the ground. You must have a great deal of patience to create topiary. For example, if you want to make a simple double-balled shape, count on five years for boxwood and ten years for yew. If you want to shape a more complex animal form, count on twice that long.

The easiest topiary to shape is the double ball or "poodle." After pruning the lower portion into a ball shape, select several strong branches and let them grow at least 2 feet above the first ball. Then strip the foliage off the bottom foot to form the separating stem and begin to shape the top foot of growth into the second ball. See Ortho's book, *All About Pruning*, for detailed instructions.

Espaliers

Espaliers are shrubs or trees that are trained to grow flat against a vertical plane. Almost any shrub with fairly limber growth can be espaliered. All shrubs should have 6 inches between themselves and the wall or fence. Wire or wooden supports fixed at that distance will allow both for air movement and room for the branches to develop.

Start with a shrub that has a strong central stem. After planting the shrub, run the wires (or supports) horizontally at intervals of 18 inches across the wall or fence. Cut the central stem off at 18 inches, just below the height of the first wire. This will activate shoots to appear just below the cut.

During the first growing season, allow

only three new shoots to develop. Train two shoots horizontally onto the wire, and let the other one grow vertically as an extension of the central trunk. Rub off all the growth from the lower trunk.

Later on, cut the new trunk off a little below the second 36-inch-high wire. This will activate a second set of shoots. Train these as you did the first set. Continue training the shrub in this manner until all the wires are covered with branches. When you have formed the frame you want, keep new growth restricted with frequent pinching during the summer.

Hedges

Hedge plants should be pruned when they are first set out. Bare-root plants, intended to produce a dense hedge, should be pruned to about ½ of their original height. Plants from containers, and other plants that will naturally produce an open hedge, should be pruned back by about ⅓, both the tops and the sides.

Let a newly planted hedgerow grow without shearing for a full growing season to give the roots a chance to become established.

The second year, trim the hedge lightly to keep it dense as it grows. Don't try to achieve the hedge height you want too quickly. Keep shearing lightly to keep the hedge thick, without gaps, as it grows to the desired height. Once the hedge is as tall as you want it, your pruning technique should change.

Shear *small-leafed hedges*, such as boxwood or yew, whenever they look ragged from uneven new growth, and take off almost all of the new growth. Just let the hedge retain a little bit of new growth each time you shear by cutting about ¼ inch farther out than you cut at the last shearing. In this way, you will avoid bare spots and clusters of cut branches. Allowing this slow growth ensures that your hedge will always have a fresh new layer of leaves to present to the world. When, after 10 or 15 years of this slow growth, the hedge becomes too large, cut it back very hard early one spring and let it begin its slow growth again.

If you shear a *large-leafed hedge*, leaves will be cut in half, giving the hedge a butchered look. So, if you have the time, it is better to prune these hedges one branch at a time with a pair of hand shears. Make your cuts inside the layer of foliage so that they will be hidden, leaving only fresh, uncut leaves on the surface.

To avoid "bare bottom"—to keep a hedge leafed out to the ground, shape your hedge so that the top is narrower than the bottom, letting light to the whole side of the hedge. Leaves that do not get enough light will drop off. Shaping a hedge in this way is especially important on the northern side, or on any portion of the hedge that is in the shade of a tree.

Solving hedge problems

Hedges that have been allowed to go their own way for a number of seasons develop several common problems. Usually they have grown too tall and spindly, have bare, unattractive spots, or lean into the neighbor's yard. All of these maladies can

The bottom of this Pittosporum *hedge is bare because it is shaded by the wide top.*

be taken care of with corrective pruning.

■ **Hedges that have grown too tall and floppy** have usually been allowed to grow too fast. Hedges should be "built" carefully. Regular pruning to encourage a sturdy structure will strengthen a mass of wispy stems. If the structure of the hedge is very weak, it can be cut back to the ground and allowed to grow up again, this time at a more sensible growth rate.

Espalier

Pinch the young plant at the height of the first wire. Let three shoots develop from this pinch. Tie the middle shoot to the second wire, and train the other two along the first wire.

Continue this pinching and tying until six shoots are trained along the wires. Maintain this form by pinching any vigorous shoots as soon as they appear.

Hedges

Hedges are formed by repeated shearings. Each shearing of a fine-textured hedge should be ¼ inch higher than the previous one.

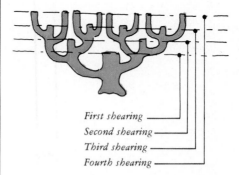

First shearing ———
Second shearing ———
Third shearing ———
Fourth shearing ———

Each time you shear a little higher, more buds break, increasing the density of the hedge. The surface is composed of fresh, new growing points, even in an old hedge. The cut stubs are buried in foliage as the hedge grows.

■ **Hedges with bare, leafless undersides** develop because there is not enough light at the bottom of the hedge. The problem may also be aggravated by a lack of water and nutrients. The solution? Cut the hedge back heavily to stimulate new growth at the bottom, then shape it properly as it grows. Water it regularly and see that it has enough fertilizer for vigorous growth.

■ **A hedge that leans into the neighbor's yard** is often caused by the fact that you are more than likely keeping your side of the hedge trimmed, while your neighbor is letting his or her side grow. One solution is to reduce the height and width of the hedge dramatically, and let it grow back with an even, strong structure. The three- or five-year system of renewal also works well in this case. See page 46. If necessary, plan to prune your neighbor's side when you prune your own to keep the hedge balanced.

■ **Bare spots in a hedge** are caused by old age and repeated shearings without allowing the hedge to grow. The problem can be alleviated by cutting away the dead twigs, branch by branch and then by shearing 1/4 inch outside the last cut in the future.

Revitalizing Old Shrubs

Many times neglected shrubs will need imaginative and dramatic pruning to make them attractive parts of the landscape again. This is often the case with a mature garden that you inherit with a formerly owned house. Look at these shrubs as a natural resource, albeit one that you have to make the best of, and you may be surprised: Many overgrown shrubs can be transformed into valuable landscape assets with sensitive pruning.

Start revitalizing an older shrub by clearing away all weak, thin shoots to open up the plant and allow sunshine to reach the center of the shrub. What this leaves behind are the more massive, older branches, which usually have considerable character. Cut away any branches that point inward or that cross other branches.

Once that phase is complete, step back and take a look at the plant's new form. Does it make an interesting silhouette, or does it still need errant branches trimmed away? Before cutting off any major branches, have someone pull the branch back as far as it will go without breaking it. What does the shrub look like without it? Does the shrub need additional thinning out to make it less massive, or does it need trimming around the edges to give it a more compact, neat look?

Many older shrubs act like small trees, growing to heights never mentioned in catalogs and gardening books. Mature specimens can be the focal point of an entire landscape, especially if the foliage and branches that conceal the trunk are trimmed away. Follow-up thinning the next year can help to revitalize an old specimen. If you're concerned by taking growth

Prune large-leafed hedges with hand shears, hiding the cuts inside the layer of foliage.

away, don't forget that you can plant new shrubs underneath the older ones to make up for the missing foliage. Or you may find the additional space desirable, particularly in a small garden.

If the top portion of a shrub appears hopelessly unattractive to you, cut the shrub completely to the ground. As long as the plant has the strength to push out new shoots and leaves, it will have enough strength to replace what you cut off. By cutting off the shrub as close to the ground as possible, new growth will be generated from the roots rather than from older branches. The best time to take this drastic kind of action is in late winter or early spring. The resulting new growth should be treated like that of a new shrub.

Be cautioned, however, that some shrubs will be killed by cutting them back too far. If you don't know how a shrub will respond to a radical pruning, head one branch back to a leafless stub to see how it responds. If the stub sprouts new growth, the shrub can probably be safely cut back.

This properly pruned hedge forms a neat enclosure for Pieris *shrubs.*

Renewal Pruning

Renewal pruning is a special form of pruning that can keep deciduous shrubs, particularly flowering varieties, young and vital, no matter how old they are. Using this method, many shrubs are alive and healthy today, particularly in the heritage gardens of the eastern states, after more than a century of growth. Even though the plant itself may be over 100 years old, this technique produces branches that never get more than three to five years old.

Every year or two, prune out a few of the oldest canes at ground level. Removing this old wood opens up the top to let light and air into the interior of the shrub and to encourage growth from the base, which eventually renews the top of the plant.

Three-year renewal

Each year a deciduous shrub produces many shoots from the plant's base or roots. Prune the shrub so that 1/3 of the shoots will be 1 year old, 1/3 will be 2 years old, and 1/3 will be 3 years old. When you prune, remove crossing limbs or any dead or diseased branches. Then cut out most of the three-year-old wood. This will induce new shoots to spring up, leaving the desired number to form the first-year shoots the following year.

The only other pruning necessary is to reduce the total height of the shrub to keep it within the bounds you desire, while preserving its natural form. Removing the third-year wood every year after blooming will guarantee that you always have young, healthy wood to produce the biggest and healthiest flowers. A bonus of this three-year renewal system is that it also results in healthier plants, because older wood is more susceptible to insects and disease than young, strong shoots.

Five-year renewal

This approach is the same as the three-year system, except that you spread the steps over five years. Slow-growing shrubs respond well to the two additional years of thinning. Keep in mind that you will not get as many new shoots each year with this method as you would with the three-year system.

Flowering shrubs that have a moundlike habit of growth, such as summer-flowering spireas, florists hydrangea, and vitex, should be pruned yearly by thinning out some of the weakest canes and cutting the rest back to varying heights so that the flowers will not all bloom at the same level.

Shrubs for Special Treatment

A few shrubs need special treatment. Three common ones are rhododendrons, azaleas, and roses.

Rhododendrons and Azaleas

Rhododendrons and azaleas require more grooming than pruning. The spent flower heads of rhododendrons should be removed—this is called *deadheading*. Tips

The small buds beside this rhododendron flower are next year's flowers and leaves. Be careful not to break them off when removing spent flowers.

of azaleas should be pinched out to make the plants bushier. Be careful not to take next year's buds with the flowers, though.

Your finger tips will work nicely to do most of the pruning of this group of plants. Only older plants that have become leggy, sparse, or damaged will require a few cuts from your hand pruners or loppers.

The difference between a rhododendron and an azalea lies in where the buds are placed, and this causes them to need different types of pruning. Since a rhododendron bud is always found just above the leaf rosette, you must cut there, just above the bud (see photograph). On an azalea, however, the bud is concealed under the bark along the entire branch. This means that you can cut anywhere along the branch and still be near a bud, which will then break into growth.

Rhododendrons must have their spent flowers removed. If seed pods are left on the plant, they consume much of the energy that could go into flowers or leaves. Hold the branch with the faded flower in one hand and with the other hand carefully snap off the flower head with a slight sideways pressure, taking care not to harm the growth buds below. These buds are next year's flowers and leaves. If you injure the flower buds, there will be no flowers the next year.

If your plant is too tall to handpick thoroughly, little harm will be done. Try using a hose to wash the dead petals away. Many rhododendrons tend to bloom in alternate years if they are not deadheaded.

Azaleas require even less pruning than rhododendrons. They should be tip pinched, particularly when young, to produce bush-

ier plants. Do this within a couple of weeks after the plant blooms.

When azaleas become older, stronger pruning may become necessary. Because of the distribution of buds along the entire branch, an azalea can be cut anywhere. You can even shear an azalea, although few people do so, because it destroys the natural shape of the plant. Shearing produces a crop of flowers at the sheared surface.

To rejuvenate an older azalea that has grown too woody and leggy, prune it over a period of two or three years. The first year, cut back the oldest branches to within 10 to 12 inches of the ground. The next year, do the same thing, and repeat this the third year. Never cut off more than 1/3 of the plant each year. In this way, you can safely transform the azalea into a compact, bushy plant that will produce an astonishing crop of flowers.

Roses

Roses are a varied lot, and their pruning varies with their growth patterns. But these growing patterns can be lumped into two groups for pruning purposes: those that bloom all summer and those that only bloom for a couple of weeks in the spring.

Spring-blooming roses are pruned when they finish blooming. Prune fairly heavily to encourage new growth, which will bear next year's flowers.

Roses that bloom all summer are mostly the hybrid teas, floribundas and grandifloras that are our most popular garden roses today. They are pruned when they are dormant, usually in late spring just before they begin growth.

The first step is to remove all dead wood and weak twigs. Then, open up the center of the plant by pruning out canes that cross inward. Next, remove any canes that have gotten too old to produce well. These canes make branches that are weak, twiggy, and branch frequently. The branches will be rough and dark with old bark and may show signs of decay.

At this point you must decide how vigorous the rose is. If the new canes are ¾ of an inch in diameter or more, the rose is vigorous. Slender canes indicate a weaker shrub. The general rule is, the less vigorous the rose, the harder you prune it.

This may sound backwards, but think of pruning as removing growing points (dormant buds) that will use up energy when the shrub begins growing in the spring. The fewer buds you leave, the more energy each growing point will have.

Leave about six canes on the most vigorous roses. On the least vigorous, leave only three. Head back the canes about ⅓ of their length. Heading them back more will make fewer, but larger, flowers. A lighter pruning produces more, smaller flowers and a more attractive shrub shape. Prune heavily if you want to produce flowers for cutting, lightly if you want a more attractive garden shrub.

As you pick each flower, cut its stem back to just above a leaf that has five leaflets. This leaf will have a strong dormant bud at its base to make a good replacement cane.

If your rose bush gets too high by the end of the summer, or if you want cut

When picking roses, cut the stem just above a five-leaflet leaf. This leaf will have a strong bud to make the next flower.

flowers with long stems, cut each stem back so that only the two lowest five-leaflet leaves are left. This will slow the growth of the shrub.

Climbing roses have long canes that do not flower; flowers are produced on laterals. If the climber is on a trellis, untie it

and lay it on the ground. Prune out all but the strongest three to five canes and cut all the laterals back to two or three buds. Tie the canes back up on their trellis without cutting them shorter. Instead, arch these over at the top. This will stop their upright growth and encourage laterals to form.

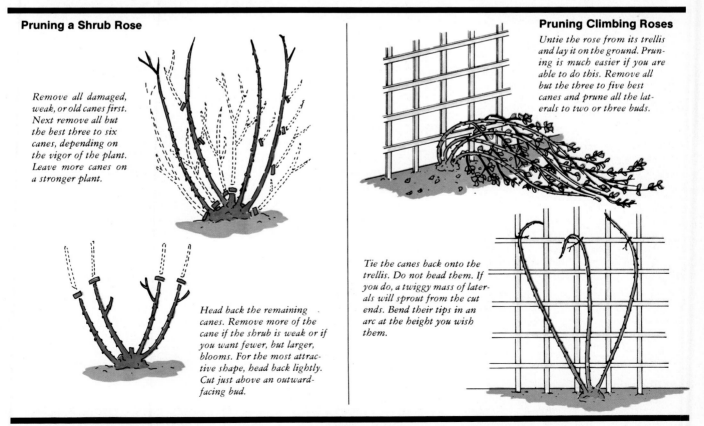

Pruning a Shrub Rose

Remove all damaged, weak, or old canes first. Next remove all but the best three to six canes, depending on the vigor of the plant. Leave more canes on a stronger plant.

Head back the remaining canes. Remove more of the cane if the shrub is weak or if you want fewer, but larger, blooms. For the most attractive shape, head back lightly. Cut just above an outward-facing bud.

Pruning Climbing Roses

Untie the rose from its trellis and lay it on the ground. Pruning is much easier if you are able to do this. Remove all but the three to five best canes and prune all the laterals to two or three buds.

Tie the canes back onto the trellis. Do not head them. If you do, a twiggy mass of laterals will sprout from the cut ends. Bend their tips in an arc at the height you wish them.

Solving Problems

The key to solving plant problems easily is to recognize the symptoms as soon as they occur and act promptly to treat the problems while they are small. Here are pictures and descriptions of some of the most common symptoms, with cures and cultural methods to keep them from returning.

Checking Up on the Garden

You can hold problems in the garden to a minimum if you are on familiar terms with the plants that are growing there. A daily stroll, with an eye for problems as well as beauty, is the most pleasant and least time-consuming way to do your trouble-shooting.

What do you look for? Anything that looks irregular: a chewed leaf, compacted soil, stunted foliage, a branch that's growing too far in the wrong direction. If you are familiar with your plants, you will be quick to see obvious clues, but you'll also be able to avoid trouble *before* problems happen.

You know things about your own garden that no book can tell you. Colors, textures, and vigor are all indicators of overall plant health, and only you know what's normal for your garden and what's not. If you make it a point to get into the garden as often as possible, you'll notice subtle but important changes that signal the current health conditions of your plants.

"At the first sign of attack" are the most important words in the business of pest and disease control. If you are in the garden on a regular basis, you'll be able to take care of the first aphids, the first brood of beetles, or the first attack of mildew.

◄

These sharpshooter leafhoppers are related to aphids and scale. Like them, they feed by piercing plant tissue and sucking the juices. The damage they do ranges from transmittal of virus diseases to nearly complete defoliation. A few leafhoppers cause little damage, but a heavy infestation can mottle leaves and even make them drop off.

Taking frequent walks through your garden keeps you up to date on potential problems. The beauty of this azalea garden lies in part with its glowing health.

Avoiding Problems

A vigorously growing shrub is less susceptible to injury from insects and diseases than one that is under stress from lack of water or nutrients—bark beetles, borers, and sucking insects do more damage during or after a drought than at any other time.

Besides having to put up with insects and diseases, plants sometimes suffer from the unwitting hand of the gardener. Sensitive gardeners are aware that plants have lives of their own. Someone who respects plants doesn't carelessly skin the bark from a trunk with a lawn mower, which could allow entrance to borers or fungi. The good gardener also makes sure that a plant is not being choked by a tie that has become too tight, and is careful not to cut the roots of nearby plants when rototilling.

Here are some common-sense steps that will help to avoid problems in your garden:

■ Keep old leaves picked up—they are often the source of infection for various diseases and a safe hiding place for many damaging insects. (Composted leaves, however, pose no problem.)

■ Keep your pruning shears *sharp,* and use them correctly (see page 43). Bark tears easily and heals slowly. Many insects and diseases will attack *only* if there is an opening in the bark.

■ Pull weeds early, before they offer competition to surrounding plants and distribute seeds for future generations of weeds. The best time to pull them is when the ground is soft from rain or watering. (See the section on page 52 for weed control.)

■ Spray at the first sign of disease or insect attack. The control you receive will be more rapid and complete and the plant will suffer less damage from pests and diseases.

■ Remove and destroy (by burning or throwing away) any diseased flowers or fruits. Disease spores can live on them from one season to the next.

■ Practice a thorough cleanup before winter sets in. Remove debris and other likely homes for overwintering insects and diseases.

■ To promote healthier plants and to keep the weed population to a minimum, keep a 3-inch layer of mulch on all open areas of ground. Cover the root zones of shrubs, as well, but keep the mulch pulled back a few inches away from stems or trunks. See page 39 on mulching.

Local Help for the Asking

Local problems in the control of pests and diseases are under constant study by the research departments of your state university. Publications on the results of their studies are available to home gardeners at the office of your county extension agent. Many are available free, others at a nominal cost.

How do you tap this storehouse of regionalized information? The office of your county extension agent is listed in your telephone book, grouped under the county government offices. A phone call will bring you a list of available publications. Or you can write the state extension office for a list of publications and the addresses of the county agents.

Local or regional arboreta and botanic gardens can be valuable resources, as well. You will find them listed in the yellow pages of your telephone book.

Problems To Look For

Small Leaves

Leaves that seem unusually small indicate low vigor, which can be caused by a number of factors. The plant may be under stress from lack of water or nutrients, it may be planted in a location not suitable to its variety, or the soil may be compacted or of poor structure.

Sometimes the problem isn't caused by a deficiency, but merely by a response to light levels. Leaves that are exposed to

These leaves came from the same shrub. The leaf on the left is from a high, outside branch exposed to full sun. The leaf on the right is from a bottom branch that never received full sun. Sun leaves are smaller and lighter colored than shade leaves. Shade leaves are darker, larger, thinner, and more delicately textured.

the direct rays of the sun are smaller, thicker, and a lighter green than leaves that grow in the shade. Shade leaves tend to be large, thin, and dark green. Here, the "problem" is a phenomenon of nature, and nothing to worry about.

Solutions: Aside from the quantity of light, small leaf growth derives from cultural reasons, which means that once good gardening practices are followed, the symptoms will disappear. Pages 36 to 39 offer good advice on watering and fertilizing procedures. Before you purchase a plant for a specific location, be sure its needs match the conditions of the site. To match up plants and locations, check the Plant Selection Guide starting on page 54.

To avoid the problems of poor soil, read up on soil types on page 20.

Sudden Wilting

If a whole shrub suddenly wilts, the cause may be a gopher. Gophers eat roots, bulbs, and tubers. Occasionally, whole plants will disappear into their holes. Gophers tunnel 6 to 12 inches under the soil and push the excavated dirt out to the surface, leaving small mounds of finely particled earth behind.

If gophers are not the problem, make sure the water you apply is getting down to the roots of the plants. The soil can

Armillaria root rot on a daphne.

often look damp on the surface, but be dry just a few inches below. See page 36.

If the shrub is healthy, except for a single branch that is wilted, it may have been physically damaged in some way. Check to see if the branch is broken.

The damage may also be caused by insects that bore into stems and trunks. Some plants, such as junipers and lilacs, are more susceptible to borer damage than others. If you suspect borers, look at the base of the damaged branch for small holes.

Some wilt, crown rot, and root rot diseases also cause severe wilting.

Solutions: Gophers are best controlled by traps, available at your local garden center. Follow the directions carefully. Gas bombs and poisoned bait are also available for gopher control; they should be used only with the greatest caution.

If a branch has been physically damaged, but has not been completely broken off, it can often be saved. Mend the break with stretch tape or budding rubbers (used for grafting), available at your nursery or garden center. Or you can make a splint by tying a stick to the branch to hold the pieces together; you may even be able to nail the break closed. Then cover the broken area with a thick coat of grafting compound to keep the tissue from drying out. If the branch cannot be saved, prune it off. New branches will quickly grow to fill in the gap.

Control borers with sprays containing lindane. Contact your local extension agent for recommended spraying times in your area.

If the problem is a wilt disease or root rot, a radical pruning will sometimes save the shrub. See pages 45 and 46.

Dead Spots on Tips and Edges of Leaves

Tan or light brown spots on the tips and edges of leaves are usually caused when a plant becomes so dry at one point that the extremities of the leaves become burned. If the dead tips and edges are dark or black, the burn is probably caused by excess fertilizer, deicing salts, or other salts in the soil.

Solutions: If the problem was caused by the plant drying out in the past, there is nothing that will restore the green color to the old burned leaves. If the leaves are too unsightly, you can prune them off. In most cases, new leaves will replace the old ones. Avoid the problem by following a good watering program in the future.

If burning is caused by a build-up of salts or too much fertilizer, leach them from the soil by applying unusually large quantities of water to the root zone at a moderately slow rate. Simply place a hose at the base of the plant and let it run slowly for several hours.

New Leaves Turn Yellow

When new leaves are abnormally yellow, it's a clear signal that the shrub is not getting something it needs. The most common reason for yellow new growth is an iron deficiency. Sufficient iron is usually in the soil, but it may be fixed into insoluble compounds that are unavailable to the

An iron deficiency symptom in an azalea.

plant. This problem frequently occurs to azaleas and other acid-loving plants that are growing in neutral or alkaline soil and to many plants that have highly alkaline soil or water.

Solutions: Apply a chelated iron fertilizer. Chelating agents are synthetic organic substances that have the property of maintaining copper, manganese, zinc, and iron in a water-soluble form so that they can be readily absorbed by plants.

At the same time, apply sulfur or iron sulfate to help make the soil more acid. Use an acid-reaction fertilizer like azalea food or ammonium sulfate to keep the soil from becoming alkaline again.

Holes in Leaves

Holes are the telltale signs that a hungry insect has been feeding on your plant. Some of the most common pests are caterpillars, beetles, and snails and slugs.

Caterpillars are the larvae of moths and butterflies. They come in all sizes and

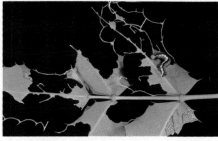

Barberry looper on a mahonia.
Snails are a problem especially in the West.

colors, either naked or hairy—some are even decorated with tufts and spines. Their names usually correspond to their appearance, their hosts, or their way of life, such as leafrollers, bagworms, and leaf skeletonizers.

Leafrollers and tiers are caterpillars that feed inside leaves that are rolled or tied together. The banded woolybear is the larva of the tiger moth. Touch it and it rolls into a ball. Webworms and tent caterpillars build unsightly "tents" in forks and crotches of plants, and crawl from these protected places to feed on foliage. Or they web together needles or leaves, usually at the ends of branches, and feed beneath the webs.

Loopers, inchworms, measuring worms, cankerworms are all caterpillars with the same movement. They double or loop when they crawl. These worms usually feed on new foliage in the spring.

Beetles are a huge and diverse group of insects that includes many beneficial as well as destructive species. Ladybird beetles (ladybugs) and black ground beetles feed on aphids, grubs, and other harmful insects, and should be protected.

If you see the holes, but cannot see what is doing the damage, either the insects have left or they do their eating at night. Check with a flashlight when it is dark to see if you can catch the pests in action. Prime suspects are *snails or slugs,* which hide in damp places during the day and feed at night or in wet weather.

Solutions: Spray with orthene or malathion. If snails or slugs are the problem, use snail and slug bait.

No Flowers

A flowering shrub that doesn't flower is a real disappointment to its owner. Some shrubs may simply need to grow a few more years before they are mature enough to flower. Another cause is the lack of enough sunlight. Most flowering shrubs bloom better when they receive more light. If the location is too dark, the foliage may look admirably healthy and lush, but there won't be enough light to promote blooming.

If some shrubs are overfertilized or fertilized at the wrong time of year, their flower production goes down. The nitrogen in a complete fertilizer is used by the plant primarily to promote green vegetative growth. The foliage may be lush, but it is thriving at the expense of the flowers. Shrubs that flower on the sides of branches, rather than at the tips, are most likely to respond in this way.

Fewer flowers may also appear if plants are pruned during the wrong season or simply if they don't receive enough water.
Solutions: If the plant is not receiving enough light, is it possible to prune overhanging branches that block the sun? If not, you should probably move it to a lighter location. See page 31 for techniques of transplanting.

Check to make sure that your fertilizer applications are timely—the general principles of when to add nutrients are discussed on page 38. If you suspect the problem is too much nitrogen, switch to a fertilizer that has a lower percentage of nitrogen, or use one without any nitrogen at all, at least for a year. Several different formulations (0–10–10, 5–10–10) are available specifically to promote better blooming. For more about fertilizer formulations, see page 38.

If you think you have been limiting flower production by pruning at the wrong time, read the section on when to prune your shrubs (pages 41 to 47), and check for the specific pruning needs of your plants in the "Plant Selection Guide." As for watering, see pages 36 and 37 for helpful tips on watering practices.

Green or Brown Hopping Insects

Pass your hand near a shrub infested with leafhoppers, and these little wedge-shaped, green or brown pests will jump out at you. They have piercing mouth parts and feed on all kinds of plants and trees. Usually they suck the sap from the undersides of leaves, causing a loss of color; a stippled, wilted appearance; and a general loss of health and vigor. Some species inject a toxic substance as they feed, causing leaves to wilt. Leafhoppers are also carriers of many plant virus diseases.

Solutions: Spray leafhoppers with orthene or malathion.

Leafhoppers are common in most parts of the country, and a few does not usually harm a shrub. But if they swarm in great clouds when disturbed, they should be controlled.

White Clouds of Insects

When you shake or disturb a plant that's infected with adult whiteflies, what appear to be little clouds of snowflakes will billow out at you. Adult whiteflies are 1/16 inch long, wedge shaped, and pure white. But it's the pale green, brown, or black nymphs that do most of the damage. Whitefly nymphs are small, flat scales that suck juices from the undersides of leaves and secrete honeydew. In time, infested leaves become pale, mottled, and may turn yellow and die. Whiteflies are a year-round pest in warm-winter areas, and a summer pest where winters are cold.

Solutions: The whitefly larvae may be controlled in the winter with an oil-based dormant spray. Follow the directions on the label carefully. At other times, orthene or malathion are effective.

Oldest Leaves Drop Off

Some shedding of the oldest leaves is natural, but if it occurs at an alarming rate, it could be caused by a number of factors. The most common one is insufficient sunlight. It may be that the location does not receive enough light or that the way the plant is shaped inhibits the sun from reaching the bottom leaves. This is often the case with hedges that have been allowed to grow wider at the top than the bottom. Other causes include the stress caused by lack of water or insufficient nutrients.

It is normal for many evergreen plants in dry climates to lose some of their older leaves at the beginning of summer. After the new leaves have grown, older leaves turn yellow and drop, usually in May or June.

Solutions: If the plant just doesn't receive enough light where it is, the only solution is to move it. If the plant's shape is causing the problem, judicious pruning can make the difference. Selectively prune the top growth to allow sunlight to reach the entire plant. Avoid plant stress with good watering practices and by fertilizing regularly. See pages 36 and 38.

Older Leaves Turn Yellow

A lack of nitrogen causes the older leaves on a shrub to yellow. The growing tips usually remain green, but the new leaves are smaller than normal. Nitrogen, in varying amounts, is a component of all complete fertilizers. During the growing season there must be an adequate supply of nitrogen in the soil for normal growth to take place and to give leaves and stems their characteristic healthy, green color. Another possible source of yellowing is a lack of good drainage.

Solutions: If a lack of nitrogen is the cause, regularly fertilize the plants with a complete fertilizer (one that contains the three primary nutrients—nitrogen, phosphorus, and potassium). If poor drainage is the problem, it may be necessary to move plants to another location. Follow the transplanting directions on page 31 carefully.

Black Smudges or a Sticky Secretion on Leaves

An unsightly black, sooty covering on branches and leaves is called sooty mold. It is not a leaf disease, and the damage it does is chiefly in its appearance. Sooty mold is a secondary problem, caused by the presence of scale or aphids. This mold does not obtain nourishment from the plant, but rather from a sugary secretion called honeydew left by aphids and scale insects.

Scales are tiny sucking insects that have shells. They can be white, red, brown, or black. Eventually, scale insects can seriously reduce a plant's vitality. Foliage will pale and needles or leaves drop off prematurely. Heavy infestations may even kill branches, and sometimes an entire shrub.

*Left: Kuno scale on a pyracantha.
Right: Aphids on a rose bud.*

Aphids are usually green or brown and frequently cluster at the growing tips of leaves to suck the plant's juices. The honeydew they secrete attracts ants. Left to their own devices, aphids can be very debilitating.

Solutions: The mold is hard to wash off and most gardeners resort to pruning away affected branches and leaves. The best defense against sooty mold is to get rid of scale and aphids before they can secrete quantities of honeydew.

Except when they are in their "crawler stage," usually in the spring, scale insects are immobile, protected by their shells from predators and most insecticides. When deciduous plants are out of leaf, when the daytime temperature is above 50° F, and when no frost is forecast for the next 24 hours, scale can be smothered with an oil-based dormant spray. In most regions, these conditions are met in the winter, but in colder regions, oil spray may be applied in late fall or early spring. Whatever the season, plants must be completely dormant. Follow the directions on the label—some plants can be damaged by oil-based sprays.

Scale can also be controlled with orthene or malation during the crawler stage. Spray three times at 7- to 10-day intervals in May and June.

To control aphids, use orthene, diazinon, or malathion. Spray three times at two-week intervals to catch the eggs as they hatch.

Weeds Around and Under Shrubs

Weed control around mature shrubs is rarely a problem—the area under properly tended shrubs is usually too shaded for most weeds to grow. However, in parts of the garden that are newly planted, you may have a weed problem for the first couple of seasons.

Solutions: The best way to control most weeds that grow under shrubs is to keep a year-round mulch on top of the soil. See page 39 for mulching procedures. Any weeds that do push through will be easy to pull.

There are two kinds of herbicides that deal with weeds. One is used before weeds occur, or after you have cleaned the area completely of existing weeds; and the other kills existing weeds. Follow the directions carefully when using weed control chemicals. If misused, they can kill or damage your shrubs and other plants.

Chemicals that stop weeds from sprouting are called *pre-emergence* products, and usually come in a dry, granular form. They have no effect on existing weeds, but keep seeds from sprouting for up to a full growing season.

Sprays that kill existing weeds come in many formulations, and perform several different functions. Some products kill any vegetative growth they touch. They are called *nonselective* weed killers. Others are *selective* weed killers that kill one type of vegetation but don't harm another.

White Powder on Leaves

Powdery mildew looks just like its name: a white, powdery mass that usually affects young leaves, shoots, and buds. Heavy infestations can distort young shoots and

Powdery mildew on rosebuds.

stunt foliage. The disease is spread by wind and encouraged by warm, humid days, followed by cool nights. The fungus overwinters on fallen leaves, inside stems, and on bud scales.

Solutions: Sulfur dust or other fungicides will usually control powdery mildew. Treatment should be started at the first sign of the disease and continued routinely.

It is also helpful to do a thorough garden cleanup in the fall. Rake up and destroy or dispose of fallen leaves and stems.

You can also help to avoid this problem by not wetting the leaves of plants in the late afternoon or evening; give the plants a chance to dry off before evening settles in.

Spots on Leaves

Spots on leaves can be the symptom of a fungus disease or, more rarely, a bacterial infection. The spores of the fungus are carried by the air or in water, and are made worse by humid spring and summer weather. The spots may appear in different colors: red, brown, black, or yellow.

Leaf spot on an ash.

Solutions: Leaf spot diseases are usually not serious; they can be controlled with fungicides applied on a regular basis, according to the manufacturer's directions.

Because the sources of some of these diseases live in plant debris—leaves, refuse, fruits, and the like—a thorough and regular garden cleanup can help to avoid leaf spot. Burn or remove refuse from your garden.

Fungus diseases can be largely prevented by pruning and spacing plants to allow for good air circulation and by allowing enough time between sprinkler irrigation and nightfall for plants to dry out.

Hose-end sprayers are particularly good for spraying large or tall shrubs.

Spraying Equipment

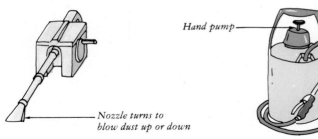

Nozzle turns to blow dust up or down

Dusters: *A fan blows a stream of air that carries the dust into the foliage. They are the simplest of pesticide applicators, requiring no mixing or washing.*

Hand pump

Pressure sprayers: *An air pump builds up pressure in the tank that forces the spray from the nozzle. Because of the slow application, they are best for restricted areas and small shrubs.*

Spoons and bowls are needed for measuring and mixing concentrates. Use a sieve to strain lumps before pouring diluted wettable powders into the sprayer.

Precautions When Using Chemicals

Many pesticides, fungicides, and herbicides are available for the control of pests, diseases, and weeds. The two most important steps in pest and disease control are proper identification of the pest or disease and correct application of the product. Whenever you use a chemical spray, be sure to follow the steps outlined below.

Mixing

For your safety and for best results, read and be sure you understand the *entire* label before using any garden chemical, and follow the directions faithfully.

When mixing these chemicals, always work on a clean, firm surface near a water source. Measure all products carefully to ensure their proper dilution. Never make up more of a solution than you need at one time.

Do not eat or smoke while mixing or spraying, and wash your hands thoroughly when you're done.

Spraying

With pesticides, application is at least half the battle. You must be sure to cover the pests and their hiding places adequately, as the label directs.

Never spray any plant that is suffering from a lack of moisture. Water deeply and thoroughly a day before spraying.

Avoid spraying altogether if the air temperature is above 85° F or if it is exceptionally windy. In hot weather, some chemical formulations may burn the foliage; and when it is windy, it is difficult to keep the spray from drifting to areas where it is not wanted.

The label will instruct you either to spray just enough to wet the foliage or to spray to the drip point, where the leaf surfaces are holding all the spray they can, and any more will drip off. In either case, be sure to cover all plant surfaces thoroughly. Don't forget the bottoms of leaves and both sides of stems and twigs.

Cleaning Up

Thoroughly rinse the sprayer before putting it back on the shelf. Also, rinse out empty chemical containers that you intend to dispose of—never burn empty containers. Allow the sprayer to drain upside down for 30 seconds. Then rinse thoroughly with water and allow to dry before storing.

Plant Selection Guide

One of the most valuable tools for a gardener is a good plant list. Here are 20 lists, including a special list of dwarf shrubs for small-space gardening, followed by complete descriptions and pictures of each shrub. Select shrubs for special effects, for particular uses in the garden, or for problem locations.

When faced with a new catalog, list, or encyclopedia of plants, the avid gardener is like a child at a candy shop—breathless and overwhelmed at the delightful variety of choices. There are well over 6,000 shrubs in horticultural commerce, and more are being added to the list every day. We have tried to simplify this vast array somewhat, and have narrowed our guide down to a mere 500 or so shrubs that we consider the best or most popular. Flip through it to enjoy the breadth of beauty available to you, noting the selections that catch your eye the most. Let our handy shrub selection lists guide you quickly to the best shrub for your particular problem. Turn to a single plant entry when you have a question about a particular shrub. Or read the "Plant Selection Guide" from beginning to end to become intimately aware of the infinite variety within the beautiful world of shrubs.

Plant Names

There are two major types of names used to refer to plants: common names and botanical names. Common names, while they are in some cases more charming or easier to pronounce, have the disadvantage of lacking a central authority to keep them straight. One plant can have many different common names, varying from region to region, even person to person. Or the same common name in one part of the country may refer to an entirely different plant in another.

◀

From top to bottom: Pinus mugo *var.* mugo Euonymus japonica *'Aureomarginata',* Juniperus horizontalis, *and* Nandina domestica *'Nana Purpurea'.*

Since anyone can (and they do!) make up new common names for plants at whim, some standard is necessary to sort out the inevitable chaos. The International Code of Nomenclature for Cultivated Plants is the worldwide authority for horticultural names. The code ensures that every plant has one, and only one, correct identification: the botanical name. Always in Latin, this name is divided into two parts. The *genus* is analogous to a human surname, indicating a general group of plants. For example, *Acer* is the generic name for a maple. The *species* is a more specific category within a genus, and is indicated by a specific epithet following the genus: *Acer palmatum* is a specific maple, Japanese maple.

A *variety* is a further subdivision of a species, and is distinguished by the ability to pass on its identifying traits through its seed. It is usually discovered by accident or in the wild. Botanical varieties are indicated in Latin, follow the species name, and are preceded by the abbreviation "var." *Acer palmatum* var. *dissectum* is the laceleaf Japanese maple.

A *cultivar* is similar to a variety, except that it passes on its particular traits either through seed or vegetative reproduction, such as cuttings or grafting. It is usually the product of deliberate horticultural development. Cultivars are set off by single quotation marks (or the abbreviation "cv."), are rarely in Latin, and either follow the name of the species or the variety, as in *Acer palmatum* var. *dissectum* 'Crimson King'. When referring to a generalized group of plants, often the term "varieties" refers both to botanical varieties and cultivars: "Many varieties of the Japanese maple are not shrubs."

The pleasing complements of foliage color and texture, flower color, and overall form in this garden are the result of careful selection.

In this book all plants are listed alphabetically by their botanical names. You can cross-refer to them from the common names listed in the index. Don't be surprised, however, if you have difficulty finding a particular common name—it is impossible to list them all. Some plants have several hundred!

Selecting a shrub

In the heading for each plant entry, you will find a range of hardiness zones, indicating the northern and southern limits of the parts of the country in which it can be grown. A slightly modified version of the USDA Plant Hardiness Zone Map is below. Locate your zone on it and use it as a reference when you conslut this guide. This kind of information should be used with discretion, however. Local conditions of temperature, rainfall, and other hardiness factors can vary radically from the norms of the surrounding region. Even within a single garden, microclimates can make the difference of an entire zone. In general, however, if we err, it is on the conservative side.

In order to simplify the process of shrub selection, we have treated only lightly the range of cultivars a particular plant may offer to the gardener. Many plants (junipers and other dwarf conifers, for example) present such a huge number of cultivars that an entire volume might not even cover them all. Moreover, cultivars are best selected on a highly regional basis. This can best be accomplished by using the expertise and experience of your local nursery, which is tailored to the exact requirements of your area.

Most of the shrubs included in this guide are popular enough to be offered by most nurseries in regions where they can be grown. A few, however, may be too new, too difficult to propogate, or too expensive to be widely available, and this is indicated in the description. In such cases, you may need to search a bit harder to find them. Your nursery may be able to special-order them for you (usually quite expensive), or you may be able to locate them in mail-order or specialty firms. Your local university, arboretum, or botanic garden may be further sources of assistance.

Climate Zones of the United States

Use this zone map to find your climate zone. Zone recommendations with a B after the zone number refer to the warmer part of that zone. Remember that these zones are approximate, based on average data, and that your local climate can be warmer or colder, especially in mountain regions.
This map is based on the USDA map of climate zones.

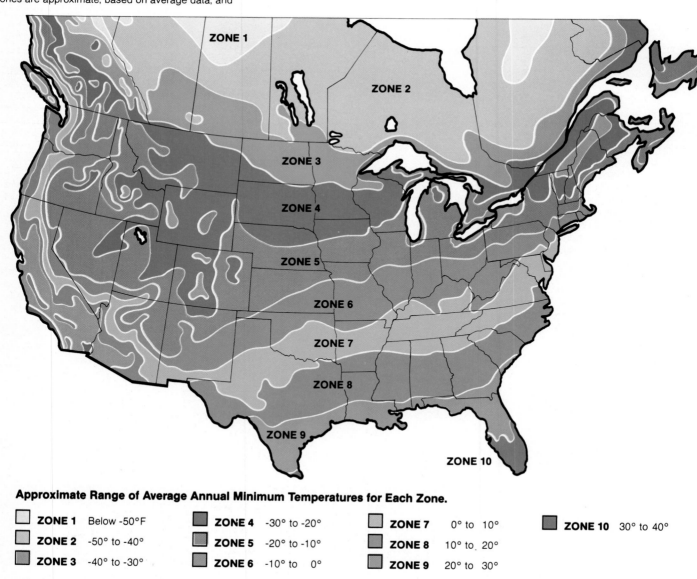

Approximate Range of Average Annual Minimum Temperatures for Each Zone.

ZONE 1 Below -50°F	**ZONE 4** -30° to -20°	**ZONE 7** 0° to 10°	**ZONE 10** 30° to 40°
ZONE 2 -50° to -40°	**ZONE 5** -20° to -10°	**ZONE 8** 10° to 20°	
ZONE 3 -40° to -30°	**ZONE 6** -10° to 0°	**ZONE 9** 20° to 30°	

Plant Selection Lists

When searching for that "just right" shrub to answer a particular problem or need, organized lists can be particularly helpful. Use the lists that follow to direct you to the appropriate description in the Plant Selection Guide.

Shrubs with Colorful Foliage the Year Around

Bright golds, reds, purples, and blues can be available in your garden all year long if you shop for shrubs with colorful foliage. Deciduous plants are included in the list below, and evergreen varieties are marked with an asterisk. All should be located with care, since brightly colored leaves usually make a very bold statement in the landscape.

Acer palmatum var. *dissectum* Laceleaf Japanese Maple, cultivars 'Crimson King', reddish; 'Flavescens', yellowish-green; 'Garnet', reddish; 'Ornatum', reddish; 'Ozakazuki', yellowish; 'Purpureum', deep red; and 'Reticulatum', green, yellow, and pink

Aucuba japonica Japanese Aucuba, cultivars 'Crotonifolia', green and yellow*; 'Picturata', green and yellow*; 'Sulphur', green and yellow*; and 'Variegata', green and yellow*

Berberis thunbergii Japanese Barberry, cultivars 'Aurea', yellow; 'Crimson Pygmy', reddish; 'Sheridan's Red', red; and 'Variegata', white and green

Berberis thunbergii var. *atropurpurea*, purple

Chamaecyparis lawsoniana—Lawson False Cypress, cultivars 'Forsteckensis', gray-green, and 'Pygmaea Argentea', yellow*

Chamaecyparis obtusa Hinoki False Cypress, 'Mariesii', green tipped with white*

Chamaecyparis pisifera Japanese False Cypress, cultivars 'Aurea Nana', yellow*; 'Boulevard', gray*; 'Golden Mop', yellow*; 'Nana Variegata', green and white*; and 'Plumosa Rogersii', yellow*

Cornus alba 'Argenteo-marginata' —Variegated Tartarian Dogwood, cultivar, 'Spaethii', green and yellow

Cotinus coggygria Smoke Tree, cultivars 'Daydream' and 'Velvet Cloak', both purple

Daphne odora Winter Daphne, cultivar 'Marginata', green and yellow

Eleagnus pungens Silverberry, cultivars 'Maculata', green and yellow*; 'Marginata', green and white*; and 'Variegata', green and yellow*

Euonymus fortunei Winter Creeper, cultivars 'Emerald and Gold', green and yellow*; 'Emerald Gaiety', green and white*; 'Golden Prince', green and yellow*; and 'Gracilis', green and white*

Euonymus japonica Evergreen Euonymous, cultivars 'Albomarginata', green and white*; 'Aureomarginata', green and yellow*; 'Gold Center', green and yellow*; 'Golden', green and yellow*; 'Microphylla Variegata', green and white*; 'President Gauthier', green and white*; 'Silver King', green and white*; and 'Silver Queen', green and white*

Hydrangea macrophylla Bigleaf Hydrangea, cultivar 'Tricolor', green, white, and yellow

Juniperus chinensis Chinese Juniper, cultivars 'Armstrong', gray*; 'Blaaw', gray*; 'Old Gold', yellow*; 'Pfitseriana Aurea', yellow*; and 'Plumosa Aureovariegata', yellow*

Juniperus chinensis var. *sargentii*, gray*

Juniperus communis Common Juniper, cultivar 'Depressa Aurea', yellow*

Juniperus conferta Shore Juniper, gray-blue*

Juniperus horizontalis Creeping Juniper, gray or blue*

Juniperus procumbens Japanese Garden Juniper, gray*

Juniperus sabina Savin Junipera, cultivars 'Broadmoor', gray*; 'Skandia', gray*; and 'Variegatus', gray and white*

Juniperus scopulorum Rocky Mountain Juniper, cultivars 'Lakewood Globe', gray-blue*; and 'Table Top Blue', blue-gray*

Kerria japonica Japanese Kerria, cultivars 'Aureovariegata', green and yellow; 'Aureo-vittata', green and yellow stems; and 'Picta', green and white

Leptospermum scoparium New Zealand Tea Tree, cultivars 'Gaiety Girl', reddish*; and 'Waringi', reddish*

Leucothoe fontanesiana Drooping Leucothoe, cultivar 'Girard's Rainbow', green, white, and pink*

Ligustrum × ibolium Ibolium Privet, cultivar 'Variegata', green and yellow

Ligustrum japonicum Japanese Privet, cultivar 'Silver Star', green and white*

Ligustrum ovalifolium California Privet, cultivar 'Aureum', green and yellow*

Ligustrum × vicaryi Golden Privet, yellow

Myrtus communis Myrtle, cultivars 'Compacta Variegata', green and white*; and 'Variegata', green and white

Nandina domestica Nandina, cultivar 'Nana Purpurea', purplish*; and 'Variegatus', green and white

Osmanthus heterophyllus Holly Olive, cultivars 'Purpureus', purplish*; and 'Variegatus', green and white

Photinia × fraseri, red*

Pieris forestii, Chinese Pieris, red new growth*

Pieris japonica Japanese Pieris, reddish new foliage*; and cultivar 'Variegata', green and white

Pittosporum tobira 'Variegata',—Japanese Pittosporum 'Variegata', green and white*

Platycladus orientalis Oriental Arborvitae, cultivars 'Aurea Nana', yellow*; and 'Compacta', gray-green*

Prunus cistena Purple-leafed Sand Cherry, purple

Rosmarinus officinalis Rosemary, gray*

Taxus baccata English Yew, cultivars 'Aurea', yellow*; 'Elegantissima', green and yellow*; and 'Washingtonii', yellow*

Taxus cuspidata Japanese Yew, cultivar 'Aurescens', yellow*

Thuja occidentalis American Arborvitae, cultivars 'Aurea', yellow*; 'Lutea', yellow*; and 'Umbracilifera', gray-blue*

Aucuba japonica 'Crotonifolia'

Cornus alba 'Sibirica'

Shrubs for Winter Interest

There are those who say you can never know the true inner beauty of a plant until it drops its leaves. A shrub's structure, bark, stem, twigs, and buds offer a kaleidoscope of winter textures to look at. The effects may be delicate and subtle or bold and dramatic, but the shrubs listed here are worth braving the cold for a stroll through the winter landscape, or at least staring out the window.

Acer palmatum var. *dissectum* Laceleaf Japanese Maple

Aronia arbutifolia Red Chokeberry

Cornus alba Tartarian Dogwood

Cornus sericea Red-osier Dogwood

Corylus avellana 'Contorta'—Harry Lauder's Walkingstick

Cytisus × praecox Warminster Broom

Genista species—Broom

Hamamelis species—Witch Hazel

Ilex decidua Possum Haw

Ilex verticillata Common Winterberry

Kerria japonica Japanese Kerria

Lagerstroemia indica Crape-myrtle

Magnolia species

Myrica pensylvanica Northern Bayberry

Rhus copallina Flameleaf Sumac; Shining Sumac

Rhus typhina Staghorn Sumac

Rosa hugonis Father Hugo Rose

Rosa virginiana Virginia Rose

Fuchsia × hybrida

Shrubs that Tolerate Shade

There are many qualities of shade, and some plants adapt especially well to a particular one. Most shrubs can tolerate the partial shade of high tree branches, even though they might prefer full sun. In the following list, however, you will find shrubs that do well in the shade more than most. Most of these plants perform best in partial shade; the few that tolerate deep shade are marked with an asterisk (*). Realize that "deep shade" does not mean total darkness—all plants require a minimum of light to survive.

Aesculus species—Horse Chestnut; Buckeye
Aucuba japonica Japanese Aucuba*
Calycanthus floridus Carolina Allspice; Strawberry Shrub
Camellia japonica Common Camelia
Camellia japonica Common Camellia
Chamaecyparis species—False Cypress
Choisya ternata Mexican Orange
Clethra alnifolia Summersweet; Sweet Pepperbush
Coprosma species
Cornus alba Tartarian Dogwood
Cornus sericea Red-osier Dogwood

Euonymus species
Euonymus alatus Burning Bush; Winged Euonymus
Fuchsia × hybrida Common Fuchsia
Fuchsia magellanica Hardy Fuchsia
Gardenia jasminoides Gardenia
Hamamelis species—Witch Hazel
Hydrangea species
Ilex species—Holly
Kalmia latifolia Mountain Laurel
Kerria japonica Japanese Kerria*
Leucothoe fontanesiana Drooping Leucothoe
Ligustrum species—Privet
Mahonia species—Oregon Grape; Holly Grape*
Myrtus communis Myrtle
Nandina domestica Nandina; Heavenly Bamboo
Osmanthus species—Devilweed*
Pieris species*
Pittosporum species
Prunus laurocerasus English Laurel
Rhododendron species—Rhododendron; Azalea
Taxus species—Yew*
Tsuga canadensis 'Pendula'— Sargent's Weeping Hemlock
Viburnum davidii David Viburnum
Viburnum × juddii Judd Viburnum
Viburnum tinus Laurustinus
Viburnum trilobum American Cranberrybush Viburnum

Cytisus hybrids

Shrubs for the Coldest Winters

If you live in the northern Plains States, the mountains, or in northern latitudes where a more limited plant selection is the rule, the following list will direct you immediately to the appropriate shrubs. You may be surprised to find a wider selection than you thought possible.

Arctostaphylos uva-ursi Kinnikinick, Zone 2
Caragana arborescens Siberian Peashrub, Zone 2
Clethra alnifolia Summersweet; Sweet Pepperbush, Zone 3
Cornus alba Tartarian Dogwood, Zone 2
Cornus sericea Red-osier Dogwood, Zone 2
Genista tinctoria Common Woadwaxen, Zone 2
Ilex glabra Inkberry, Zone 3
Juniperus communis Common mon Juniper, Zone 2
Juniperus horizontalis Creeping Juniper, Zone 3
Juniperus virginiana Eastern Redcedar, Zone 2

Lonicera tatarica Tatarian Honeysuckle, Zone 3
Myrica pensylvanica Northern Bayberry, Zone 3
Picea species—Spruce, Zone 2
Pinus mugo var. *mugo*—Dwarf Mugo Pine, Zone 2
Potentilla fruticosa Bush Cinquefoil, Zone 2
Prunus cistena Purple-leafed Sand Cherry, Zone 2
Prunus tomentosa Nanking Cherry; Manchu Cherry, Zone 2
Rhododendron canadense Rhodora, Zone 2
Rhododendron lapponicum Lapland Rhododendron, Zone 3
Rosa rubrifolia Redleaf Rose, Zone 2
Rosa rugosa Rugosa Rose; Saltspray Rose, Zone 2
Syringa vulgaris Common Lilac, Zone 3B
Tamarix ramosissima Fivestamen Tamarix, Zone 2
Thuja occidentalis American Arborvitae, Zone 2
Viburnum trilobum American Cranberrybush Viburnum, Zone 3

Potentilla fruticosa 'Goldfinger'

Drought-tolerant Shrubs

In many parts of the United States, watering is the gardener's most time-consuming chore. Whether your garden is in the arid deserts of the Southwest, the Mediterraneanlike, summer-drought climates of the West Coast, or the dry plains of the Prairie States, planting shrubs from the following list can help to make your gardening easier.

Arctostaphylos species—Manzanita
Aronia arbutifolia Red Chokeberry
Aucuba japonica Japanese Aucuba
Berberis species—Barberry
Callistemon citrinus Lemon Bottlebrush
Caragana arborescens Siberian Peashrub
Ceanothus species—Wild Lilac
Cistus species—Rockrose
Coprosma species
Cotinus coggygria Smoke Tree
Cotoneaster species
Cytisus × praecox Warminster Broom

Eleagnus species
Euonymus japonica Evergreen Euonymus
Genista species—Broom
Hypericum species—St. Johnswort
Juniperus species—Juniper
Lagerstroemia indica Crapemyrtle
Leptospermum scoparium New Zealand Tea Tree
Ligustrum species—Privet
Myrica pensylvanica Northern Bayberry
Myrtus communis Myrtle
Nandina domestica Nandina; Heavenly Bamboo
Nerium oleander Oleander
Osmanthus species—Sweet Olive
Photinia species
Potentilla fruticosa Bush Cinquefoil
Punica granatum Pomegranate
Raphiolepis indica India Hawthorne
Rhus species—Sumac
Rosmarinus officinalis Rosemary
Tamarix species Tamarisk
Xylosma congestum Shiny Xylosma

Hibiscus rosa-sinensis

Shrubs for City Dwellers

Consider the following shrubs if you live in areas that have high atmospheric pollution. Most of these shrubs are also fairly tolerant of the restricted sunlight, reduced air circulation, and poor soils of the urban garden.

Aesculus parviflora Bottlebrush Buckeye

Aronia arbutifolia Red Chokeberry

Berberis thunbergii Japanese Barberry

Caragana arborescens Siberian Peashrub

Chaenomeles speciosa Common Flowering Quince

Cornus alba Tartarian Dogwood

Cornus sericea Red-osier Dogwood

Eleagnus species

Forsythia species

Hamamelis virginiana Common Witch Hazel

Hibiscus rosa-sinensis Chinese Hibiscus

Hibiscus syriacus Shrub Althea; Rose of Sharon

Hydrangea species

Hypericum species—St. Johnswort

Ilex crenata Japanese Holly

Ilex glabra Inkberry

Juniperus species—Juniper

Kerria japonica Japanese Kerria

Lagerstroemia indica Crapemyrtle

Ligustrum species—Privet

Lonicera species—Honeysuckle

Magnolia stellata Star Magnolia

Mahonia aquifolium Oregon Grapeholly

Malus sargentii Sargent's Crabapple

Myrica pensylvanica Northern Bayberry

Nerium oleander Oleander

Philadelphus coronarius Sweet Mockorange

Pittosporum tobira Tobira; Japanese Pittosporum

Potentilla fruticosa Bush Cinquefoil

Pyracantha coccinea Scarlet Firethorn

Rhus species—Sumac

Ribes alpinum Alpine Currant

Rosa rugosa Rugosa Rose; Saltspray Rose

Rosa wichuraiana Memorial Rose

Spiraea × bumalda Bumalda Spirea

Spiraea vanhouttei Vanhoutte Spirea

Syringa vulgaris Common Lilac

Taxus baccata English Yew

Taxus cuspidata Japanese Yew

Vaccinium corymbosum Highbush Blueberry

Viburnum opulus European Cranberrybush

Syringa

Shrubs with Fall Foliage Color

Many deciduous shrubs are very striking in the fall when their foliage changes to various shades of red, orange, yellow, and bronze. Frequently, their colors are brighter and longer lasting than many flowers. Consult the list that follows for some of the more spectacular choices.

Abelia × grandiflora Glossy Abelia

Acer palmatum var. *dissectum* Laceleaf Japanese Maple

Aronia arbutifolia Red Chokeberry

Berberis thunbergii Japanese Barberry

Clethra alnifolia Summersweet; Sweet Pepperbush

Cornus alba Tartarian Dogwood

Cornus sericea Red-osier Dogwood

Cotinus coggygria Smoke Tree

Cotoneaster divaricata Spreading Cotoneaster

Cotoneaster horizontalis Rockspray Cotoneaster

Enkianthus campanulatus Redvein Enkianthus

Euonymus alatus Burning Bush; Winged Euonymus

Fothergilla major Large Fothergilla

Hamamelis species—Witch Hazel

Hydrangea quercifolia Oakleaf Hydrangea

Lagerstroemia indica Crapemyrtle

Mahonia aquifolium Oregon Grapeholly

Nandina domestica Nandina; Heavenly Bamboo

Paxistima canbyi Canby Paxistima

Punica granatum Pomegranate

Shrubs with Fragrant Flowers

For those who love the beautiful fragrances that only flowers can bring, the following list should prove helpful. Many more shrubs in the "Plant Selection Guide" are fragrant, but these are the most powerful ones. One tip: To experience most intensely fragrance in your garden, take a stroll on days that are humid and mild. Early to mid-morning and evening hours can be especially delightful times for the nose.

Buddleia davidii Summer Lilac; Orange-eye Buddleia

Calycanthus floridus Carolina Allspice; Strawberry Shrub

Ceanothus Wild Lilac, western species

Choisya ternata Mexican Orange

Clethra alnifolia Summersweet; Sweet Pepperbush

Daphne species

Eleagnus species

Escallonia species

Fothergilla major Large Fothergilla

Gardenia jasminoides Gardenia

Hamamelis species—Witch Hazel

Leucothoe fontanesiana Drooping Leucothoe

Rhus copallina

Rhododendron arborescens Sweet Azalea

Rhododendron kaempferi

Rhododendron Knapp Hill-Exbury Hybrids

Rhododendron schlippenbachii Royal Azalea

Rhododendron vaseyi Pinkshell Azalea

Rhus species—Sumac

Rosa virginiana Virginia Rose

Vaccinium corymbosum Highbush Blueberry

Viburnum × carlcephalum Fragrant Snowball Viburnum

Viburnum dilatatum Linden Viburnum

Viburnum × juddii Judd Viburnum

Viburnum opulus European Cranberry Bush

Viburnum plicatum var. *tomentosum* Doublefile Viburnum

Viburnum trilobum American Cranberrybush Viburnum

Lonicera species—Honeysuckle

Magnolia stellata Star Magnolia

Malus sargentii Sargent's Crabapple

Osmanthus species—Devilweed

Philadelphus species—Mockorange

Pittosporum napaulense Golden Fragrance Plant

Pittosporum tobira Tobira; Japanese Pittosporum

Prunus tomentosa Nanking Cherry; Manchu Cherry

Rhododendron arborescens Sweet Azalea

Rhododendron × 'Loderi'—Loderi Hybrid Rhododendron

Rhododendron nudiflorum Pinxterbloom Azalea

Rhododendron vaseyi Pinkshell Azalea

Rhododendron viscosum Swamp Azalea

Rosa spinosissima Scotch Rose

Rosa wichuraiana Memorial Rose

Syringa vulgaris Common Lilac

Viburnum × burkwoodii Burkwood Viburnum

Viburnum × carlcephalum Fragrant Snowball Viburnum

Viburnum carlesii Koreanspice Viburnum

Viburnum × juddii Judd Viburnum

Viburnum tinus Laurustinus

Rosa gallica 'Officinalis'

Fast-growing Shrubs for Quick Solutions

Patience is one of the most difficult traits for a gardener to practice. The shrubs listed below can help ease the wait, since they grow more quickly than most. Don't expect them to leap up into their adult size overnight, however. Most will still take at least two seasons before they resemble a mature effect. Understand that many are not for more permanent solutions: In general, the faster a shrub grows, the shorter it lives.

Abelia × grandiflora Glossy Abelia

Berberis species—Barberry

Callistemon citrinus Lemon Bottlebrush

Caragana arborescens Siberian Peashrub

Ceanothus species—Wild Lilac

Choisya ternata Mexican Orange

Cistus species—Rockrose

Coprosma species

Cornus alba Tartarian Dogwood

Cornus sericea Red-osier Dogwood

Cotoneaster dammeri Bearberry Cotoneaster

Cotoneaster divaricata Spreading Cotoneaster

Cytisus × praecox Warminster Broom

Eleagnus species

Escallonia species

Forsythia species

Fuchsia × hybrida Common Fuchsia

Hydrangea macrophylla Bigleaf Hydrangea

Hypericum calycinum Aaronsbeard St. Johnswort

Kerria japonica Japanese Kerria

Kolkwitzia amabilis Beautybush

Ligustrum species—Privet

Lonicera species—Honeysuckle

Nerium oleander Oleander

Philadelphus species—Mock-orange

Prunus laurocerasus English Laurel

Pyracantha species—Firethorn

Rhus copallina Flameleaf Sumac; Shining Sumac

Rhus typhina Staghorn Sumac

Rosa species—Rose

Salix species—Willow; Osier

Spiraea species—Spirea

Tamarix species—Tamarisk; Salt Cedar

Weigela florida Old-fashioned Weigela

Shrubs that Attract Birds

Nearly all shrubs, except for the low dwarfs, provide attractive habitats and protection for birds. The ones on this list provide an especially valuable nesting or hiding environment, or else tasty fruits in different seasons.

Arctostaphylos species—Manzanita

Aronia arbutifolia Red Chokeberry

Berberis species—Barberry

Buddleia species—Butterfly Bush

Callistemon citrinus Lemon Bottlebrush

Ceanothus species—Wild Lilac

Cornus species—Dogwood

Cotoneaster species

Eleagnus species

Escallonia species

Fuchsia species

Ilex species—Holly

Juniperus species—Juniper

Ligustrum species—Privet

Lonicera species—Honeysuckle

Mahonia species—Oregon Grape; Holly Grape

Malus sargentii Sargent's Crabapple

Myrica pensylvanica Northern Bayberry

Photinia species

Prunus species

Pyracantha species—Firethorn

Rhus species—Sumac

Rosa species—Rose

Rosmarinus species—Rosemary

Salix species—Willow; Osier

Symplocos paniculata Sapphireberry; Asiatic Sweetleaf

Vaccinium species—Blueberry; Huckleberry

Viburnum species

Viburnum dilitatum

Shrubs for Containers

Some shrubs adapt more easily to container culture than others. They may be naturally small, with a relatively contained root system. Or, they may dwarf more easily by judicious pruning of roots and shoots. The shrubs that usually do best in containers already have a naturally neat and compact growth habit, or else can easily be kept that way. Use the following list as a guide for adding greenery and color to your deck or patio. Also see the list of dwarf shrubs on page 64 for more ideas about shrubs that are suitable for container gardening.

Acer palmatum var. *dissectum* Laceleaf Japanese Maple

Aucuba japonica Japanese Aucuba

Buxus microphylla Littleleaf Boxwood

Buxus sempervirens Common Boxwood

Camellia species

Chamaecyparis species—False Cypress

Corylus avellana 'Contorta'—Harry Lauder's Walking Stick

Cotoneaster horizontalis Rockspray Cotoneaster

Euonymus fortunei Winter Creeper

Fuchsia × hybrida Common Fuchsia

Gardenia jasminoides Gardenia

Hydrangea macrophylla Bigleaf Hydrangea

Ilex cornuta Chinese Holly

Ilex crenata Japanese Holly

Ilex vomitoria 'Nana'-Yaupon

Kalmia latifolia Mountain Laurel

Lagerstroemia indica Crapemyrtle

Leptospermum scoparium New Zealand Tea Tree

Leucothoe fontanesiana Drooping Leucothoe

Ligustrum species—Privet

Lonicera nitida Box Honeysuckle

Mahonia bealei Leatherleaf Mahonia

Mahonia lomariifolia

Myrtus communis Myrtle

Nandina domestica Nandina; Heavenly Bamboo

Rhododendron

Nerium oleander Oleander

Osmanthus species—Devilweed

Picea species—Spruce, dwarf varieties

Pieris japonica Japanese Pieris

Pinus Pine, dwarf varieties

Pittosporum tobira Tobira; Japanese Pittosporum

Prunus laurocerasus English Laurel

Punica granatum Pomegranate

Pyracantha species—Firethorn

Raphiolepis indica India Hawthorn

Rhododendron species—Rhododendron and Azalea

Rosmarinus officinalis Rosemary

Taxus species—Yew

Thuja species—Arborvitae, dwarf varieties

Tsuga canadensis 'Pendula'—Sargent's Weeping Hemlock

Shrubs with Evergreen Foliage

Evergreen shrubs, whether broad-leafed or coniferous, add their own special warmth to the garden. Their presence is especially appreciated in the winter, when the landscape might otherwise feel bleak and uninviting. In the following list, the abbreviation SE following an entry indicates that a plant is semievergreen—partially or totally dropping its leaves in the northern limits of its hardiness range.

Abelia × *grandiflora* Glossy Abelia, SE
Arctostaphylos species—Manzanita
Aucuba japonica Japanese Aucuba
Berberis darwinii Darwin Barberry
Buxus species—Boxwood
Callistemon citrinus Lemon Bottlebrush
Calluna vulgaris Scotch Heather
Camellia species
Ceonothus Wild Lilac, western species
Chamaecyparis species—False Cypress
Choisya ternata Mexican Orange
Cistus species—Rockrose
Coprosma species
Cotoneaster dammeri Bearberry Cotoneaster
Cotoneaster horizontalis Rockspray Cotoneaster, SE
Cytisus × *praecox* Warminster Broom
Daphne species
Eleagnus pungens Silverberry
Erica species—Heath
Escallonia species
Euonymus fortunei Winter Creeper

Euonymus japonica Evergreen Euonymus
Euonymus kiautschovicus Spreading Euonymus
Gardenia jasminoides Gardenia
Genista species—Broom
Hypericum calycinum Aaronsbeard St. Johnswort
Hypericum × *moseranum* Goldflower St. Johnswort
Hypericum patulum Goldencup St. Johnswort, SE
Iberis sempervirens Evergreen Candytuft
Ilex cornuta Chinese Holly
Ilex crenata Japanese Holly
Ilex glabra Inkberry
Ilex × *meserveae* Meserve Hybrid Holly
Ilex vomitoria Yaupon Holly
Juniperus species—Juniper
Kalmia latifolia Mountain Laurel
Leptospermum scoparium New Zealand Tea Tree
Leucothoe fontanesiana Drooping Leucothoe
Ligustrum × *ibolium* Ibolium Privet, SE
Ligustrum japonicum Japanese Privet
Ligustrum lucidum Glossy Privet
Ligustrum ovalifolium California Privet, SE
Ligustrum 'Suwanee River'
Lonicera nitida Box Honeysuckle
Mahonia species—Oregon Grape; Holly Grape
Myrtus communis Myrtle
Nandina domestica Nandina; Heavenly Bamboo
Nerium oleander Oleander
Osmanthus delavayi Delavay Osmanthus
Osmanthus fragrans Sweet Olive
Osmanthus heterophyllus Holly Olive
Paxistima canbyi Canby Paxistima
Photinia × *fraseri*

Pittosporum tobira 'Variegata'

Photinia serrulata Chinese Photinia
Picea species—Spruce
Pieris species
Pinus species—Pine
Pittosporum species
Prunus laurocerasus English Laurel
Pyracantha coccinea Scarlet Firethorn, SE
Rhododendron carolinianum Carolina Rhododendron
Rhododendron catawbiense Catawba Rhododendron
Rhododendron, Gable Hybrids Gable Hybrid Azalea, SE
Rhododendron impeditum Cloudland Rhododendron
Rhododendron, Indica Hybrids Indian Hybrid Azalea
Rhododendron kaempferi, SE
Rhododendron keiskei Kiesk Rhododendron
Rhododendron lapponicum Lapland Rhododendron

Rhododendron × 'Loderi'—Loderi Hybrid Rhododendron
Rhododendron maximum Rosebay Rhododendron
Rhododendron obtusum Hiryo Azalea
Rhododendron, PJM Hybrids
Raphiolepis indica India Hawthorne
Rosa wichuraiana Memorial Rose, SE
Rosmarinus officinalis Rosemary
Taxus species—Yew
Thuja species—Arborvitae
Tsuga canadensis 'Pendula'—Sargent's Weeping Hemlock
Viburnum × *burkwoodii* Burkwood Viburnum, SE
Viburnum davidii David Viburnum
Viburnum tinus Laurustinus
Xylosma congestum Shiny Xylosma

Thorny Shrubs for Barriers

Beware of these thorny shrubs! Use them wherever you want to keep people away—including yourself. Don't plant them near public places where they will scratch passers-by, lodge in the feet of barefoot children, or attack your knees and hands as you weed beds. As barriers, each of

the following shrubs will prove to be impenetrable.
Berberis species—Barberry
Chaenomeles speciosa Common Flowering Quince
Eleagnus pungens Silverberry
Ilex cornuta Chinese Holly
Osmanthus heterophyllus Holly Olive
Pyracantha coccinea Scarlet Firethorn
Rosa species—Rose

Berberis darwinii

Shrubs for Acid Soils

While most shrubs will tolerate a moderately acid soil (pH 6), many shrubs *require* acid soil in order to thrive. The following shrubs should be considered only if you have, or intend to create and maintain, soil with a pH of 6 or less.

Arctostaphylos uva-ursi Kinnikinick
Calluna vulgaris Scotch Heather
Camellia species
Choisya ternata Mexican Orange
Clethra alnifolia Summersweet; Sweet Pepperbush
Enkianthus campanulatus Redvein Enkianthus
Erica species—Heath
Exochorda species—Pearlbush
Fothergilla species—Fothergilla
Gardenia jasminoides Gardenia
Hydrangea quercifolia Oakleaf Hydrangea
Ilex species—Holly
Juniperus communis Common Juniper
Kalmia latifolia Mountain Laurel

Rhododendron

Leucothoe fontanesiana Drooping Leucothoe
Magnolia species—Magnolia
Mahonia species—Oregon Grape; Holly Grape
Paxistima canbyi Canby Paxistima
Rhododendron species—Rhododendron; Azalea
Tsuga canadensis 'Pendula'—Sargent's Weeping Hemlock
Vaccinium corymbosum Highbush Blueberry

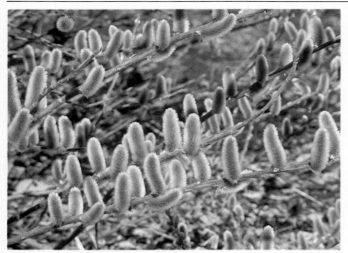
Salix gracilistyla

Shrubs for Wet Soils

For many gardeners, a serious problem is having to work with heavy soil with poor drainage. Often, the low spots in such gardens collect water, which remains for a long time. The following list contains shrubs that perform well in standing water, along with other plants that tolerate a low amount of soil aeration.

Aronia arbutifolia Red Choke-berry

Calycanthus floridus Carolina Allspice; Strawberry Shrub

Clethra alnifolia Summersweet; Sweet Pepperbush

Cornus alba Tartarian Dog-wood

Cornus sericea Red-osier Dogwood

Hamamelis vernalis Vernal Witch Hazel

Hypericum densiflorum Dense Hypericum

Ilex glabra Inkberry

Ilex verticillata Common Winter-berry

Myrica pensylvanica Northern Bayberry

Potentilla fruticosa Bush Cin-quefoil

Rhododendron canadense Rhodora

Rhododendron viscosum Swamp Azalea

Salix gracilistyla Rosegold Pussy Willow

Viburnum cassinoides Witherod Viburnum

Viburnum opulus European Cranberry Bush

Viburnum trilobum American Cranberrybush Viburnum

Shrubs for Ground Covers

Many woody shrubs make excellent ground covers. The selections that follow represent the best of the low, spreading forms. Consider them for covering a steep bank where a lawn is difficult to maintain and where a solution to erosion is needed. Some of them do well in large beds, all to themselves. The list of dwarf shrubs on page 64 indicates by asterisks (*) which ones are suitable for ground covers.

Abelia × grandiflora 'Prostrata'

Abelia × grandiflora 'Sherwoodii'

Arctostaphylos uva-ursi Kinni-kinick

Berberis thunbergii Japanese Barberry, selected varieties

Calluna vulgaris Scotch Heather

Ceanothus Wild Lilac, selected varieties

Chaenomeles, selected varieties

Cistus species—Rockrose

Coprosma × kirkii

Cotoneaster dammeri Bearberry Cotoneaster

Cotoneaster horizontalis Rock-spray Cotoneaster

Erica species—Heath

Hypericum calycinum Aarons-beard St. Johnswort

Iberis sempervirens Evergreen Candytuft

Ilex glabra 'Compacta'

Juniperus chinensis Chinese Juniper, selected varieties

Juniperus horizontalis Creeping Juniper

Juniperus procumbens Japanese Garden Juniper

Juniperus sabina Savin Juniper, selected varieties

Leptospermum scoparium New Zealand Tea Tree, selected varieties

Leucothoe fontanesiana Droop-ing Leucothoe

Lonicera × xylosteoides 'Clavey's Dwarf'

Paxistima canbyi Canby Paxis-tima

Potentilla fruticosa Bush Cin-quefoil

Pyracantha coccinea Scarlet Firethorn, selected varieties

Rosa wichuriana Memorial Rose

Rosmarinus officinalis Rose-mary

Xylosma congestum Shiny Xylosma

Pyracantha coccinea

Shrubs with Showy Fruit

The wise gardener is aware of the all-season values that shrubs can bring, a chief one being attractive fruit. While flowers often last only a week or so, the spectacular fruits of many shrubs can last an entire winter. The following list presents some of the more lavishly beautiful examples of ornamental fruits.

Arctostaphylos species—Manzanita

Aronia arbutifolia Red Chokeberry

Aucuba japonica Japanese Aucuba

Berberis darwinii Darwin Barberry

Berberis koreana Korean Barberry

Berberis thunbergii Japanese Barberry

Chaenomeles speciosa Common Flowering Quince

Cotoneaster dammeri Bearberry Cotoneaster

Cotoneaster divaricata Spread-ing Cotoneaster

Cotoneaster horizontalis Rock-spray Cotoneaster

Cotoneaster multiflora Many-flowered Cotoneaster

Eleagnus species

Euonymus fortunei Winter Creeper, selected varieties

Ilex cornuta Chinese Holly

Ilex verticillata Common Winterberry

Ilex vomitoria Yaupon

Lonicera tatarica Tartarian Honeysuckle

Mahonia species—Oregon Grape; Holly Grape

Malus sargentii Sargent's Crab-apple

Myrica pensylvanica Northern Bayberry

Nandina domestica Nandina; Heavenly Bamboo

Photinia species

Prunus maritima Beach Plum

Prunus tomentosa Nanking Cherry; Manchu Cherry

Punica granatum Pomegranate

Pyracantha coccinea Scarlet Firethorn

Rhus copallina Flameleaf Sumac; Shining Sumac

Rhus typhina Staghorn Sumac

Rosa hugonis Father Hugo Rose

Rosa virginiana Virginia Rose

Symplocos paniculata Sapphire-berry; Asiatic Sweetleaf

Vaccinium corymbosum High-bush Blueberry

Viburnum davidii David Viburnum

Viburnum dilatatum Linden Viburnum

Viburnum × juddii Judd Viburnum

Viburnum opulus European Cranberry Bush

Viburnum plicatum var. *tomentosum* Doublefile Viburnum

Viburnum tinus Laurustinus

Viburnum trilobum American Cranberrybush Viburnum

Erica species

Shrubs that Are Easy To Care For

Any shrub is easy to maintain once the correct conditions for growth are met. The trick is in knowing and creating those conditions. Certain plants can ease that difficulty somewhat, because they are not very finicky. The shrubs listed here adapt to a wide variety of conditions and are pest resistant. While they can almost be left alone, even these plants will benefit from an occasional shot of fertilizer and deep watering during drought.

Abelia × *grandiflora* Glossy Abelia

Aesculus parviflora Bottlebrush Buckeye

Arctostaphylos uva-ursi Kinnikinick

Aronia arbutifolia Red Chokeberry

Aucuba japonica Japanese Aucuba

Berberis species—Barberry

Callistemon citrinus Lemon Bottlebrush

Calycanthus floridus Carolina Allspice; Strawberry Shrub

Caragana arborescens Siberian Peashrub

Chaenomeles speciosa Common Flowering Quince

Cistus species—Rockrose

Clethra alnifolia Summersweet; Sweet Pepperbush

Coprosma species

Cornus alba Tartarian Dogwood

Cornus sericea Red-osier Dogwood

Corylus avellana 'Contorta'—Harry Lauder's Walking Stick

Cotinus coggygria Smoke Tree

Cotoneaster species

Cytisus species—Broom

Deutzia species

Eleagnus species

Euonymus alatus Burning Bush; Winged Euonymus

Exochorda species—Pearlbush

Fothergilla major Large Fothergilla

Genista species—Broom

Hamamelis species—Witch Hazel

Hypericum species—St. Johnswort

Ilex species—Holly

Juniperus species—Juniper

Kerria japonica Japanese Kerria

Kolkwitzia amabilis Beautybush

Lagerstroemia indica Crapemyrtle

Leptospermum scoparium New Zealand Tea Tree

Ligustrum species—Privet

Lonicera nitida Box Honeysuckle

Lonicera × *xylosteoides*

Malus sargentii Sargent's Crabapple

Myrica pensylvanica Northern Bayberry

Myrtus communis Myrtle

Nandina domestica Nandina; Heavenly Bamboo

Nerium oleander Oleander

Osmanthus species—Devilweed

Paxistima canbyi Canby Paxistima

Philadelphus species—Mockorange

Pinus species—Pine

Pittosporum species

Potentilla fruticosa Bush Cinquefoil

Prunus cistena Purple-leafed Sand Cherry

Prunus tomentosa Nanking Cherry; Manchu Cherry

Raphiolepis indica India Hawthorne

Rhus species—Sumac

Rosa species—Rose

Rosmarinus officinalis Rosemary

Spiraea species—Spirea

Symplocos paniculata Sapphireberry; Asiatic Sweetleaf

Taxus species—Yew

Thuja species—Arborvitae

Viburnum species

Xylosma congestum Shiny Xylosma

Nerium oleander

Shrubs for Hedges and Other Formal Shapes

Consider the following shrubs when you plan for a hedge, topiary, or other formal planting. All of them will take close shearing and clipping well.

Abelia × *grandiflora* Glossy Abelia

Berberis thunbergii Japanese Barberry

Buxus species—Boxwood

Chamaecyparis species—False Cypress

Eleagnus pungens Silverberry

Euonymus fortunei Winter Creeper, shrub cultivars

Euonymus kiautschovicus Spreading Euonymus

Euonymus japonica Evergreen Euonymus

Ilex cornuta Chinese Holly, small cultivars

Ilex crenata Japanese Holly

Ilex glabra Inkberry

Ilex vomitoria Yaupon

Juniperus Juniper, selected cultivars

Ligustrum species—Privet

Lonicera nitida Box Honeysuckle

Lonicera × *xylosteoides*

Myrtus communis Myrtle

Osmanthus species—Devilweed

Pittosporum crassifolium

Pittosporum eugenoides

Prunus laurocerasus English Laurel

Prunus tomentosa Nanking Cherry; Manchu Cherry

Pyracantha coccinea Scarlet Firethorn

Rhododendron maximum Rosebay Rhododendron

Rosmarinus officinalis Rosemary

Taxus species—Yew

Viburnum tinus Laurustinus

Xylosma congestum Shiny Xylosma

Buxus sempervirens

Leptospermum scoparium

Shrubs for the Seacoast

Seacoast gardens have their own unique problems—from harsh, constant winds to sandy soil and saline spray. The plants in the list below perform well under these conditions. Usually, they also make excellent choices for desert gardens; see our list for drought tolerance.

Arctostaphylos species—Manzanita

Callistemon citrinus Lemon Bottlebrush

Ceanothus species—Wild Lilac

Cistus species—Rockrose

Coprosma species

Cotoneaster dammeri Bearberry Cotoneaster

Cotoneaster divaricata Spreading Cotoneaster

Cotoneaster horizontalis Rockspray Cotoneaster

Cytisus × *praecox* Warminster Broom

Eleagnus species

Escallonia species

Genista species—Broom

Hibiscus syriacus Shrub Althea; Rose of Sharon

Hydrangea macrophylla Bigleaf Hydrangea

Juniperus Juniper, especially *J. conferta* Shore Juniper

Leptospermum scoparium New Zealand Tea Tree

Lonicera nitida Box Honeysuckle

Myrica pensylvanica Northern Bayberry

Pittosporum crassifolium

Prunus maritima Beach Plum

Raphiolepis indica India Hawthorne

Rosa rugosa Rugosa Rose; Saltspray Rose

Rosa virginiana Virginia Rose

Rosmarinus officinalis Rosemary

Tamarix species—Tamarisk; Salt Cedar

Dwarf Shrubs

The trend toward increased urban dwelling and smaller property lots in the suburbs, coupled with a rising demand for plants that are easy to maintain, has resulted in the increasing importance of an unusual type of plant in the landscape: the dwarf shrub. The term *dwarf* is used in many different ways. Here we mean it to be a small, generally slow-growing shrub that matures to a height of 3 feet or less under normal growing conditions. This eliminates from our consideration the man-made dwarfs created by pruning and restricting root growth—such as container, bonsai, and topiary plants—or by grafting. Dwarf shrubs can have many origins. Some, like heather *(Calluna vulgaris)*, are naturally low growing. Often these plants have evolved under harsh environmental conditions where survival favored those low dwarfs that could evade cold and drying winds by hiding under snow or behind hillocks or rocks. Many alpine plants fall into this category.

Some dwarfs occur as seedling mutations. These mutants can occur in nature—the dwarf Alberta spruce *(Picea glauca* 'Conica'), for example, was accidentally discovered on a walk through the woods. Others, and this is more common, are discovered in a nursery seedling bed. Dwarf shrubs can also originate as bud mutations, called sports, that are vegetatively propagated. A particular type of sport is called a *witches' broom*, in which a dense, compact, and slow-growing mass of twigs arises from a single bud mutation.

Some dwarf shrubs are actually the result of a virus disease that is carefully perpetuated by vegetative propagation. And some are produced by propagating a slow-growing side branch of a larger plant, resulting in a slow-growing dwarf with a prostrate habit. Many of the plants included in our list of dwarf shrubs, especially forms of the coniferous evergreens, are actually trees. Selections of junipers, false cypress, spruces, pines, arbovitae, and hemlock are examples.

Regardless of their origin, the usefulness of dwarf shrubs is virtually limitless. Where garden space is at a premium, they are ideal. Frequently, the unusual character of many varieties inspires the gardener to think of them only as specimens, but don't feel this is the only way dwarf shrubs can be used. Integrate and blend them as you would their larger forms. Dwarfs are excellent in foundation plantings, where their slow, restrained growth provides an easy-care answer to the transition from vertical walls to horizontal lawns and beds. Many dwarf shrubs stay low but spread wide, and are a good choice for that difficult, steep bank. Others have restrained growth in all directions that makes them a perfect choice for edging along drives, walks, borders, and beds—anywhere, in fact, that a neat, low, formal or informal hedge or demarcation is desired.

The generally slow-growing habit of dwarf shrubs can make them easier to care for in the landscape. Pruning and shearing need to be done much less frequently, and feeding requirements are usually fewer. For those dwarf shrubs that are propagated from side branches or juvenile growth parts, special care must be taken to ensure that they do not revert to their more vigorous, upright antecedents. Immediately remove any branches that exhibit a larger growth habit or foliage. This is particularly a problem with some forms of *Euonymus*, false cypress, and juniper. Beware of overfeeding slow-growing dwarfs; they require much less fertilizer than their forbears. For the most part, however, the care of dwarf shrubs is the same as their larger form.

All species in the list that follows have a complete description in the "Plant Selection Guide," where you will find pertinent information on maintenance. The descriptions of the species are generally appropriate to the dwarf forms, except for the element of size.

An asterisk (*) indicates wide-spreading and rapid-growing shrubs that are suitable for ground covers.

Abelia × grandiflora 'Prostrata'

Arctostaphylos uva-ursi Kinnikinick*

Berberis darwinii 'Corallina Compacta'

Berberis thunbergii 'Crimson Pigmy'

Buxus microphylla var. *koreana* 'Tide Hill'

Buxus sempervirens Common Boxwood, cultivars 'Bullata'; 'Suffruticosa', 'Vardar Valley'

Calluna vulgaris Scotch Heather

Caragana arborescens 'Nana'

Ceanothus gloriosus Point Reyes Ceanothus*

Ceanothus griseus var. *horizontalis*

Chamaecyparis lawsoniana Lawson False Cypress, cultivars 'Minima Glauca' and 'Nidiformis'

Chamaecyparis obtusa Hinoki False Cypress, cultivars 'Kosteri', Lycopioides', 'Nana'

Chamaecyparis pisifera 'Squarrosa Minima'

*Coprosma × kirkii**

Cornus sericea 'Isanti'

Cotoneaster dammeri Bearberry Cotoneaster*

Cotoneaster horizontalis Rockspray Cotoneaster, cultivars 'Little Gem' and 'Perpusilla'

Daphne cneorum Garland Flower

Erica carnea Spring Heath

Erica vagans Cornish Heath

Euonymus fortunei Winter Creeper, cultivars 'Azusa', 'Emerald Cushion', and 'Kewensis'

Euonymus fortunei var. *coloratus**

Euonymus japonica Evergreen Euonymus, cultivars 'Microphylla' and 'Microphylla Variegata'

Fothergilla gardenii Dwarf Fothergilla

Fuchsia × hybrida Common Fuchsia

Gardenia jasminoides 'Radicans'

Genista tinctoria Common Woadwaxen

Genista pilosa Silky-leafed Woadwaxen

Genista sagittalis Arrow Broom

Hypericum calycinum Aaronsbeard; St. Johnswort*

Hypericum frondosum 'Sunburst'

Hypericum kalmianum Kalm St. Johnswort

Iberis sempervirens Evergreen Candytuft

Ilex cornuta Chinese Holly, cultivars 'Berries Jubilee', 'Carissa', 'Dazzler', and 'Dwarf Burford'

Ilex crenata Japanese Holly, cultivars 'Border Gem', 'Golden Gem', 'Green Island', 'Kingsville Green Cushion'

Ilex vomitoria 'Nana'

Juniperus chinensis Chinese Juniper, cultivars 'Alba', 'Armstrong', 'Blue Vase', 'Fruitland', 'Mint Julep', 'Pfitzeriana Arctic', 'Pfitzeriana Kallay'

Juniperus chinensis var. *sargentii,** and cultivars 'Compacta',* 'Glauca,*' and 'Viridis'*

Juniperus communis Common Juniper, cultivars 'Compressa', 'Depressa',* 'Gold Beach', and 'Hornibrookii'

Juniperus conferta Shore Juniper,* cultivars 'Blue Pacific' and 'Emerald Sea'

Juniperus horizontalis Creeping Juniper*

Juniperus procumbens Japanese Garden Juniper,* especially 'Nana'

Juniperus sabina Savin Juniper, cultivars 'Arcadia', 'Broadmoor',* 'Buffalo', and 'Skandia'

Juniperus sabina var. *tamariscifolia**

Juniperus virginiana 'Silver Spreader'

Lagerstroemia indica Crapemyrtle, petite series

Leptospermum scoparium New Zealand Tea Tree, cultivars 'Horizontalis', 'Nanum', 'Snow White', and 'Waeringi'

Leucothoe fontanesiana 'Nana'

Lonicera tatarica Tartarian Honeysuckle, cultivars 'Nana' and 'LeRoyana'

Lonicera × xylosteoides, cultivars 'Clavey's Dwarf' and 'Emerald Mound'

Myrtus communis Myrtle, cultivars 'Compacta', 'Compacta Variegata', and 'Microphylla'

Paxistima canbyi Canby Paxistima

Pieris japonica Japanese Pieris, cultivars , 'Crispa', and 'Pygmaea'

Pinus mugo var. *mugo*, Dwarf Mugo Pine, cultivars 'Compacta', 'Gnome', and 'Slavinii'

Pittosporum tobira 'Wheeler's Dwarf'

Platycladus orientalis Oriental Arborvitae, cultivars 'Aurea Nana', 'Bonita', and 'Raffles'

Potentilla fruticosa Bush Cinquefoil

Prunus laurocerasus English Laurel, cultivars 'Mt. Vernon', 'Nana', and 'Otto Luyken'

Punica granatum Pomegranate, cultivars 'Chico' and 'Nana'

Pyracantha Firethorn, cultivars 'Lodense', 'Red Elf' and 'Tiny Tim'

Raphiolepis indica India Hawthorn

Rhododendron canadense Rhodora

Rhododendron impeditum Cloudland Rhododendron

Rhododendron lapponicum Lapland Rhododendron

Rosmarinus officinalis Rosemary, cultivars 'Collingwood Ingram'* and 'Prostratus'*

Spiraea albiflora Japanese White Spirea

Spiraea × bumalda Bumalda Spirea

Spiraea japonica var. *alpina* Japanese Spirea, alpine variety

Taxus baccata English Yew, cultivars 'Nana', 'Pygmaea', and 'Repandens'

Taxus cuspidata Japanese Yew, cultivars 'Aurescens', 'Densa', 'Intermedia', and 'Nana'

Taxus × media 'Berryhilli'

Thuja occidentalis American Arborvitae, cultivars 'Aurea', 'Boothii', 'Ericoides', 'Little Gem', and 'Umbraculifera'

Viburnum davidii David Viburnum

Viburnum opulus European Cranberrybush, cultivars 'Compactum' and 'Nanum'

Viburnum trilobum—'Compactum'

Weigela florida Old-fashioned Weigela, cultivars 'Foliis Purpuriis' and 'Variegata Nana'

Xylosma congestum—'Compacta'

Vibernum opulus 'Nanum'

A Gallery of Shrubs

No description or photograph can be a perfect substitute for a live plant when you are selecting a shrub for your landscape. But locating a mature specimen of a shrub in which you are interested is often difficult or impossible. Consider this guide to be a sort of tour through different regions of the country, whose purpose is to provide a capsule introduction to a wide variety of shrubs. Remember that any plant's requirements are flexible. Indeed, the challenge of proving the "experts" wrong is, for some, one of the greatest joys of gardening. When you run across a shrub that sounds particularly interesting, try to locate a mature, healthy example. Ask your gardening friends who have grown it how satisfied they are with its performance. Best of all, talk it over with your nurseryperson. Most likely, he has had direct experience with your choice, and has probably received considerable feedback over the years from satisfied (or dissatisfied) customers. Don't hesitate to take advantage of his knowledge to answer any question about local adaptation and usefulness that this guide does not answer.

Abelia × grandiflora

Abelia × grandiflora
(uh-BEEL-ee-yuh grandi-i-FLO-ra)

Glossy Abelia

ZONES 6 to 10

Broad-leafed evergreen

(Deciduous in the North)

The hardiest and most free flowering of the abelias, this hybrid makes an effective specimen, informal hedge, grouping, or mass, combining particularly well with broad-leafed evergreens. Showy, pinkish-white flowers cover the plant from July until frost. The finely textured, glossy, deep green summer foliage turns an attractive bronze in the fall. It is deciduous to semievergreen in the North and increasingly evergreen the further south it is grown. The habit is graceful, rounded, and arching. It grows at a medium to fast rate, reaching 4 to 8 feet high and wide. Give it well-drained soil, ½ to full sun, and average watering, and it will prove to be an easy-to-grow, pest-free plant. While it can be sheared easily into formal shapes, doing so seriously reduces flowering. It is probably best to allow it to achieve its natural, graceful shape. Expect frequent winter dieback in northern Zone 6, although the new growth will come back quickly. Older, overgrown shrubs can be renewed by cutting back hard, almost to the ground, in late winter or early spring. Lower forms, such as 'Prostrata' and 'Sherwoodii', make excellent, large-scale ground and bank covers.

Acer palmatum var. dissectum
(AY-sir pawl-MAY-tum)

Laceleaf Japanese Maple

ZONES 6 to 10

Deciduous

For that refined, aristocratic touch, few shrubs can beat this dwarf tree. An open, picturesque form—growing quite slowly 6 to 8 feet in height and width—soft, wispy foliage available in a variety of shades and variegations, and consistently showy fall color all make this an outstanding specimen plant. Consider using it as a focal point for an entryway, near a patio, or naturalized in a woodland understory. Performing beautifully in containers, it makes an excellent bonsai subject.

In Zone 6 the roots of container plants should be given extra protection in the winter—mulch and add extra insulation to the container, or sink it into the ground in a protected spot. Transplant from a container in winter or early spring into well-drained, acid soil (pH 5.5 to 6.5) that is rich in organic matter. Filtered shade is preferable, especially in hot climates, as well as protection from drying winds—especially the cold, drying winds and late frosts of spring—due to this plant's susceptibility to leaf scorch.

Be aware that not all varieties of the Japanese maple are the lace-leafed dwarfs. Some are 15- to 25-foot trees with an extensive range of different foliage qualities. If a shrublike plant is desired, always ask for the lace-leafed types. Some of the better cultivars are 'Crimson King', 'Garnet', 'Flavescens', 'Ornatum', 'Ozakazuki', 'Purpureum', and 'Reticulatum'. Native to Japan, China, and Korea.

Aesculus parviflora

Aesculus parviflora
(ES-kew-lus par-vi-FLO-ruh)

Bottlebrush Buckeye

ZONES 5 to 8

Deciduous

Spectacular late-season flowers, trouble-free foliage (unusual for the buckeyes), and adaptability to heavy shade make this shrub an excellent subject for a specimen, massing and clumping in problem shady areas, such as under large shade trees. Not a shrub for small areas, its open, wide-spreading (8 to 15 feet), suckering habit can be troublesome if not given enough room to grow. The flowers are profuse, large, erect clusters that grow 8 to 12 inches long, are white with red anthers, and bloom from early to late July. *Aesculus parviflora* prefers moist, well-drained soil that is high in organic matter, and it tolerates full sun to heavy shade. Bottlebrush buckeye is native to rich, moist woods from South Carolina to Alabama.

'Roger's' is a superior cultivar that is worth seeking out: It produces huge flower clusters, 18 to 30 inches long, two weeks later than the species, and does not exhibit the suckering habit.

Aesculus pavia (Red Buckeye; Zones 6 to 8), like bottlebrush buckeye, is relatively resistant to most of the leaf diseases that plague the buckeyes. Mildew can still be a problem. However, it will not affect this shrub's long-term vigor. Red buckeye differs largely from bottlebrush buckeye by having bright red flowers in early spring and being less hardy. In size and form it is much the same. *A. pavia* 'Atrosanguinea' has darker red flowers, while 'Humilis' is a low, often prostrate form. Red buckeye is native to the coastal-plain woods, from southeast Virginia to Florida, west to Texas, and north to southern Illinois.

Arctostaphylos uva-ursi

Arctostaphylos uva-ursi
(ARK-toe-STAFF-i-loes OO-va-ER-see)

Bearberry Manzanita; Kinnikinick

ZONES 2 to 8A

Broad-leafed evergreen

A low, mat-forming ground cover with evergreen foliage of pleasing, fine texture, bearberry manzanita is especially useful for poor, sandy soil. Drooping, tiny, bell-shaped flowers —not particularly showy, but attractive—are followed by bright red berries. Relatively slow growing, set plants from containers or flats 2 feet apart for complete cover in about 2 seasons. Bearberry is salt tolerant and therefore makes an excellent beach plant. It is native to northern and arctic Europe, Asia, and North America, where it is found south to Virginia, northern Mexico, and northern California.

In addition to *Arctostaphylos uva-ursi*, over 60 species of *Arctostaphylos* are native to western North America, from southern California to British Columbia. Most are large (10 to 20 feet), open, picturesque shrubs with beautiful gnarled, smooth trunks; startlingly red or reddish bark; grayish-green to deep green, leathery, evergreen foliage; and mildly to quite showy white to deep pink clusters of flowers. Useful as drought-tolerant natives in gardens west of the Rockies, all are quite particular to soil and habitat. Check with your local nursery for the species and cultivar best suited to your garden.

Aronia arbutifolia

Aronia arbutifolia
(a-ROAN-ee-a ar-bute-i-FOAL-ee-a)
Red Chokeberry
ZONES 5 to 8
Deciduous

In addition to spectacular bright red berries in profusion and consistently showy red to purple fall color, the red chokeberry is an easy plant to grow. A distinctly leggy, upright shrub that grows slowly 6 to 10 feet high and 3 to 5 feet wide, this plant is best used in masses and large groups that serve to accentuate the fruit display and diminish its legginess. Naturalized at the edge of woodlands and around ponds and other wet areas, a large planting is like an ocean of red in fall and winter. While tolerant of dry soils and prairie drought, it is also an excellent choice for that problem wet area, and performs admirably in heavy soil. Fruiting is best in full sun, although partial shade is tolerated well. Adaptable and little troubled by pests, the red chokeberry is a care-free plant. Native to thickets in bogs, swamps, wet woods, and occasionally dry soils from Nova Scotia to Florida, and west to Michigan, Missouri, and Texas.

Aucuba japonica

Aucuba japonica
(aw-KEW-ba ja-PON-i-ca)
Japanese Aucuba
ZONES 7B to 10
Broad-leafed evergreen

Valued for its tolerance of heavy shade; its leathery, large, evergreen leaves; and its adaptability to adverse growing conditions, the Japanese aucuba also makes an excellent container plant. Use it in that problem shady area, such as a dim, north-facing entryway, or under densely foliaged trees—it competes well with tree roots. Unpruned, the shrub becomes a leggy, open plant that grows 6 to 10 feet or more tall. Prune to keep it a dense, rounded

shrub by selectively cutting branches back to a leaf node. Bright red berries can be attractive in the fall and winter, but both male and female plants are required to set fruit. Performing well in any soil, and drought tolerant once established, Japanese aucuba still benefits from additional organic matter in the soil when it is planted. This is not a plant for hot, sunny, exposed locations. Native from the Himalayas to Japan. Numerous cultivars are available for different foliage colors, variegations, and shapes.

Berberis darwinii
(BER-ber-iss dar-WIN-ee-eye)
Darwin Barberry
ZONES 8 to 10
Broad-leafed evergreen

This is undoubtedly the showiest barberry in flower, literally covered with bright yellow-orange flowers in early March. It will grow rapidly into an arching, loose shrub, 5 to 10 feet high and 4 to 7 feet wide, with small, evergreen leaves. Its dark blue berries are a decided asset, since they are both beautiful and attract birds. It has a tendency to spread by underground stolons, and will become loose and open in old age unless pruned regularly. Like all barberries, it is not particular to soil and withstands drought well. 'Corallina Compacta' is an especially beautiful cultivar that is valuable for its neat, dense, compact, and rounded shape. Native to Chile.

Berberis koreana

Berberis koreana
(BER-ber-iss kor-ee-AY-na)
Korean Barberry
ZONES 5 to 8
Deciduous

This is the showiest hardy barberry for flower and fruit, bearing spectacular luminous yellow flowers in 3- to 4-inch-long drooping racemes from early to mid-May, followed by profuse bright red berries that persist well into winter. Like the Japanese barberry, it makes an excellent thorny barrier, and is extremely adaptable and trouble free. An individual plant is relatively small, growing to a dense, oval 4 to 6 feet high with slightly less spread. Unfortunately, Korean barberry suckers prolifically from the roots, occasionally outgrowing its bounds and forming large colonies. As such, it is best reserved for large informal hedges, borders, and masses. As a flowering specimen its suckering habit should be well considered. Native to Korea.

Berberis thunbergii
(BER-ber-iss thun-BER-jee-eye)
Japanese Barberry
ZONES 5 to 9
Deciduous

As an extremely easy plant to grow, with impenetrable thorns and dense, shearable foliage, the Japanese barberry is one of the most popular hedge and barrier plants around. Outstanding fall color and mildly effective winter fruits are additional plus points, as are the numerous red-, yellow-, and variegated-leafed cultivars. The plant tends to collect trash, which is particularly unsightly in the winter and irksome to remove due to the vicious thorns. And this is not a plant to garden around: Weeding near it is a thorn-ridden and painful task. Growing at a moderate rate, 3 to 6 feet high and 4 to 7 feet wide, the natural outline of this shrub is upright, arching, and rounded, with a dense profusion of thorny stems and finely textured foliage. Easily transplanted, this barberry is extremely adaptable to nearly any soil, withstands drought well, and performs admirably in full sun or partial shade. Cultivars with colored foliage generally retain their color only if grown in full sun. The cultivar 'Crimson Pygmy' makes a good ground cover for a hot, sunny area, as well as a low hedge. Native from southern Europe across Asia to central China and the Himalayas.

Buddleia davidii
(BUD-lee-a da-VID-ee-eye)
Butterfly Bush
ZONES 5 to 10
Deciduous

An old-time favorite for pretty, fragrant, mid-summer flowers that attract multitudes of butterflies, this shrub is unfortunately wild and unruly in its growth habit. With extremely large leaves and coarse texture, it grows very rapidly into an open, rangy 6 to 10 feet. The flowers are fragrant, 6- to 12-inch-long spikes that appear in July and August on the current season's growth. It is best to treat this shrub as an herbaceous perennial in the rear of a perennial border, pruning it after it flowers each fall by cutting it to within a few inches of the ground. This helps to keep it manageable and increases the number of flowering shoots. While *Buddleia* is susceptible to many different pests, remember that spraying will also eliminate the visitation of any butterflies. Numerous cultivars are available for flower color, ranging from white through pinks and reds to the blues. Native to China.
Buddleia alternifolia (Fountain Buddleia) is hardy to Zone 6, where it does not exhibit the dieback of *Buddleia davidii*. It is also much more graceful and refined, its arching sprays of lilac like flowers appearing in mid-May to June on the previous year's wood. Native to northwestern China.

Buxus sempervirens
(BUX-us semp-er-VYE-rens)
Common Boxwood
ZONES 6 to 10
Broad-leafed evergreen

Shaped as globes and cubes and teddy bears, this is the plant most commonly used in formal gardens to shear into fantastic shapes. Besides topiary and trimmed hedges, the common boxwood also makes an uncommonly beautiful specimen in old age, since it grows

Buxus microphylla 'Compacta'

quite slowly into a gnarled, spreading, and open treelike shrub, 10 to 20 feet in height and width. Most of us know it as a young plant, however, when it is a dainty, rounded, compact shrub. Unfortunately, its usefulness is limited to warm, moist climates that do not exhibit extremes of heat and cold, and it is subject to a wide variety of insect and disease pests. Plant boxwood in a well-drained, moist soil that has been generously amended with organic matter, and mulch heavily to provide a cool, moist root run. Each year prune out the inner dead twigs and remove the fallen leaves that accumulate in the branch crotches. This will help to prevent twig canker disease, which is common in the East. Never cultivate around boxwoods, because they root close to the surface. They will not tolerate drought. Protect them from drying winds and extreme temperatures, and give them partial shade in hot climates, full sun or partial shade elsewhere. Many cultivars are available for increased hardiness and different forms and sizes. 'Northern Find' and 'Vardar Valley' are two of the hardiest (Zone 5). Native to southern Europe, northern Africa, and western Asia.

Buxus microphylla (Littleleaf Boxwood; Zones 6 to 10) is similar to the common boxwood, except that it is slightly hardier and more finely textured, and its foliage usually turns yellow-brown in cold weather. However, 'Tide Hill', 'Wintergreen', and others are cultivars of *Buxus microphylla* var. *koreana* (Korean Boxwood) that are hardy to Zone 5 and retain excellent green foliage all winter long. Cultural instructions and landscape uses are the same as for the common boxwood. Native to Japan.

Callistemon citrinus
(kal-i-STEE-mon si-TRY-nus)

Lemon Bottlebrush

ZONES 9 to 10

Broad-leafed evergreen

Common in the gardens of southern California and Florida, this evergreen, drought-tolerant plant displays bright red, brushlike flowers throughout most of the year, which are effective in the landscape and attractive to hummingbirds. Its fragrant leaves are lemon scented. A massive shrub, growing 10 to 15 feet in height and width into a round-headed, open form, the lemon bottlebrush is best used either as a screen or a tall, informal hedge, or possibly a specimen. It is an excellent choice for the desert landscape, since it tolerates drought and a wide range of soils, including those that are alkaline and saline. Both good drainage and full sun are preferred. Select named varieties from your nursery, since this plant is quite undependable when grown from seed. Cultivars vary according to flower color,

Callistemon citrinus

flower size, and compactness. Native to Australia.

Bank of Calluna vulgaris

Calluna vulgaris
(ka-LOON-a vul-GARE-is)

Scotch Heather

ZONES 5 to 7 (milder on coasts)

Narrow-leafed evergreen

While its finely textured, evergreen foliage; dainty, colorful flowers; and low, restrained habit make this one of the most treasured ground covers or rock garden plants available, the famous Scotch heather can be a finicky, difficult plant to grow. It *must* have perfectly drained soil that also retains moisture well. The best soil is acid (pH 6 or less); sandy or high organic (most authorities recommend ½ coarse sand and ½ peat—volcanic sand is best, if you can get it); and infertile. Too rich a soil causes heather to stretch and decrease flower production. Best in full sun, it will do well in partial shade but will flower less. Mulch well and do not cultivate around the shallow roots. Heather will not tolerate drought. Prune or shear each fall after flowering to maintain compactness and encourage heavier blooming. Dense, many stemmed, mat-forming shrubs with tiny, needlelike evergreen leaves, many cultivars are available for size variation (4 to 24 inches high by 2 feet or more wide), flower color (whites, pinks, purples), time of bloom (midsummer to fall), and foliage color (deep green to yellow or bronze). Native to Europe and Asia Minor.

Calycanthus floridus

Calycanthus floridus
(kal-i-KAN-thus FLOR-i-dus)

Carolina Allspice; Strawberry Shrub

ZONES 5 to 9

Deciduous

For fragrance in bloom and easy care, the Carolina allspice is hard to beat. Plant it wherever you can enjoy the fragrance—near outdoor living areas, under windows, beside screen doors, in the shrub border. The 2-inch, dull, reddish-brown flowers, while merely "interesting" to look at, gloriously permeate the garden with a sweet strawberry scent in mid-May, and often sporadically into July. The shrub grows slowly to a neat, rounded outline, 6 to 9 feet high and 6 to 12 feet wide. It will grow in nearly any soil, but performs best in deep, moist loam. While adaptable to sun or shade, it will not grow as tall in full sun. The shrub transplants readily and is highly resistant to pests. Prune after flowering. Native to moist woods, from Virginia to Florida.

Calycanthus fertilis, another eastern native occasionally mistaken for Carolina allspice, and *Calycanthus occidentalis*, a western native, are similar species, but do not have the pleasing floral fragrance of the Carolina allspice. Since fragrance is the chief motive for acquiring *Calycanthus floridus,* purchase it while it is in flower to ensure positive identification.

Camellia japonica 'Pink Perfection'

Camellia japonica
(ka-MEE-lee-a ja-PON-i-ka)

Common Camellia

ZONES 8 to 10

Broad-leafed evergreen

Beloved by southern gardeners for its large, beautiful flowers in winter and early spring and its dense, polished, dark evergreen foliage, the camellia makes a fine specimen, either standing alone or in a mixed shrub border. It is especially effective when massed or in groups in shady woodland gardens, and blends nicely with other broad-leafed evergreens.

While its size can vary according to cultivars, a height of 6 to 12 feet is common; occasionally in great age it can reach 20 feet or so. Often single trunked and branching well up from the ground, the effect is usually a roundish, densely foliaged mass that is nearly as broad as it is tall.

The flowers are extremely variable—there are over 3,000 named varieties—and normally last for about a month. The blooming season differs according to cultivar, from early (October to January), to mid-season (January to March) and late (March to May). The form of the flower varies from single to double with various degrees of flutes and frills. The colors range from white to red, and the size from 2½ inches to 5 inches in diameter.

Often camellias are lumped with rhododendrons when cultural requirements are discussed, but this is not quite fair. Camellias are not nearly as touchy about soil, and withstand heavy soils better than rhododendrons, but they still appreciate plenty of organic matter and slight acidity (pH 6). Guard against overfertilization and salt build-up in the soil, and give them average watering. Avoid cultivating around their shallow roots.

When necessary, prune immediately after flowering. Many varieties set too many flower buds. If large blossoms are sought, it is best to disbud in midsummer by removing all but 2 flower buds on each branch end, and 1 for every 2 to 4 inches of branch along the stems (the flower buds are the fat round ones; the slender ones are leaf buds).

Petal blight is a serious, disfiguring disease that causes petals to turn an ugly brown. Sanitation is the best control. Remove all fallen petals immediately and dispose of them, and replace the mulch every year. Native to China and Japan.

Camellia sasanqua (Sasanqua Camellia; Zones 7B to 10) is similar to the common camellia, except that it blooms earlier, from autumn to early winter. Again, tremendous variety is available for flower and form. Some are low-growing, sprawling shrubs that are useful for ground covers and espaliers, while others make good hedges or screens. All make good specimens. Native to China and Japan.

Caragana arborescens
(kar-a-GAY-na ar-bor-ESS-enz)

Siberian Peashrub

ZONES 2 to 7

Deciduous

Valuable for a hedge, screen, or windbreak where growing conditions are difficult—especially in the Northern Plains States—the Siberian peashrub contributes bright yellow flowers to the early to mid-May landscape. A large shrub, growing rapidly into a 15-foot high and 12-foot wide sparse, angular and open structure, it is often trained as a small tree. Shearing encourages denser growth, but if a neat, formal hedge is desired, another plant choice would be better. The Siberian peashrub resists most pests, although leafhoppers can be damaging. It grows well in dry, rocky soils and exposed, windy sites, making it an effective answer to a difficult spot. 'Nana', a dwarf form with contorted branches, and 'Pendula', with angular, weeping branches grafted to a standard, are two interesting cultivars. Native to Siberia, Manchuria, and Mongolia.

Caryopteris × clandonensis 'Azure'

Caryopteris × clandonensis
(kare-ee-OP-ter-is klan-doe-NEN-sis)

Blue Spirea; Bluebeard

ZONES 6 to 8

Deciduous

Valuable for a subtle, unusual, blue haze of flowers from mid-August to frost, the blue spirea is most striking when contrasted against white or yellow flowers or massed in large groups. Otherwise, its gray-blue, misty effect can easily get lost in the landscape. The blue spirea usually dies to the ground each winter, growing each year to a loose, open, airy 2- to 3-foot shrub. In milder climates where it does not die back, it will become a gangly, floppy, unattractive shrub. In either case, it is best to plant blue spirea as a perennial in the border, cutting it back to the ground each winter to keep it compact and increase the blooms. Give it average water and good garden soil. 'Azure' has bright blue flowers, as does 'Heavenly Blue', although it is slightly more tender. 'Blue Mist' has light blue flowers.

Caryopteris incana is inferior to *Caryopteris × clandonensis,* although still commonly sold. It is more tender (Zone 7) and has less effective flowers.

Ceanothus griseus var. horizontalis 'Yankee Point'

Ceanothus species
(see-a-NOH-thus)

Wild Lilac

ZONES 8 to 10 in the West

Some broad-leafed evergreen; some deciduous species

This genus of shrubs is generally most useful in West Coast gardens, where over 40 species can be grown. Two deciduous species, *Ceanothus americanus* and *C. ovatus,* are native to eastern North America, but the western evergreen natives are the ones that have the most ornamental interest. Their hallmarks are beautiful, fragrant blue or white flowers and usually glossy, dark evergreen leaves.

Many species and varieties are available, from 8-inch ground covers to 30-foot small trees. The evergreen varieties are intolerant of heavy soils and too much water. Plant them in very rocky, sandy soil and away from sprinklers. Except for the initial season or two of establishment, do not overwater. Plant wild lilac only in full sun. Prune only during the dry summer months to avoid transmitting a deadly canker disease. These shrubs are most effective in large masses, either as ground or bank covers on large, rocky slopes, or as higher, billowing masses. Occasionally, they are used as specimens because of the striking, blue flowers of some cultivars. However, *Ceanothus* tends to become rangy with age, and most live for a relatively short time. Check with your nursery for the species or cultivar most useful to you.

Chaenomeles speciosa
(keen-NOM-uh-leez spee-see-OH-sa)

Common Flowering Quince

ZONES 5 to 9

Deciduous

While this shrub is the most ornamental of the quinces, it still remains a single-season plant whose only assets are early spring flowers that are quite showy for about ten days and a thorniness that is good for barriers. For the other 50 weeks of the year it is mediocre at best. Variable in habit, it is usually a rounded, dense shrub 6 to 10 feet high and as wide, but cultivars are available from prostrate to open to erect forms, some of which are thornless. The plant has an annoying habit of collecting trash, which is painful to extract from the thorny twigs, and which is particularly unsightly in exposed winter branches.

The flowers are effective in late March (late February in the South), especially when massed, and are available in a confusing array of very similar cultivars, from red and scarlet to pink and white. The fruits make good jams and jellies. Common flowering quince is easy to grow and adaptable to a wide variety of conditions and soils, including dry soils and prairie drought. This quince flowers the most prolifically when it is placed in full sun and when it is pruned annually to about 6 inches from the ground immediately after spring bloom. Leaf spots, particularly in wet climates, and scale can be problems, as well as chlorosis in alkaline soils. It will not flower as prolifically in warm winter climates. Native to China.

Chamaecyparis species
(kam-uh-SIP-a-ris)

False Cypress

ZONES 4 to 8, according to the species

Conifer

While the species are all large trees, each is available in a huge variety of dwarf cultivars that can be used as well as coniferous evergreen shrubs. Many *Chamaecyparis* adapt primarily to moderate and moist coastal climates, while a few perform well in the harsher conditions of the Midwest. Care should be taken to match the selection to the climate. With evergreen foliage similar to the juvenile leaves of junipers, cultivars vary according to foliage color—bright yellows, deep greens, grays, and blues—and habit—from tiny, inches-high tufts to open, picturesque small trees. Transplant false cypress into rich, well-drained soil in the spring, and give it full sun in moist, mild climates, and partial shade elsewhere. Pruning to control form is best accomplished just before the new foliage emerges in the spring. Most forms have a tendency to die out in the center and lose lower branches with age—a strong jet of water is the easiest way to remove this foliage. Protect all *Chamaecyparis* from hot, drying winds.

Chamaecyparis lawsoniana 'Minima Aurea'

Chamaecyparis lawsoniana (Lawson False Cypress; Zones 6 to 8). The most adapted to coastal, moist climates, this false cypress is not suitable for midwestern conditions. Root rot appears to be a significant problem in this species on the West Coast. Yellow-leafed varieties are particularly susceptible to burn from hot sun and drying winds. Native to southwestern Oregon and northwestern California.

Chamaecyparis obtusa (Hinoki False Cypress; Zones 5 to 8). Tolerating neutral soils somewhat better than other false cypresses, this is probably the best choice for midwestern conditions. It is available in a wide variety of dwarf forms. Native to Japan and Formosa.

Chamaecyparis pisifera (Japanese False Cypress; Zones 4 to 8). The hardiest of the false cypresses, this one is notorious for losing its inner and lower foliage with age, and distinctly prefers acid soil. Native to Japan.

Choisya ternata

Choisya ternata
(SHOY-zia ter-NAH-ta)

Mexican Orange

ZONES 8B to 10

Broad-leafed evergreen

The early, deliciously scented white flowers of this shrub are a delight near entryways, outdoor living areas, windows, walkways, and paths—wherever fragrance can be enjoyed. The evergreen, fan-shaped foliage is produced densely at the ends of branches, creating an interesting layered, sculptured texture that is effective as an informal hedge or screen. The Mexican orange is touchy about soil conditions, needing well-drained acid soil that is rich in organic matter, and is intolerant of alkaline or high-salt soils. It will tolerate full sun on the coast, but needs partial shade in hot summer climates. In too deep shade it will become leggy and straggly and be particularly prone to insect attacks. Water infrequently but deeply, and prune yearly to maintain a compact, dense form about 4 to 5 feet high and wide. Native to Mexico.

Cistus × 'Elma'

Cistus species
(SISS-tus)

Rockrose

ZONES 8 to 10

Broad-leafed evergreen

Useful in the Mediterraneanlike climates of the West, the rockroses make an excellent large-scale bank and ground cover that is low in maintenance and big in spring color. An added asset is foliage that is fragrant, especially on hot days. Drought resistant and adaptable to salt spray, ocean winds, and desert heat, rockroses are bushy, dense, rounded shrubs that generally grow 3 to 4 feet tall and 4 to 5 feet wide. When massed they give the effect of a billowing dark or gray-green sea of foliage. Give them fast-draining soil, and pinch the tips of young plants to encourage denser growth. Don't try to move them once they're established—they won't transplant well. Native to the Mediterranean region.

Clethra alnifolia
(KLETH-ra al-ni-FOL-ee-a)

Summersweet; Sweet Pepperbush

ZONES 3 to 9

Deciduous

In addition to extremely fragrant, cool white spikes that bloom in July and August when flowers are scarce, summersweet is particularly useful in those difficult wet, shady areas of the garden, although it will thrive in nearly any soil. Once established, it will grow slowly to a broad, oval mass 3 to 8 feet high and 4 to

Clethra alnifolia 'Rosea'

8 feet wide. It is cloaked in handsome, dark green, pest-free foliage that inconsistently turns a clear yellow in the fall before dropping.

While quite tolerant of salty, sandy coastal conditions, its best garden performance is in moist, acid soil that is heavily supplemented with organic matter. Reputedly difficult to establish, try planting balled and burlapped or containerized plants in early spring, and water profusely. Though native to swamps, nursery grown clethras are usually grown in well-drained soils. Thus, the roots are no longer adapted to swampy soil conditions. When transplanting into wet soils, ease the transition by planting 3 to 4 inches higher than the soil level and mulching heavily.

While rarely necessary, pruning should be done in early spring. It is best to allow this shrub to attain its naturally clean, dense, oval shape. *Clethra* is intolerant of drought, and will attract great quantities of bees while in flower.

'Paniculata' is a cultivar with longer flowered spikes, and is superior to the typical species. 'Rosea' has clear pink buds that open into flowers of white tinged with pink. Native to swamps and moist, sandy soils from Maine to Florida.

Coprosma repens 'Coppershine'

Coprosma repens
(kop-ROZ-ma REE-penz)

Mirror Plant

ZONES 9 to 10

Broad-leafed evergreen

When pruned to restrain its rapid, sometimes awkward upright growth to 10 feet high and 6 feet wide, the extremely shiny, glossy leaves of this plant make it an excellent quickly forming hedge, screen, foundation plant, or espalier. Since the flowers and fruits are inconspicuous, and its habit is rangy and open when neglected, use this shrub for its attractive evergreen foliage where you don't mind occasionally having to train it. It adapts particularly well to seashore conditions and is drought tolerant once established. Give it full sun on the coast or partial shade in hot inland areas. It will perform well in nearly any soil. As a rapid grower, it will need regular pruning to keep it dense and neat. Several forms have yellow-or white-variegated leaves. *Coprosma × kirkii* is a wide-spreading, 2- to 3-foot-high shrub that makes a tough evergreen ground cover, particularly on banks where erosion may be a problem. Native to New Zealand.

Cornus alba 'Sibirica'
(KOR-nus AL-ba sy-BEER-i-ka)
Siberian Dogwood
ZONES 2 to 8
Deciduous

The screaming red, winter stems of this dogwood distinguish it from all other landscape plants—none other is so bright, nor, as some think, as difficult to integrate into the garden. Its loose, open, and very erect branches grow rapidly to a height of 8 to 10 feet, with lateral branching occurring only in the upper ⅓ of the shrub. The spread is quite variable, usually ranging from 5 to 10 feet. Extremely vigorous and apt to overgrow neighboring shrubs, the Siberian dogwood is also difficult to use as a single specimen. It can be effective in the shrub border, however, and is especially beautiful when massed on a large scale, such as along drives, on banks, or naturalized around a pond. Siberian dogwood transplants easily and is adaptable to nearly any soil when it has sun or light shade. Like most dogwoods, it is beset by a host of insect and disease pests. Maintaining a vigorous plant is the best protection. In order to encourage vigorous new growth each year, on which the winter stem color is most evident, prune hard every spring by removing at least ⅓ of old wood—more if a compact plant is desired. Don't be afraid to cut it completely back to the ground each spring. Native from Siberia to Manchuria and North Korea.

Cornus sericea 'Flaviramea'

Cornus sericea, also listed as *C. stolonifera* (Red-osier Dogwood; Zones 2 to 8). This is the North American counterpart to *Cornus alba*, differing chiefly in its more muted, and some consider more effective, dark red winter stem color, and its preference for moist, water-logged soils. *Cornus sericea* 'Flaviramea' has

an unusual bright yellow winter stem color, but is notoriously susceptible to cankers and twig blights. These are generally not a problem, however, if the shrub is pruned heavily each spring. Dwarf forms, such as 'Isanti', have recently appeared on the market. Native to wet places from Newfoundland to Manitoba and south to Virginia and Nebraska.

Corylus avellana 'Contorta'
(KOE-ri-lus a-ve-LA-na kon-TOR-ta)
Harry Lauder's Walking Stick
ZONE 5
Deciduous

A thoroughly distinctive shrub with uniquely curled and twisted stems, twigs, and leaves that imparts a decidedly oriental flavor, Harry Lauder's walking stick is a definite loner in the landscape. Use it as an accent or focal point in an entryway or courtyard. It is especially effective against a light-colored wall because of its interesting winter silhouette. A rapid grower, it will form a rounded mass of contorted, snaking branches 8 to 10 feet in height and width (which is usually larger than anticipated), and can even become a 20-foot small tree. The flowers are pendulous yellowish or tan catkins that are quite unusual and showy in March before the leaves appear. Adaptable to a wide range of soils, acidity, and sunlight, it is an easy plant to grow. Try to select plants in the nursery that are propagated by cuttings, and thus are growing on their own roots. If you happen to get a grafted plant, immediately prune out any suckers that arise from below the graft union—the more vigorous understock has a tendency to overtake the contorted top growth. Give it average water.

Continus coggygria 'Folius Purpureus'

Cotinus coggygria
(ko-TINE-us ko-GIG-ree-a)
Smoke Tree
ZONES 6 to 8 (can be grown in ZONES 4 and 5 with winter dieback)
Deciduous

A long-lasting, cloudlike pinkish or whitish display in midsummer, along with several good purple-leafed cultivars, have made this plant a long-time favorite in the low-maintenance garden. Quite large—often a small tree grows to 25 feet high—the smoke tree is usually a

loose, open shrub with many upright stems 10 to 15 feet in height and greater in width, creating a rounded and irregular appearance. Most useful for the shrub border as a textural and color accent, and in massings and groups, this is not a plant for single specimen use, a common and unfortunate sight. The foliage on the species is an attractive blue-green with occasionally outstanding fall color in the reds, yellows, and purples.

Many of the purple-leafed cultivars fade to green as the season progresses. An exception is 'Velvet Cloak', one of the best selections, because it retains its purple color throughout the season. The floral display varies from pink to whitish, and is only showy on predominantly female plants, so purchase only named varieties. 'Daydream' is an especially floriferous form with pink pedicels.

The smoke tree is easily transplanted and adaptable to a wide variety of soils, including dry, rocky ones. Give it full sun. It must have frequent and deep watering when young, but is prairie-drought tolerant once established. Resist the temptation to prune this plant, except to remove dead branches, since each pruning cut will stimulate several long, slender shoots into growth, ultimately creating a ragged, unkempt-appearing plant. Native from southern Europe to central China.

Cotoneaster dammeri
(ko-TONE-ee-ass-ter DAM-er-eye)
Bearberry Cotoneaster
ZONES 6 to 9
Broad-leafed evergreen

The glossy, dense leaves; good fruiting color; rapid growth rate; and low, prostrate habit make this one of the best hardy, broad-leafed evergreens for ground covering. It can be used on banks and slopes, in masses, in a shrub border, or as a low facing plant for tall, leggy shrubs. The bearberry cotoneaster will spread rapidly to 6 feet or more wide, since its branches root where they touch the ground, and will remain under 1½ feet high. The finely textured, lustrous, dark green leaves are speckled with white flowers in late May, followed in late summer by bright red, berrylike pomes like tiny apples. Some cultivars, such as 'Coral Beauty', flower and fruit more freely than species plants. 'Lowfast' is hardier to southern Zone 5. *Cotoneaster dammeri* transplants easily from containers and is adaptable to many soils, although it prefers fast drainage. It is an excellent choice for dry, rocky soil in an exposed, sunny location. Fireblight and aphids can be problems. Native to central China.

Cotoneaster divaricata
(ko-TONE-ee-ass-ter di-var-i-KAY-tuh)
Spreading Cotoneaster
ZONES 5B to 9
Deciduous

This is one of the most handsome cotoneasters for summer and fall foliage, fruit, and graceful form. Use it in a shrub border where it will blend well with other shrubs, and consider it for informal hedges, masses, and groupings as a refined textural asset. It will grow rapidly 5 to 6 feet high and 6 to 8 feet wide. While the rose-colored flowers that bloom in May are nothing to get excited over, the bright to dark red fruits that nearly cover the plant from September through November are spectacular. The finely textured foliage is a beautiful dark, glossy green in summer, changing in the fall

Cotoneaster divaricata

to brilliant florescent yellow and red combinations that last for a long time, since it is one of the last shrubs to defoliate. Preferring well-drained, moist, and fertile soils, spreading cotoneaster nevertheless performs well in dry, rocky ones. The shrub is wind tolerant, adapts to various pH levels, and is a good choice for seashore conditions. Give it full sun or light shade. *C. divaricata* is one of the most trouble free of the cotoneasters. Native to western and central China.

Cotoneaster horizontalis

Cotoneaster horizontalis
(ko-TONE-ee-ass-ter hor-i-zon-TAL-iss)

Rockspray Cotoneaster

ZONES 5B to 9

Deciduous (semievergreen in mild climates)

Spilling over walls, down slopes, and over rocks, the angular, layered form and herringbone branches of the rockspray cotoneaster add an unusual texture to the garden. Often used as a large-scale bank or ground cover for excellent erosion control, this 2- to 3-foot high shrub will spread 5 to 8 feet or more. The attractive but not overwhelming pink flowers can be abundant from late May to early June, attracting prodigious numbers of bees. Red berries dot the plants from late August through November and are frequently quite showy. The plant's glossy, semievergreen foliage is deciduous in northern areas, where it turns orange and red before dropping. In mild climates, the leaves usually remain a glossy green all winter. See *C. dammeri* for cultural suggestions. Many cultivars are available for differences in form and foliage color. Native to China.

Cotoneaster multiflora
(ko-TONE-ee-ass-ter mul-ti-FLO-ra)

Many-flowered Cotoneaster

ZONES 6 to 9

Deciduous

One of the most trouble free of the cotoneas-

Cotoneaster multiflora

ters, this shrub is happily also one of the most beautiful. Its white early to mid-May flowers are quite spectacular, and are followed by abundant bright red berries that last from late August into October. In habit it is a graceful, arching, mounded, or fountainlike shrub that grows 8 to 12 feet or more high and 12 to 15 feet wide. In flower and form it is similar to, and a good substitute for, a large Vanhoutte spirea. It is definitely not a shrub for the small landscape—use it in the shrub border and for massing in spacious areas where it has plenty of room to grow. The foliage is an interesting blue-green with a medium-fine texture, and has little or no coloration before dropping in the fall. Plant container-grown plants in well-drained soil in a sunny, airy location. It is best to root-prune the plants as you set them out to help develop a strong, fibrous root system. Native to China.

Cytisus × praecox

Cytisus × praecox
(SIT-i-sus PREE-cox)

Warminster Broom

ZONES 6 to 10

Deciduous (with evergreen stems)

While not strictly evergreen, the Warminster broom has that effect by virtue of its dense, vertical stems that remain green all winter long. Even in the summer, foliage is sparse or nonexistent; nearly all the photosynthesis takes place in the green stems, which in all seasons are the plant's main textural asset. In May, the addition of profuse, pale yellow flowers creates an extremely showy display. Use this plant as a specimen in a shrub border, in large rock gardens, where dry, poor soil presents a problem, or where an interesting textural evergreen accent in winter and a showy spring display are desired. Under most conditions this shrub will grow 4 to 6 feet high with an equal or greater spread, forming a rounded mass of many parallel, mostly vertical stems.

Move only young, container-grown plants in the spring into perfectly drained soil. Bacteria on the roots of this plant fix nitrogen from the atmosphere and it actually prefers infertile and poor soil. Young plants can be tip pinched, but older plants do not respond well to pruning of any kind—it is best to allow them to develop their natural form.

Many other cytisus species are available, but most become rampant, naturalizing, self-sowing pests. Particularly notorious is Scotch broom (*Cytisus scoparius*), which has wrought much ecological damage on the West Coast and in parts of the Northeast. Unfortunately, it is one of the most commonly available brooms. Some cultivars, such as *Cytisus scoparius* 'Carla', and most hybrids, such as *C. × praecox,* are generally not a weed problem. Native to the Mediterranean region.

Daphne cneorum
(DAFF-nee nee-OR-um)

Garland Flower

ZONES 5 to 7

Broad-leafed evergreen

Few can forget the penetrating, delicious fragrance of daphne once they experience it. This one has finely textured evergreen foliage with rosy-pink clusters of flowers at the ends of the branches in April and May. It will grow slowly 6 to 12 inches high and 2 feet or more in spread, forming a low, loose trailing mass. Use it as a small-scale ground cover, in a rock garden, in shady spots, or in groupings where its fragrance can be most appreciated. Always plant daphne from containers into well-drained, moist soil. While much controversy surrounds the issue of pH levels, most experts agree that neutral soil is best. Protect the plants from hot sun and drying winds, mulch to keep the roots cool and moist, and don't disturb it after it is established by cultivating or trying to move it. It is best to plant daphne fairly high to reduce the chances of crown rot. Native to Central and Southern Europe.

Daphne cneorum

Daphne × burkwoodii (Burkwood Daphne; Zones 6 to 8) is a larger daphne with extremely fragrant flowers in May that open white and fade to pink. It grows to a compact 3 to 4 feet high and wide. 'Somerset' is a larger cultivar, growing 4 to 5 feet wide, and is reputed to be the easiest daphne to grow.

Daphne odora (Winter Daphne; Zones 8 to 10), more than any other daphne, is responsible for its reputation of being unpredictable and frustrating—full-grown plants often suddenly die for no discernible reason. Despite this, it is the most popular daphne in mild regions. Rosy-pink flowers that bloom in February and March adorn the lustrous, dark green,

Daphne odora

Elaegnus pungens 'Maculata'

3-inch-long leaves. The fragrance is legendary. This daphne *must* have perfect drainage and be planted high. Water infrequently during the summer months to increase flowering and prevent root rot. 'Marginata' is a popular variegated form reputedly hardier and easier to grow. Native to Japan and China.

Deutzia gracilis
(DOOT-zee-a gra-SIL-is)
Slender Deutzia
ZONES 5 to 8
Deciduous

Deutzia is another of the old-fashioned, popular favorites that is showy for a short time in the spring, but has little to offer the rest of the year. There are many deutzia species and cultivars, but this one is probably the most graceful in form and the most dependable for flower. A low, broadmounded shrub 2 to 6 feet high and 3 to 6 feet wide with gracefully upright-arching branches and dull green foliage, this shrub is best used in a shrub border, where its nondescript appearance when not in flower can blend with other shrubs. In mid- to late May, pure white flowers literally cover the shrub like a bank of new snow. Easy to grow, *Deutzia gracilis* transplants readily in the spring into any reasonably good garden soil, and will take full sun to light shade. Severe winter dieback is frequently annoying, and should be pruned out annually. Deutzia flowers on old wood, so prune immediately after flowering. Native to Japan.
Deutzia × rosea 'Carminea' is more dwarf in habit, with a great abundance of rosy-pink flowers.
Deutzia × lemoinei is a twiggy, erect shrub 5 to 7 feet tall, with white flowers that appear after those of slender deutzia. 'Avalanche' is a more compact form that grows 4 feet high and wide.

Eleagnus pungens
(el-ee-AG-nus PUN-jenz)
Silverberry
ZONES 7 to 10
Broad-leafed evergreen

The inconspicuous but powerfully fragrant flowers that bloom in October and the evergreen, olive-colored foliage are this tough shrub's hallmarks, along with adaptability, thorny branches, and edible red fruit in the spring. Good in problem areas of heat, wind, and drought, this shrub actually prefers poor, infertile soil, because it fixes its own nitrogen from the atmosphere. It responds well to shearing, which increases its density. This is an excellent hedge plant, and its thorny branches

will present an impenetrable barrier. Without pruning it will rapidly become a rigid, sprawling, angular shrub growing anywhere from 6 to 15 feet tall. Cultivars are available for variegated foliage. Native to Japan.

Enkianthus campanulatus
(en-key-AN-thus cam-pan-yu-LAY-tus)
Redvein Enkianthus
ZONES 5 to 9
Deciduous

Redvein enkianthus is a treasured, refined shrub with many ornamental features, including delicate, yellowish clusters of bell-like flowers in May that become veined with red, spectacular orange and red fall color, and an interesting horizontal branching structure. It is an excellent specimen plant and combines well with rhododendrons. Use it where it can be appreciated up close, such as around entryways or in outdoor living areas. A narrow, upright shrub or small tree with stratified branches and tufted foliage, it grows slowly 6 to 8 feet high in northern climates, and can reach 20 to 30 feet high in mild ones. Culture is similar to rhododendrons; plant in moist, well-drained, acid soil that is rich in organic matter, in a location that has full sun to partial shade (shade is preferred in hot summer climates). Enkianthus will not tolerate drought or salts. Native to Japan.

Erica veitchii

Erica species
(AIR-i-ka)
Heath
ZONES 4 to 8, varying according to species
Narrow-leafed evergreen

Quite similar to *Calluna* (heather), these evergreen shrubs have a more variable size, a generally greater tenderness, and an earlier spring bloom. The smaller forms make outstanding ground covers and masses, facing

plants for a shrub border, and rock garden specimens. The larger forms make striking textural and color accents in the spring. All are most effective when grown in large masses or beds. Like heather, *Erica* is a culturally finicky plant—refer back to the description of *Calluna vulgaris* (page 67) for its growing requirements. Many of the species listed below have a large number of cultivars.

Heaths native to northern Europe

Erica carnea (Spring Heath; Zones 6 to 8). A dwarf, spreading form growing 6 to 16 inches high and 2 to 6 feet wide, this shrub tolerates more alkaline soils than most heaths. An annual pruning or shearing just after blooming will give it its best look.
Erica vagans (Cornish Heath; Zones 6 to 8). A bushy shrub that grows 2 to 3 feet tall and 3 to 4 feet wide, its flowers are the latest of the heaths to bloom—from July until September.

Heaths native to southern Europe

Erica arborea (Tree Heath; Zones 9 to 10). A rather awkward shrub or small tree that grows 10 to 20 feet high, its fragrant white flowers bloom from March to May.
Erica canaliculata (Christmas Heath; Zones 9 to 10). A bushy shrub growing 6 to 8 feet tall with irregular spires of foliage, this is often sold in containers around Christmastime.
Erica mediterranea (Biscay Heath; Zones 8 to 10). With upright growth 4 to 7 feet high, this finely textured shrub is good strictly for background foliage, with inconsequential flowers.

Escallonia × exoniensis 'Frades'

Escallonia rubra
(ess-ka-LON-ee-a ROO-bra)
Red Escallonia
ZONES 8 to 10
Broad-leafed evergreen

Fast-growing, producing attractive red, fragrant flowers in the summer and fall (year-round in milder climates), and tolerant of the wind and salt spray of coastal gardens, escallonia makes an excellent screen or windbreak, and is useful for massing and integrating into the shrub border. Its dark, evergreen foliage responds well to pruning, although with a corresponding reduction in blooming. A light annual pruning will maintain a compact form, but left to itself it will quickly grow to 6 to 15 feet tall with a dense, rounded, and upright habit. Escallonia will not tolerate highly alkaline soils, and needs partial shade in hot inland gardens. It can tolerate short periods of drought, but performs best with adequate water. Escallonia is native to South America, principally Chile.
Escallonia × exoniensis 'Balfouri' (Zones 9 to 10), will grow as high as 10 feet, with graceful, drooping branchlets and pink blossoms.
Escallonia × exoniensis 'Frades', (Zones 9

to 10) produces more abundant pink flowers and retains a more compact 5- to 6-foot habit.

Euonymus alatus 'Compactus'

Euonymus alatus
(yoo-AWN-i-mus a-LAY-tus)

Burning Bush; Winged Euonymus

ZONES 4 to 7

Deciduous

Popular especially for its brilliant scarlet fall color, *Euonymus alatus* displays a neat, vase-shaped habit and clean, pest-free foliage. It will eventually get quite large and open, however—15 to 20 feet high and as wide—and this should be considered before it is used. Burning bush is easily transplanted and adaptable to many soils and growing conditions, except to very wet ones. Pruning will destroy the naturally neat outline of the plant, causing "witches' brooms" and uneven growth. It adapts equally well to full sun or heavy shade, where it still develops good fall color, although its brightest hues are in full sun. Use it as an unclipped hedge or screen, in groups, in the shrub border, or as a specimen. The cultivar 'Compactus' is a slightly smaller form, growing 10 to 15 feet in height and spread. It is often sold as a cute little dwarf, which it most certainly is not. Native from northeastern Asia to central China.

Euonymus fortunei
(yoo-AWN-i-mus for-TOON-ee-eye)

Wintercreeper

ZONES 5 to 8

Broad-leafed evergreen

While popular as one of the hardiest broad-leafed evergreens, the shrub forms of wintercreeper should be used with caution due to their susceptibility to several serious diseases and insects. Be aware that many of the *Euonymus fortunei* cultivars are spreading, semi-prostrate ground covers. The shrub forms are quite variable in habit and ultimate size, so check at your nursery when in doubt. Some cultivars, propagated from "juvenile" growth, do not fruit; others bear heavy crops of bright orange fruits in fall and winter. Euonymus transplants easily, is tolerant of all but the wettest soils, and withstands full sun to heavy shade. In harsh, exposed locations, the foliage is prone to yellowing and browning in winter. In moist, humid climates and sites with poor air circulation, mildew is a serious problem. Anthracnose, crown gall, and scale are even more serious, often decimating entire plantings. Leaf spots, aphids, and thrips cause problems, too. Native to China.

Euonymus kiautschovicus (Spreading Euonymus; Zones 6 to 9). While this is generally an evergreen shrub growing 8 to 10 feet high, in areas that have cold winters the foliage often turns a ghastly yellow-brown and hangs on interminably. It has the same pest problems as *Euonymus fortunei*. 'Dupont' is a hardier, more compact form. 'Manhattan' is similar to 'Dupont'. 'Sieboldiana' has cleaner foliage and is more resistant to scale.

Euonymus japonica (Evergreen Euonymus; Zones 8 to 10). A shrub or small tree that grows to a 15-foot width and an 8-foot spread, this is a popular low-maintenance, tough plant for harsh situations and poor soils. Notoriously susceptible to mildew and a range of sucking insects—especially scale, aphids, mites, and thrips—plant this shrub where air circulation is good and where water does not stand. Many cultivars are available, the more popular being the strongly variegated golden and white forms.

Exochorda racemosa

Exochorda racemosa
(EX-o-kor-da ray-suh-MO-sa)

Pearlbush

ZONES 5 to 8

Deciduous

Popular from time immemorial for its white, pearllike buds that open into showy bloom in mid-May, this is another single-season plant that has little value the rest of the year. Pearlbush will grow 9 to 15 feet in height and spread. This upright, irregular shrub becomes quite unruly as it gets older. Pruning the shrub annually just after flowering will help it to maintain a more compact habit. Plant it in well-drained, acid soil, give it full sun to partial shade and average watering, and it will attract no serious pests. Native to eastern China.

Exochorda x macrantha 'The Bride' is a superior hybrid cultivar worth seeking; it is lower growing and more compact, growing 3 to 4 feet in height and spread.

Forsythia × intermedia
(for-SITH-i-a in-ter-MEE-dee-a)

Border Forsythia

ZONES 5 to 9

Deciduous

Few have witnessed the bright yellow burst of forsythia at the close of a harsh winter and not been pleased at this harbinger of spring. Spectacular pale to deep yellows in late March or early April (February to March in mild climates) are, unfortunately, this shrub's only

Forsythia × intermedia 'Spectabilis'

attribute. An upright, arching, and vigorous shrub that constantly needs grooming, it will rapidly grow 8 to 10 feet high and 10 to 12 feet wide. Plant forsythia in nearly any soil, but give it plenty of water and feeding. A location in full sun will maximize flowering. Prune forsythia annually, right after it completes flowering, by removing 1/3 of the oldest canes. Give it plenty of room and allow it to grow in its natural form; do not shear. Older, overgrown plants can be renewed by cutting them almost entirely to the ground. While the roots are reasonably hardy, the flower buds are often killed by late freezes as far south as mid-Zone 6. Select flower-bud hardy varieties, like 'Karl Sax' and the Farrand hybrids, and plant in protected areas if you live in northern zones. Many cultivars are available for growth habit and for quantity, color, and size of bloom, from pale to deep yellow.

Forsythia suspensa (Zones 5 to 8). While not as free-flowering as *Forsythia × intermedia*, it displays a graceful, pendulous form excellent for cascading over banks and sides of streams. Native to China.

Forsythia ovata (Zone 4B). While ornamentally inferior, this forsythia is useful in those northern, borderline areas where the flower buds of *Forsythia × intermedia* are often killed. Native to the mountains of Korea.

Fothergilla major

Fothergilla major
(fa-ther-GILL-a MAY-jor)

Large Fothergilla

ZONES 6 to 8

Deciduous

Fothergilla is one of the most attractive and desirable of the southeastern native shrubs. Its honey-scented, profuse white blooms resemble small, round bottlebrushes, and flower in late April to early May. And its clean, dark green, and pest-free foliage consistently provides an extremely showy fall display of electric yellow, orange, and scarlet. It is an extremely neat, rounded shrub that grows 6 to 10 feet high with a slightly narrower spread. Use fothergilla in groups, masses, and foundation planting. It is especially attractive as a specimen or integrated into the shrub border. Although an acid, well-drained soil is a must, fothergilla is a relatively adaptable plant that is entirely pest free. While it will grow well in partial shade and dry, rocky soils, full sun and soils rich in organic matter will improve flowers and fall color. Native to dry, sunny ridges in the southern Appalachians from Virginia to South Carolina.

Fothergilla gardenii (Dwarf Fothergilla; Zones 6 to 8). Differing from the large fothergilla in smaller size (to 3 feet) and flowers that bear *before* the leaves, this is an excellent shrub for small spaces. Unfortunately, it is rarely available in nurseries.

Fuchsia × hybrida
(FYOO-shya HYE-brid-a)
Common Fuchsia
ZONE 10
Deciduous to evergreen

Fuchsias are common evergreen (in frost-free areas), deciduous, or perennial shrubs in Zone 10, and are often seen as houseplants elsewhere. Fuchsias are a widely variable group of plants that displays bright, multi-colored flowers and has a trailing to upright habit. Blooming from early summer until frost, the flowers attract hummingbirds. Some forms make excellent trailing cascades for hanging baskets or stream banks; others can be used as upright specimens or integrated into the shrub border, and are often espaliered.

Fuchsias definitely perform best in areas with cool summers, high atmospheric moisture, filtered shade, and moist, rich soil that's high in organic matter. In dry climates especially, they should be mulched heavily, misted and watered frequently, and protected from hot, searing winds. Give them light applications of liquid fertilizer every 10 to 14 days throughout the growing season, spray regularly to control sucking insects, and pinch them back frequently to encourage dense growth. Prune annually in the early spring before new growth starts by removing about the same amount of wood as was formed the previous season. Always leave at least two healthy buds on each branch.

Fuchsia magellanica 'Alba'

Fuchsia magellanica (Hardy Fuchsia; Zones 6 to 10). In northern areas this shrub is a pe-

rennial, dying to the ground and growing to a rounded 3-foot shrub each year. In the deep South it commonly reaches 4 to 8 feet high. The flowers are bright red with blue inner petals, and are smaller than those of the common fuchsia. They bear profusely from late June until frost. A graceful shrub with attractive foliage, it performs best in partial shade and rich, well-drained but moist soil (although it is not as finicky as *Fuchsia × hybrida*). Native to Chile where it forms thickets in low, moist areas near water.

Gardenia jasminoides

Gardenia jasminoides
(gar-DEE-nee-a jazz-mi-NOI-deez)
Gardenia
ZONES 8 to 10
Broad-leafed evergreen

The legendary fragrance of gardenia flowers is a treasured asset to any garden, but the superb, glossy, evergreen leaves should not be discounted. Use gardenias as specimens in containers and raised beds, as hedges and low screens, or as espaliers. Most varieties will grow 3 to 6 feet high and wide. Lower-growing forms, such as 'Radicans', make effective ground covers on a limited scale.

Unfortunately, gardenias are quite finicky in their growing requirements. They will not tolerate alkaline soil, saline water, poor drainage, or drought. Plant their crowns high in an acid soil rich in organic matter. They prefer a protected location of partial shade, full sun in foggy areas. Late frosts can be quite damaging, especially in the northern limits of their range. Mist the foliage regularly in the early mornings while the plant is not in bloom, and feed every 3 to 4 weeks during the growing season with an acid plant food. Spray regularly to control sucking insects. Gardenias will not bloom well in cool summer areas. Native to China.

Genista tinctoria
(Jen-ISS-ta tink-TOR-ee-a)
Common Woadwaxen
ZONES 2 to 9
Deciduous

This is the hardiest of the *Genista* and features spectacular yellow flowers in June and a small, neat, rounded habit that is 2 to 3 feet high, composed of strongly vertical, nearly leafless, evergreen stems. All genistas require full sun and sharp drainage, but beyond that they are easy to grow and adaptable, actually preferring poor, dry, infertile soil. They tolerate drought and coastal conditions well. Leave genistas alone after they become established —they do not move easily. All genistas are native to the Mediterranean region.

Genista tinctoria 'Plena'

Genista hispanica (Spanish Gorse or Spanish Broom; Zones 6B to 9), has bright yellow flowers in early June. The shrub grows 1 to 2 feet high and spreads quite wide.

Genista monosperma (Bridal Veil Broom; Zones 9 to 10), has white, fragrant flowers in both winter and spring. It is a large, upright shrub, growing 20 feet high and 10 feet wide.

Genista pilosa (Silky-leafed Woadwaxen; Zones 6 to 10), has yellow flowers in late May and grows 1 to 1½ feet tall and 7 feet wide. It has silvery leaves.

Genista sagittalis (Arrow Broom; Zones 5 to 10), is a rapidly growing prostrate shrub that has outstanding yellow flowers in May and June. It grows 6 to 12 inches high and 7 feet wide.

Hamamelis × intermedia 'Primavera'

Hamamelis × intermedia
(ham-a-MEE-lis in-ter-MEE-dee-a)
Hybrid Witch Hazel
ZONES 6 to 8
Deciduous

All witch hazels are delightful for their spicily fragrant, delicately showy winter flowers. During periods of extreme cold, the flower petals curl up into a tight ball, and thus can withstand prolonged periods of being covered with ice in 0° weather. While this hybrid is not as fragrant or restrained in size as others it is the showiest of all the witch hazels available in the United States. As early as February its leafless branches are covered with deep yellow blossoms that last about a month. The red-flowered cultivars, such as 'Jelena' (which is actually a coppery-orange), while interesting, are not as outstanding from a distance as the ones with yellow flowers. This is not a shrub for small gardens—it will eventually reach 15 to 20 feet in height with a comparable spread. Expect an outstanding show of fall color in reds, oranges, and yellows before the leaves drop.

Plant witch hazels in deep, rich, soils that have an abundant supply of moisture. While they will not tolerate drought, you will find little need to pamper them—they are virtually pest free. Use them as screens, backgrounds, or large focal points. Or train them into small trees. They make an excellent choice for a naturalized woodland understory. Consider planting them near windows, where they can be seen from indoors on a cold, wintry day.

Hamamelis vernalis (Vernal Witch Hazel; Zones 6 to 9). With powerfully fragrant, small, yellow flowers in January and February, this witch hazel has a neater, smaller habit (6 to 10 feet high and usually much taller) that is round and dense. The leaves turn a clear yellow in the fall. Native to gravelly, often-flooded stream banks in the Ozark Mountains.

Hamamelis virginiana (Common Witch Hazel; Zones 5 to 9). This is the hardiest but also the largest and rangiest of the witch hazels, growing 20 to 30 feet high and wide. Its yellow flowers in November and December often coincide with clear yellow fall foliage, reducing their effectiveness; but they are quite fragrant. Native to forest understories from Canada to Georgia and west to Nebraska.

Hibiscus syriacus

Hibiscus syriacus
(hi-BISS-kuss seer-ee-AY-kuss)

Shrub Althea; Rose of Sharon

ZONES 6 to 9

Deciduous

An old-fashioned favorite for its late-summer-to-frost flowers, the shrub althea has unfortunately been used traditionally as a focal specimen, although it has little to offer when not in flower and is much more effective when grouped or massed in the shrub border. It is a large, very erect and round-topped shrub or small tree that grows at a medium rate 8 to 12 feet tall and 6 to 10 feet wide. A large variety of cultivars is available for flower color—whites, reds, purples, violets, and combinations in between. It is extremely tolerant of the salts and wind of coastal gardens, and prefers a hot summer. Wet weather will tend to rot the flower buds. While not particular about soils, the shrub althea will not do well in wet or dry ones. Best in full sun, it will tolerate partial shade. If left unpruned the flowers will be profuse but small. For larger flowers, prune hard each spring—it flowers on the current year's growth—to 2 to 3 buds per stem. Its leaves are among the last to appear in the spring, which frequently causes worry for gardeners new to this shrub. The leaves are also among the first to drop in the fall. Spray regularly for Japanese beetles, scale, aphids, and whiteflies. In addition to insects, this shrub is susceptible to a wide range of diseases in humid climates. Native to China and India.

Hibiscus rosa-sinensis (Chinese Hibiscus; Zones 9 to 10). Popular in Florida, California, Texas, and Hawaii, this shrub will grow rapidly to 30 feet high. Literally thousands of cultivars are available, with large, platelike flowers in whites, pinks, reds, and yellows. Hibiscus should have good drainage; abundant moisture, sun, and heat; and protection from wind and frost. They will seldom bloom in cool summer areas. Feed them monthly during the growing season and protect them from aphids. Prune out about ⅓ of the old wood each spring to keep older plants vigorous and tip pinch to increase bloom. Native to China.

Hydrangea macrophylla

Hydrangea macrophylla
(hy-DRAN-jee-a mak-roh-FY-la)

Bigleaf Hydrangea

ZONES 7 to 10

Deciduous

While this hydrangea has an excellent late summer floral display (July to August) and lustrous, neat foliage in mild winter areas, this is also the hydrangea commonly grown in pots by florists. Generally, however, varieties suitable as container plants are not as satisfactory in the garden. Outside it is a round shrub with many erect, infrequently branched stems reaching 4 to 8 feet in height (sometimes 12 feet) and spreading indefinitely, due to its tendency to sucker vigorously. Many cultivars are available, and are generally divided between the *hortensias,* with all sterile flowers forming large globular heads, and the *lace-caps,* which have a delicate ring of large, sterile flowers surrounding a cluster of tiny, fertile ones. Flowers can be single or double; are available in white, pinks, and blues; and are generally clustered in heads that are 5 to 10 inches in diameter. The bigleaf hydrangea seems to *prefer* rather than just tolerate seashore conditions, where it can be planted in full sun. Otherwise, plant it in partial shade and in moist, rich, well-drained soil that's high in organic matter. Soil acidity affects the uptake of aluminum by the plant, which in turn determines whether the flowers will be pink or blue. Blue flowers result from a pH of 5 to 5.5, while pink flowers occur in soils with a pH of 6 to 6.5 or higher. Apply aluminum sulfate to the soil to increase acidity and provide aluminum for blue flowers; apply lime to decrease the acidity for pink flowers. Either must be accomplished well before blooming to achieve the color desired. Bigleaf hydrangeas flower on old wood, so pruning should occur just after flowering. If the plant dies back from a hard winter, it will not produce flowers that season. Native to Japan.

Hydrangea quercifolia

Hydrangea quercifolia
(hy-DRAN-jee-a kwer-si-FO-lee-a)

Oakleaf Hydrangea

ZONES 6 to 9

Deciduous

The lacy, delicate white flowers and deep red or purplish fall leaves make this shrub an attractive one, but the foliage texture is often the chief feature in the garden. Its attractively coarse, clean foliage is useful in the shrub border for an accent in large masses, in difficult shady places, or as a specimen. An upright and irregular shrub that grows slowly, 6 to 8 feet high and 4 to 6 feet wide, it has a tendency to sucker from the roots and form large colonies. The conical flower clusters appear in late June through July and are white and lacy, as the large, sterile flowers surround the tiny, fertile ones in a ring. They persist on the shrub for a long time, fading to pink, then to purplish pink, and finally to brown. Plant it in moist, fertile, well-drained soil on the acid side, in sun or half shade. If necessary, it will tolerate dense shade quite well, although the fall leaf color will be less and fewer flowers will be produced. Mulch well in dry climates to maintain a cool, moist root run. Because this shrub flowers on old wood, it is strictly a foliage plant where winters reach 0°F or colder; severe weather causes serious dieback. Native to Georgia and Florida, west to Mississippi.

Hypericum patulum 'Hidcote'

Hypericum prolificum
(hy-PURR-i-kum pro-LIF-i-kum)

Shrubby St. Johnswort

ZONES 5 to 9

Deciduous

The pert, bright yellow flowers of this hardiest *Hypericum* are a welcome addition to any garden, effective over a long season from mid-

June through August. Fresh, clean, blue-green foliage covers this dense, rounded shrub that grows 1 to 4 feet high and wide. If you have a location in bright sun with well-drained, light soil, *Hypericum* will prove to be a tough, durable plant that's easy to maintain and free from pests. It tolerates poor, dry, sterile soil, city air pollution, and partial shade beautifully. Although seldom necessary, pruning should be accomplished in the late spring after new growth hardens off. Use shrubby St. Johnswort in the border, for large-scale masses or small groupings, as foundation plantings or as a low, informal hedge. Native from New Jersey to Iowa and Georgia.

Hypericum frondosum (Golden St. Johnswort; Zones 6 to 9) grows 3 to 4 feet high and wide. It has very handsome blue-green foliage and large, bright yellow flowers. 'Sunburst' is a lower-growing form (2 to 4 feet high and wide) that is excellent for a low facing shrub.

Hypericum patulum (Goldencup St. Johnswort; Zones 7 to 10) is a semievergreen or evergreen species growing as high and wide as 3 feet. Variety *H.p. henryi* is more vigorous and has larger flowers. 'Hidcote' is a smaller, 18-inch shrub with large, fragrant, yellow flowers that bloom from June to October. 'Sungold' is supposedly more hardy.

Hypericum calycinum (Aaronsbeard St. Johnswort; Zones 6 to 10) is a low-growing, deciduous, spreading kind of shrub that is suitable for ground covering. It tends to become a weedy pest that is difficult to control. It should be mowed to the ground every few years when appearance warrants it.

Hypericum × moseranum (Goldflower St. Johnswort; Zones 8 to 10) is a low, evergreen shrub. This is one of the few plants that will do well under eucalyptus trees.

Iberis sempervirens 'Pygmaea'

Iberis sempervirens
(eye-BEER-iss sem-per-VY-renz)
Evergreen Candytuft
ZONES 5 to 10
Broad-leafed evergreen

A handsome, mat-forming evergreen shrub that produces generous drifts of pure white flowers in April or May, use iberis as a ground cover interplanted with woody shrubs and in combination with spring bulbs. Extremely showy in bloom, the neat, 6-to 12-inch-high shrub will spread wide at a medium to rapid rate, and is covered in all seasons by dark green, finely textured foliage. It transplants easily, either from containers or as seedlings, into light soil that has average fertility. Do not overfertilize or it will become loose and rangy. Prune hard each year after flowering. Removal of spent flowers is important to increase

next year's bloom and to keep plants dense. Unless given excellent drainage, refrain from overwatering. Excessive moisture encourages several severe disease problems. 'Christmas Snow' repeats its bloom in the fall. 'Little Gem' is more of a dwarf and hardier than the species. 'Purity' is similar, but has larger flower clusters. Native to southern Europe and western Asia.

Ilex cornuta 'Rotunda'

Ilex cornuta
(EYE-lex cor-NOO-ta)
Chinese Holly
ZONES 7 to 10
Broad-leafed evergreen

While the species is a large, upright shrub 10 to 15 feet tall, many smaller, denser cultivars of this shrub are available. The leaves are an extremely handsome, dark, polished green in all seasons, and are larger and coarser than the Japanese holly. The fruits are normally a brilliant red and bear profusely. Unlike other hollies, the fruits apparently develop without fertilization, so having both male and female plants is not necessary. 'Dwarf Burford', 'Carissa', and 'Dazzler' are heavy fruiting forms that have a slow-growing, dwarf habit. 'Rotunda' is especially dense and low growing. 'Burfordii' is a reputedly hardier cultivar said to perform well in Zone 6. See Japanese holly (following) for cultural recommendations. Native to eastern China and Korea.

Ilex crenata 'Helleri gold'

Ilex crenata
(EYE-lex cre-NAH-ta)
Japanese Holly
ZONES 6B to 10
Broad-leafed evergreen

This holly is commonly mistaken for boxwood due to its neat, rounded shape and dark green, dense, lustrous, and finely textured foliage. A slow-growing shrub that responds well to

pruning, it will eventually reach 5 to 10 feet in height with a usually greater spread, although old specimens in arboreta often reach 20 feet or more. A wide range of cultivars is available for size, form, and hardiness. 'Black Beauty', 'Hetzii', and 'Helleri' are three of the hardiest, compact types. 'Microphylla' and 'Convexa' are larger, hardier forms. The Japanese holly makes an excellent selection for hedges, foundation planting, and massing, and for an evergreen, soft texture in the shrub border. It transplants easily into moist, well-drained, slightly acid soils, does well in sun or shade, and appears to be tolerant of pollution. Often sheared into formal shapes, prune after the new growth has matured in the spring. Unlike some hollies, the fruits on this one are black and inconspicuous. Native to Japan.

Ilex glabra

Ilex glabra
(EYE-lex GLAY-bra)
Inkberry
ZONES 3 to 10
Broad-leafed evergreen

The inkberry is the hardiest broad-leafed evergreen available to northern gardeners. The handsome, dark green foliage grows densely on younger plants in all seasons; older ones often reach 6 to 8 feet in height by 8 to 10 feet in spread and develop a leggy openness, although this is quite variable. The fruits are black and not particularly showy. 'Compacta' is a dwarf, dense clone worth looking for. *Ilex glabra* is native to swamps from Nova Scotia to Florida and west to Mississippi, where it suckers profusely, forming large clumps. When planted in moist, acid soil, it is easy to grow and pest free. It responds well to pruning; in fact, heavy pruning is an excellent way to renew leggy old plants. This shrub, and especially its cultivar 'Compacta', is excellent for massing, hedges, and foundation planting.

Ilex verticillata
(EYE-lex ver-tiss-i-LAY-ta)
Common Winterberry
ZONES 4 to 8
Deciduous

This deciduous holly is unusual for its adaptability to wet, swampy soils, to which it is native. A popular plant in the eastern United States, it is an outstanding fruiting shrub, which bears great quantities of bright red berries on bare branches far into the winter. Birds find the berries tasty, so the effective season often depends on their appetite. Winterberry can grow 20 feet high in the wild, but usually only reaches 6 to 9 feet in the garden, with a similar spread. Be sure to plant a male within a few hundred feet of each female to ensure fruiting. It will tolerate dry soil, but prefers moist, acid ones high in organic matter. Plant it in full sun to partial shade. Winterberry is particularly effective when planted in large masses, such as in the shrub border and by water. 'Winter Red' is a new cultivar that is superior for its neat, dense growth, 8 to 10 feet high and wide, and for its unbelievably abundant bright red fruits. Native from Newfoundland and Minnesota to Georgia, Tennessee, and Missouri.

Ilex vomitoria
(EYE-lex vom-i-TOR-ee-a)

Yaupon

ZONES 7B to 10

Broad-leafed evergreen

While the species is a small evergreen tree, several cultivars are available, such as 'Nana' and 'Stokes', that are effectively dwarf (18 inches or less) and compact. Popular in the southeastern United States, this holly is more tolerant of alkaline soils and drought than other hollies. Its finely textured foliage can easily be sheared into formal shapes, and while the species is considered one of the heaviest fruiting of the hollies, the dwarf forms are generally sterile. Native to the southeastern United States.

Juniperus species
(joo-NIP-er-us)

Juniper

Hardiness varies according to the species

Conifer

Few landscape gardens in North America do not have a juniper somewhere on the property. Extremely versatile, available in a perplexing array of forms and sizes, adaptable to nearly any growing condition, and one of the original low-maintenance plants, *Juniperus* is an immensely popular plant genus. "If you can't grow junipers, then don't bother planting anything else," says one authority. Commonly used, junipers are also commonly misused.

Their low-maintenance reputation masks susceptibility to a range of pests, including twig blight, bagworms, white juniper scale, spider mites, spruce mites, twig borers, root rot, and water molds. When planted in shade they quickly become spindly and loose. In wet soils they are especially susceptible to disease. And their eventual size is often disregarded, necessitating removal and replacement that is usually difficult.

While they are a common answer to the gardener's desire for a finely textured evergreen, particularly in the northern garden where such plants are usually in short supply, junipers often disappoint, since many varieties turn dull purple, gray, or dirty green in cold weather. Some gardeners, however, consider this winter color change an attractive asset.

Nevertheless, when properly located and well established, there is a juniper to solve nearly any landscape problem. While preferring sandy, well-drained soil and a sunny, open exposure, they will grow well just about anywhere, in any soil, provided it isn't waterlogged or in deep shade. Guard against overwatering junipers or planting them in the path of lawn-oriented sprinkler systems.

Most of the species whose descriptions follow are large trees with a confusing variety of shrublike, prostrate, or columnar cultivars. While it is impossible to list all of the cultivars in this book, a few of the most recommended ones follow each species description. When in doubt, the best practice is to ask your local nurseryperson which is best for your area. When inquiring, stress your desire for pest resistance and accurate ultimate size.

Juniperus chinensis (Chinese Juniper; Zones 4 to 10, although cultivars may vary in hardiness). This is an extremely diverse species, whose cultivars range from prostrate ground covers to 75-foot-high trees. Included under this species are many of the most popular shrublike forms. Most are quite susceptible to Phomopsis twig blight (especially the cultivar 'San Jose'), which can be devastating in wet years. Beware of the eventual size of many selections—the extremely common 'Pfitzeriana' and 'Hetzii' will grow 15 feet high and 30 feet wide or more. This species prefers alkaline soils. It is native to China, Mongolia, and Japan.

Some of the better varieties include:

'Armstrong', a dwarf form, 4 feet high and wide, with soft, gray-green leaves.

'Iowa', a spreading, relatively open shrub that is 6 feet high and wide and has bluish-green leaves. It is blight resistant.

'Mint Julep', a 2- to 3½-foot-high, 6-foot-wide dwarf with bright green foliage and blue fruit.

Var. *sargentii*, growing 1½ to 2 feet high and spreading 9 to 10 feet wide, with blue-green foliage. This juniper and its cultivars are resistant to Phomopsis blight.

'Sea Spray' (hardy to Zone 5) is a new cultivar that is reportedly resistant to Phomopsis blight, water molds, and root rot. Growing 1 to 2 feet high and spreading wide, with good, intense blue-gray foliage, it has been recommended as a substitute for the more disease-plagued *Juniperus horizontalis* cultivars.

Juniperus communis 'Echiniformis'

Juniperus communis (Common Juniper; Zones 2 to 10). A typical plant of this species is 5 to 10 feet high, spreading 8 to 12 feet, with spiny leaves that are gray or blue-green in the summer, turning to a yellowish- or brownish-green in winter. All forms of this plant are tremendously susceptible to Phomopsis blight. Extreme hardiness and adaptability to the poorest, driest soils make it a worthwhile choice for difficult sites.

This species is native to more places than any other tree or shrub in the world: northern and central Europe, the Mediterranean region, Asia Minor, Iran, Afghanistan, the western Himalayas, Canada, and the eastern United States from New England to Pennsylvania and North Carolina, and west to the Rockies and California.

'Compressa' is a dwarf form growing to an

erect, relatively narrow 2 to 3 feet, with silvery-green leaves.

'Depressa' rarely grows over 4 feet high, but often ranges as much as 15 feet wide. This is not a plant for the small garden.

'Depressa Aurea' is similar to 'Depressa', but has yellow foliage.

'Gold Beach' is an interesting choice for a rock garden, growing only 6 inches tall and 2 feet wide. The yellow new growth in the spring changes to green.

Juniperus conferta (Shore Juniper; Zones 6 to 10). Marked by intense, bluish-green, softly textured foliage, this procumbent shrub makes an excellent ground cover for coastal gardens. Growing 1 to 2 feet high, it will slowly spread 6 to 8 feet, forming a dense, handsome mat. It is extremely tolerant of poor, sandy soils and saline coastal conditions, but will not grow well in wet, heavy soil. 'Blue Pacific' and 'Emerald Sea' are two cultivars worth seeking out, due to their extra-low habit and clean, blue-green foliage.

Juniperus horizontalis (Creeping Juniper; Zones 3 to 10). Almost all of the many cultivars of this low, spreading ground cover plant turn an unattractive grayish-purple in winter. All forms are extremely susceptible to Phomopsis blight, which, under conditions of high humidity, can devastate entire plantings. Nevertheless, this is a popular species because of several of its intensely blue, extremely prostrate cultivars. Native from Nova Scotia to British Columbia, south to Massachusetts and Montana.

'Bar Harbor' and 'Wiltonii' (also known as 'Blue Rug') are two of the favorites. 'Blue Chip' is one of the best. Their greyish-purple winter effects should be considered when selecting these plants. 'Emerson', a slow-growing form that grows 1 foot high and 9 to 15 feet wide, has intense blue-green foliage that holds its color throughout the winter.

Juniperus procumbens 'Nana'

Juniperus procumbens (Japanese Garden Juniper; Zones 6 to 10). This is another low, spreading juniper frequently used as a ground cover that spreads over banks and hillsides and tumbles over rocks and walls. One plant will grow 1 to 2 feet high and 10 to 15 feet wide, at a slow to medium rate. Like *Juniperus horizontalis*, a planting of this juniper can be wiped out by Phomopsis blight. It is native to the mountains of Japan. 'Nana' is a dwarf, compact form that grows about half the size of the species.

Juniperus sabina (Savin Juniper; Zones 5 to 10). The stiff, distinctly vase-shaped branches of this shrub can spread 10 to 15 feet at maturity, with a height of 4 to 6 feet. It is particularly tolerant of urban pollution, and a few of its cultivars are resistant to Phomopsis blight. The lower-growing forms of this plant are excellent for massing, foundation planting, and high ground and bank coverings. The foliage is a dark green in summer, often turning a brownish-green in cold weather. This juniper is native to the mountains of central and southern Europe.

'Arcadia' is an excellent dwarf form. It grows 1 foot high by 4 feet wide and exhibits good resistance to Phomopsis blight.

'Broadmoor' grows 18 inches tall and 10 to 15 feet across in time, building up more height in the center with age. It, too, is blight resistant.

The variety *tamariscifolia* is very popular on the market, although it is susceptible to several pests.

'Skandia' is another blight resistant shrub, similar to 'Arcadia', with bluish-green foliage.

'Von Ehron' is a vase-shaped form growing 5 feet high by 5 feet wide, which is resistant to Phomopsis blight.

Juniperus scopulorum (Rocky Mountain Juniper; Zones 4 to 10). Normally a narrow, erect tree that grows 30 to 40 feet high in nature, the smaller cultivars of this plant are valued as hedges, screens, and windbreaks because of their generally upright habit, slow rate of growth, and bluish cast to the foliage. The species is native to dry ridges of the higher elevations of the Rocky Mountains, from Alberta to Texas.

Some of the more compact cultivars include:
'Lakewood Globe' becomes a round 4 to 6 feet after 10 years of growth; it has blue-green foliage.

'Table Top Blue' is a silvery-blue form that grows 5 to 6 feet high and 8 feet wide in 10 years, having a distinctly flat-topped appearance.

'Silver Star' is a wide-spreading form, 3 feet high and 6 to 8 feet wide, with silvery-gray foliage.

'Welch' is a very narrow, compact column that grows up to 8 feet high. Its gray-green new growth turns a distinctly blue-green in the summer.

Juniperus virginiana (Eastern Redcedar; Zones 2 to 10). This species is most valued for its many cultivars, all of which are resistant to Phomopsis blight, but which are more susceptible to cedar apple rust and bagworms than most junipers. The foliage ranges from deep green to gray-green, and often assumes a brownish, dull cast in the winter. The eastern redcedar grows wild throughout eastern and central North America.

Some of the better compact forms include:
'Kosteri', an extremely wide-spreading, low-growing form that reaches 3 to 4 feet high and 25 to 30 feet wide after many years. The foliage turns purplish in the winter and is grayish-blue in all other seasons.

'Nana' is an extremely hardy, narrow, upright form that grows 10 to 12 feet high.

'Skyrocket' is the narrowest blue-gray columnar form available, growing 10 to 15 feet tall in old age.

'Tripartita' is very similar to a small Pfitzer juniper. It only grows 4 feet tall and 7 feet wide, and has pale green or slightly gray leaves.

Kalmia latifolia
(KAL-mee-a lat-i-FOLE-ee-a)
Mountain Laurel
ZONES 5 to 8
Broad-leafed evergreen

For spectacular white to deep pink flowers and excellent evergreen foliage, this eastern native is an undisputed treasure in any garden where it can be grown. Use it as a specimen

Kalmia latifolia 'Clementine Churchill'

and as a companion for azaleas and rhododendrons. Slow growing, in youth it is dense, rounded, and neat, becoming gnarled, picturesque, and open in old age. In the wild it can reach 30 to 35 feet high, but under cultivation 7 to 15 feet is a more reasonable figure. In the harsher climate of the Midwest, it rarely grows over a rounded 3 to 7 feet high. Plant it from a container into acid, cool, moist, well-drained soil that is high in organic matter, and give it full sun for optimum flowering. In hot summer areas, however, partial shade is appreciated. Mulch rather than cultivate around its shallow roots. This is not a good choice for dry, Mediterraneanlike climates or areas without frost (Zones 9 to 10). Cultivars are available for flower color from white to deep, bright pink. Native from New Brunswick to Indiana and south to Florida and Louisiana.

Kerria japonica 'Pleniflora'

Kerria japonica
(KARE-ee-a ja-PON-i-ka)
Japanese Kerria
ZONES 5 to 9
Deciduous

For its bright yellow flowers in the spring and bright green stems all winter long, this deciduous shrub performs well in practically the densest shade. Use it where shade is a problem—in a border and in masses and groups. Standing alone, it tends to appear rather disorganized. It will grow slowly 3 to 6 feet high and eventually spread 6 to 9 feet. Keep this shrub away from rich, fertile soils where it becomes rank and weedy and decreases flower production. A tough, care-free shrub, plant it

in deep to partial shade, because its flowers fade quickly in full sun. A protected location with good drainage will reduce the chance of winter damage. Prune directly after flowering, since it flowers on last year's wood. 'Pleniflora' is the most popular variety, being double flowered and extremely showy—some even consider it too gaudy. Several cultivars, rarely available, have white or yellow foliage or stems. Native to western and central China.

Kolkwitzia amabilis

Kolkwitzia amabilis
(kol-KWIT-zee-a am-a-BIL-is)
Beautybush
ZONES 5 to 8
Deciduous

A low-maintenance, old-time shrub of limited value when not in flower, the beautybush is nevertheless quite a spectacle in bloom. Flowers are produced in late May in great profusion, and are a good, bright pink. It is a large shrub with medium texture in the summer and coarse texture in the winter. It grows rapidly to 6 to 10 feet high (sometimes 12 feet) and has a slightly smaller spread. The upright-arching form usually becomes quite leggy, but the reddish, peeling bark of the lower trunks and branches can be quite attractive. Nevertheless, this shrub is best used in the rear of the shrub border in large gardens. Easily transplanted, it is indifferent to soil type or pH. Give it a sunny location and plenty of room to grow, and prune out older stems every year. Old, overgrown shrubs can be renewed by cutting them completely to the ground. Prune after flowering, since it blooms on old wood. Native to central China.

Lagerstroemia indica
(lay-ger-STREEM-ee-a IN-di-ka)
Crape Myrtle
ZONES 7B to 10
Deciduous

Brilliant floral displays in late summer and early fall, spectacular fall foliage color, and intriguing, beautiful, mottled bark in the winter make this truly an all-season plant. Actually a small tree, most forms can be grown as a large upright-rounded shrub, 15 to 25 feet high and as wide, while several dwarf cultivars 5 to 12 feet tall are available. It makes a beautiful specimen or focal grouping, particularly with a ground cover planted underneath it. This shrub can also be effective integrated into a foundation planting or as a hedge or screen. New foliage is bronze, maturing to a medium green, then turning into electric reds, yellows, or oranges in the fall. Flowers are produced from July to September in great profusion. A wide variety of cultivars are available that have

Lagerstroemia indica

white, pink, deep red, and lavender blooms. Crepemyrtle flowers on the current season's growth, so it can be pruned as late as early spring and still produce flowers the same season. Plant it in well-drained, moist soil that is rich in organic matter, and in a hot, sunny location. Spray to control aphids. Try to select from the newer dwarf cultivars developed by the National Arboretum for resistance to powdery mildew. Otherwise, you will need to spray just prior to blooming every year to control this disease. Prune annually to increase flowering wood by removing flower clusters and small twiggy growth on small shrubs, or 12 to 18 inches of each branch on large ones. Older, overgrown plants can be cut clear to the ground to renew or contain them. Native to China and Korea.

Leptosperum scoparium 'Red Damask'

Leptospermum scoparium
(lep-to-SPER-mum sco-PARE-ee-um)

New Zealand Tea Tree

ZONES 9 to 10

Narrow-leafed evergreen

For an outstanding floral display from late winter to spring and an interesting accent of finely textured, fragrant evergreen foliage, the New Zealand tea tree can be an effective choice in gardens with a mild climate, particularly the Mediterraneanlike climates of the West Coast. Extremely variable from seed, a wide range of cultivars is available for flower color (in reds, pinks, and white) and habit (from 6 to 10 feet high to prostrate ground covers 8 to 12 inches high and 2 to 3 feet wide). The flowers are profuse and colorful, appearing from late winter to midsummer, depending on the variety, and are effective for about 2 to 4 weeks.

Leptospermum scoparium must have excellent drainage and prefers a location in full sun. Once established, it is drought tolerant and pest free. If you must shear or prune for a formal appearance, do so lightly. Never prune into bare wood; if you do, buds will not break into new growth. New Zealand tea is an ex-

cellent choice in seacoast gardens as a specimen, accent, or focal point in the shrub border. The prostrate forms make interesting and colorful ground covers, although you shouldn't expect their fairly open habit to suppress weeds. Native to New Zealand.

Leucothoe fontanesiana

Leucothoe fontanesiana
(lew-KO-tho-ee fon-ta-nee-zee-AN-a)

Drooping Leucothoe

ZONES 5 to 7

Broad-leafed evergreen

Most commonly planted in moist, acid, eastern gardens, the drooping leucothoe makes a terrific companion to rhododendrons, azaleas, and mountain laurel because of its evergreen, lustrous, dark foliage, and graceful form. The bright green or bronze new foliage in the spring and the purplish winter color, along with the delicate, subtle, white, fragrant flowers in spring, are important assets. Use leucothoe as a facer plant for leggy shrubs; a graceful high ground cover for shady slopes; or for massing, grouping, or integrating into the shrub border. It is a perfect shrub to naturalize in a shady, woodland, wildflower garden.

Leucothoe fontanesiana transplants easily from a container in early spring, but is fastidious about its requirements. If given an acid, moist, well-drained soil that is high in organic matter, as well as full shade, ample moisture, and protection from drought and drying winds, it will prove to be a basically trouble-free plant, although leaf spots can be a problem. Pruning should be accomplished directly after flowering, although it is seldom necessary due to its natural, graceful, fountainlike form, which grows 3 to 5 feet high and often wider. Older plants can be rejuvenated by pruning them clear to the ground.

'Girard's Rainbow' has yellow, green, and copper-variegated foliage. 'Nana' is a dwarf form that is 2 feet high and 6 feet wide. Native to streamsides in the mountains of Virginia to North Carolina and Tennessee.

Ligustrum species
(li-GUSS-trum)

Privet

Hardiness varies according to the species

Some evergreen, some deciduous species

Pest free, highly adaptable, and low in maintenance, the shrubby privets are most often used as formal and informal hedges, backgrounds, and screens. Most have white, spike-like clusters of strongly scented flowers in early summer, whose scent is variously described as offensive to pleasant. All privets transplant easily bare root, are adaptable to nearly any soil except a wet one, and take full

Ligustrum hedge

sun to partial shade. They perform well under adverse conditions of pollution and drought. If flowers are desired, prune just after blooming. Otherwise, prune any time. All privets are rapidly growing shrubs that respond well to pruning and shaping.

Deciduous Types

Ligustrum obtusifolium (Border Privet; Zones 4 to 10). In addition to being one of the hardiest privets, the border privet is also one of the most attractive because of its broad, horizontal growth habit and good, dark green foliage. It will grow 10 to 12 feet tall and 12 to 15 feet wide, although it can easily be kept much smaller. Var. *regelianum* is a low, 4- to 5-foot-high shrub with unusual, horizontally spreading branches that are most attractive if allowed to grow naturally. Native to Japan.

Ligustrum vulgare (Common Privet; Zones 5 to 10). This is a plant to avoid because of its susceptibility to anthracnose. To lose mature hedge plants is an annoyance, to say the least.

Ligustrum amurense (Amur Privet; Zones 4 to 10). Another hardy privet that is excellent for hedges, it has good, clean, medium- to finely textured foliage. Native to northern China.

Ligustrum ovalifolium (California Privet; Zones 6 to 10). Excellent glossy, semievergreen leaves often tempt gardeners to grow this plant north of its range, where it dies to the ground every winter. Where hardy it is a deservedly popular hedge plant. Native to Japan.

Ligustrum × ibolium (Ibolium Privet; Zones 5 to 10). This shrub is similar to the excellent California privet, except it is hardier.

Ligustrum × vicaryi (Golden Privet; Zones 6 to 10). In full sun the leaves of this popular plant are a glaring yellow; in shade they are yellow-green to light green. Clipped hedges will remain yellow-green, since the shaded inner leaves are constantly exposed from clipping. 'Hillside Strain' is a hardier variety that is useful in Zone 5, although it is a difficult, gaudy plant to integrate into the landscape.

Evergreen types

Ligustrum japonicum (Japanese Privet; Zones 7B to 10). Making an excellent hedge or screen in southern or western gardens because of its excellent evergreen, lustrous leaves; its dense, compact habit—it grows rapidly 6 to 12 feet high; and its responsiveness to pruning, this privet is also commonly used for training into topiary or small standards. An excellent container plant, it looks best when given plenty of water and protected from the hot sun. Many forms are available. This plant is frequently sold incorrectly in nurseries as *Ligustrum texanum*. Native to Japan and Korea.

Ligustrum lucidum (Glossy Privet; Zones 7B to 10). Often confused with the Japanese privet, this privet is more treelike, since it grows 35 to 40 feet high. To differentiate from *L. japonicum* among young nursery plants, feel the undersides of the leaves. If the veins are raised, it is *L. japonicum;* if they are sunken, it is *L. lucidum.* Native to China and Korea.

Ligustrum 'Suwanee River' is an evergreen hybrid that eventually grows 4 to 6 feet high, with a compact, tight habit. Its dark green, wavy leaves are useful as a low hedge or in a foundation planting.

Lonicera 'Zabellii'

Lonicera tatarica
(loe-NIS-ser-a ta-TARE-i-ka)
Tartarian Honeysuckle
ZONES 3B to 9
Deciduous

The chief attributes of this shrub are intensely fragrant, early May flowers that are available in the widest color range of any honeysuckle (whites, pinks, and reds), and showy, bright red berries in June. The bluish-green, dense foliage has a medium texture. Unfortunately, this shrub becomes quite leggy, requiring a facing plant, and like nearly all honeysuckles displays an impossible winter appearance. It is best used in the shrub border where these factors can be hidden. An upright and arching shrub that is 10 to 12 feet high and wide, the berries are a favorite of the birds, and they will deposit them all over the garden, so that it is soon full of seedlings. Easily transplanted and adaptable to many soils, *Lonicera tatarica* prefers full sun. Pruning should be accomplished just after flowering. Overgrown plants can be renewed by cutting them clear to the ground. 'Arnold Red' has the darkest red flowers of any honeysuckle. 'Nana' has good, pink flowers and only grows 3 feet high. Native to central Asia.

Lonicera nitida (Box Honeysuckle; Zones 7B to 10), is a finely textured evergreen with fragrant, white flowers that bloom in June. Tolerant of coastal conditions, this shrub responds well to pruning and makes an excellent hedge. Unlike other honeysuckles, it presents a neat, refined appearance.

Lonicera × xylosteoides 'Clavey's Dwarf' (Zones 5 to 10), is an excellent choice for a low hedge, forming a neat, 3- to 6-foot mound with clean, fresh green foliage. 'Emerald Mound' is a beautiful, low-growing type with excellent bluish-green leaves, becoming 3 feet high and 4 to 6 feet wide.

Magnolia quinquepeta 'Nigra'

Magnolia quinquepeta
(formerly *M. liliflora*)
(mag-NO-lee-a kwin-kwe-PAY-ta)
Lily Magnolia
ZONES 6 to 10
Deciduous

The large, showy flowers of the lily magnolia are purple on the outside with white centers, and effective from late April to early May (earlier in mild climates). A smaller, more open shrub than the star magnolia, it will grow slowly to 8 to 12 feet in height with a similar spread. Treat it the same as the star magnolia for culture and landscape use. Several cultivars are available, the most popular being 'Nigra', which has larger, deeper purple flowers and a more restrained habit. Native to China.

Magnolia stellata 'Pink Stardust'

Magnolia stellata
(mag-NO-lee-a stel-LA-ta)
Star Magnolia
ZONES 5 to 10
Deciduous

Especially when displayed against the dark background of evergreens or a brick wall, the large, white, fragrant flowers of the star magnolia are a glorious sensory experience in early to mid-April (March in the South). Actually a large shrub or small tree that grows slowly to 15 to 20 feet tall and 10 to 15 feet wide, it is often planted without due consideration for its ultimate size. Use it as a specimen, in groups, or focused in the shrub border or foundation planting. The flowers are delicate and often damaged by wind and rain, but late frosts present the most danger because of the early blooming period. Put them in a protected location, and avoid southern exposures, since

this forces the flowers out even earlier. Plant magnolias in the spring in deep, rich, well-drained and moist soil, and never cultivate around the roots—they are fleshy and close to the surface, and are easily damaged. Do not plant the crown below the soil level. Give magnolias full sun to partial shade. Pruning, although rarely necessary, should be done immediately after flowering. Native to Japan.

'Rosea' has pink buds that open into white flowers, while 'Pink Star' has flowers that remain clear pink. *Magnolia* × 'Ann' is a new hybrid worth seeking for its fragrant, lilylike, deep pink buds and clear pink flowers that open later and last longer than the star magnolia. It also displays a superior, uniform 8- to 12-foot, upright habit. While better form and flower are important considerations, its chief advantage is a later flowering period, and hence decreased susceptibility to late frosts.

Mahonia aquifolium

Mahonia aquifolium
(ma-HONE-ee-a a-kwi-FOLE-ee-um)
Oregon Grapeholly
ZONES 5 to 9
Broad-leafed evergreen

Mahonia aquifolium is an open, loose shrub with upright, heavy stems and very showy, bright yellow flowers that bloom in late April. While popularly used as an evergreen ground cover in shady areas, its irregular spreading habit and frequently high growth (3 to 6 feet and sometimes 9 feet tall) is best when integrated into a shrub border or foundation planting, and possibly as a specimen. While its spiny, hollylike leaves are evergreen, the leaves often turn a purplish-bronze at the onset of cold weather. In locations that are exposed to wind and sun, they scorch and turn brown. Inclined to spread by underground stems, the shrub's tendency to openness and straggliness can be somewhat controlled by pruning annually just after flowering to maintain a 3-foot height. Plant mahonia in a moist, acid soil and protect it from hot sun and wind. Several cultivars are available for better form, winter leaf colors, and floriferousness. Native to damp forests from British Columbia to Oregon.

Mahonia bealei
(ma-HONE-ee-a BEE-lee-eye)
Leatherleaf Mahonia
ZONES 6B to 10
Broad-leafed evergreen

Striking structural interest is the chief attribute of this plant. It often grows 10 to 12 feet high and has strongly vertical, little-branched stems and large, compound leaves that are held horizontally. The effect is exotic and tropical, especially when displayed against a wall or dramatically lit at night. In addition, it produces large, showy clusters of yellow flowers, followed by powdery blue, grapelike fruit. This mahonia will not tolerate drought, hot sun, or winter sun and wind, and should be planted in a rich, moist soil and given plenty of water. Consider its ultimate size before planting, since it is difficult to prune correctly.

Mahonia lomariifolia (Zones 8B to 10). While more tender than *Mahonia bealei,* this shrub is even more dramatic, with larger, coarser foliage. Both of these mahonias make excellent container plants. Avoid planting where the spiny foliage can scratch people. Both are native to China.

Malus sargentii

Malus sargentii

(MA-lus sar-JEN-tee-eye)

Sargent's Crabapple

ZONES 5 to 9

Deciduous

Most crabapples are thought of as trees; this one is small enough to be used as a shrub. A superb, easy-to-grow plant, it has a strongly horizontal effect, growing 6 to 8 feet tall and usually spreading twice as wide. It is graced with spectacular clouds of white, fragrant flowers in mid-May, which are the most effective in alternate years; good, dark green foliage in the summer; and profuse, bright red, pea-sized crabapples in the fall and early winter that are adored by birds. It is adaptable to a wide variety of soils, preferring full sun and average watering. Although it is seldom necessary, prune directly after flowering and before next year's buds set in mid-June. For the curious collector, 'Tina' is an extremely dwarf form, 18 to 24 inches high and 2 to 3 feet wide. 'Rosea' has clear pink buds. *Malus sargentii* is highly resistant to many of the diseases that commonly plague crabapples. Native to Japan.

Myrica pensylvanica

(MIR-i-ka pen-sil-VAN-i-ca)

Northern Bayberry

ZONES 2 to 7

Deciduous

Bayberry is one of the few plants outside of the pea family that fixes its own nitrogen from the atmosphere and that actually prefers infertile, dry, sandy soils. It is excellent for large-scale massing in poor soil and coastal areas and adapts well to difficult urban sites, where it will form rolling, billowing masses of clean, deep, lustrous green foliage, ranging 5 to 12 feet in height. It tends to sucker and form large colonies, but is also good for a shrub border, informal hedge, and to combine with broad-

Myrica pensylvanica

leafed evergreens. The fruits are grayish-white, waxy berries that are produced in great quantities along the stems of female plants and persist all winter long. All parts of the plant are aromatic—the berries have been used since Colonial times to make fragrant candles. Transplant from a container into any soil, from sand to clay, and give it full sun to partial shade. It is tolerant of salt spray and wind, and attracts no serious pests. Older, leggy plants can be renewed by pruning them down to the ground. Native to coastal areas from Newfoundland to North Carolina, and along the Great Lakes.

Myrtus communis

(MIR-tus com-MYOON-iss)

Myrtle

ZONES 9 to 10

Broad-leafed evergreen

With glossy bright green foliage that is delightfully fragrant when bruised, myrtles are commonly used in the hot, dry areas and coastal gardens of Arizona and California as formal or informal hedges, screens, masses, or backgrounds. Myrtle accepts shearing extremely well and is easily trained into a formal hedge. Unpruned, the myrtle is usually seen as a 5- to 6-foot-high and 4- to 5-foot-wide, round, bushy shrub, although it can attain treelike dimensions with great age, up to 15 feet tall and 20 feet wide. Sweet-scented, mildly attractive flowers are produced in the summer. The smooth, rusty-tan bark is showy on older specimens. Other than requiring fast drainage, it is not particular about soil. Many cultivars are available, mostly for form and foliage color. Native to the Mediterranean region.

Nandina domestica

Nandina domestica

(nan-DEE-na do-MESS-ti-ka)

Nandina; Heavenly Bamboo

ZONES 7 to 10

Broad-leafed evergreen (semideciduous in the North)

Not even remotely related to true bamboo, nandina is a deservedly popular shrub in

southern gardens for its variety of ornamental assets and easy care. A strongly vertical form contrasts nicely with delicate, wispy foliage that is evergreen in mild climates. Erect, creamy white flower spikes borne on the ends of the vertical branches in June are followed by bright red clusters of berries. Even if it only receives a few hours of sun a day, nandina frequently has brilliant crimson to purple foliage in the fall and winter. Often reaching 8 feet in height and 2½ to 3 feet in width, nandina is effective as a hedge or screen, in a mass or grouping, and as a solitary specimen in an entryway or container. It is particularly effective when backlit. Nandina will lose its leaves at 10°F, and will die back to the ground at 0°F, although it quickly recovers the following season. In the northern limits of its range, it is best used as an herbaceous perennial. Since crossfertilization seems to improve fruiting, try to plant nandina in groups. It performs well in nearly any soil, in sun or shade (although some protection is required in particularly hot climates), and established plants tolerate drought well. Prune out old, leggy canes annually to encourage density. Nandina competes well with tree roots, and is little troubled by pests, although it will exhibit chlorosis in alkaline soils. Several cultivars are offered for form, dwarf size, foliage color, and improved hardiness. Native to central China and Japan.

Nerium oleander

Nerium oleander

(NEE-ree-um OH-lee-an-der)

Oleander

ZONES 8 to 10

Broad-leafed evergreen

This is a commonly used shrub in the South and west of the Rockies, because of its coarse, evergreen foliage; attractive red, pink, white, or yellow flowers in the summer; and easy care, especially in hot, dry climates. A broad, rounded, and bulky shrub, oleander grows very rapidly to 8 to 12 feet tall and 6 to 10 feet wide, sometimes becoming open and leggy. Plant oleander in full sun, in any soil from dry sand to wet clay. Heat, salt, and drought tolerant, it is an excellent choice for desert gardens. Prune the shrub in early spring to control size and form. Remove old wood that has flowered each year. Tip pinch to encourage density, or pull off suckers from the base to encourage more open height. Oleander is plagued by many insects and diseases, particularly in shady or humid environments. Mildew, scale, and aphids are among the most severe.

All parts of the plant are violently poisonous to humans and animals. Be extremely cautious with clippings from pruning. Smoke from burning plant parts, green or dried, can cause severe skin and respiratory irritations. Contact with leaves can give some people dermatitis. And, ingesting even small amounts can cause severe illness, even death. Many cultivars are available for flower color, fragrance, and dwarf habit. Native to the Mediterranean region.

Osmanthus heterophyllus 'Variegata'

Osmanthus fragrans
(oz-MAN-thus FRAY-grans)

Sweet Olive

ZONES 8 to 10

Broad-leafed evergreen

While the powerfully fragrant nearly year-round flowers are an attraction, sweet olive is also a compact, neat plant with glossy evergreen foliage that makes an outstanding hedge, screen, background, espalier, or container plant. It is very easy to care for and quite adaptable. Plant *Osmanthus fragrans* in any soil, from sand to clay, give it partial shade, and it will grow at a moderate rate to a 10-foot-wide and -high shrub with a rounded outline. It can easily be kept lower, however, and responds well to shearing. Prune any time of the year; pinch the growing tips to encourage denseness. 'Aurianticus' has orange blossoms that concentrate their bloom in October, and will astound you with their powerful fragrance. Native to eastern Asia.

Osmanthus heterophyllus (Holly Olive; Zones 7 to 10). This is perhaps the handsomest of the *Osmanthus* species, often confused with English holly—holly has alternate leaves while *Osmanthus* always has opposite leaves. Possessing lustrous, spiny, dark green leaves and fragrant, hidden, yellow flowers in the fall, a number of cultivars are available for variegated foliage. This *Osmanthus* is unusually shade tolerant.

Osmanthus delavayi (Delavay Osmanthus; Zones 8 to 10). Small, finely textured leaves and a graceful, arching habit distinguish this *Osmanthus*, along with the largest white flowers of the genus. They are profuse and fragrant from late March to May. Particularly handsome on banks and walls where branches can cascade, it also responds well to pruning as a hedge or foundation plant.

Paeonia suffruticosa
(pee-OWN-ee-a suf-roo-ti-COH-sa)

Tree Peony

ZONES 5 to 9

Deciduous

While the curiously textured foliage on this deciduous, woody shrub is a decided asset, the tree peony is grown chiefly for its flower. And what a flower it is! Huge—6 to 10 inches or more in diameter—with exquisitely inter-graded coloring and a delicate texture, like

Paeonia 'Golden Isles'

crepe paper. An astounding array of cultivars and hybrids are available, from white, yellow, pink, and red, to maroon, violet, and purple. Usually growing to a rather open, leggy shrub, 4 feet high and wide and sometimes larger, the leaves are in proportion to the flowers—equally huge, often 18 inches long. Their deeply cut lobes, however, impart a curious mixture of coarse and fine texture to the plant. The blossoms, unfortunately, are short lived, lasting ten days at the most, and much less in excessively warm or moist weather. Single or semidouble forms are preferable; the fully double blossoms are so heavy they require individual staking.

Plant tree peonies in early fall in well-drained, moist, rich soil that has been amended with ample organic matter to make it slightly alkaline (although they tolerate slight acidity). These plants live a long time, so carefully preparing the soil in the beginning pays off in the long run. Choose their positions in the garden carefully—they transplant with difficulty. Grafted forms must be planted with the graft union at least 4 inches below the ground, so that the grafts may form their own roots. Protect from rabbits during the first year by covering them with wire cages, and mulch well. Carpenter bees are a serious pest in the East; control them by plugging entry holes or cutting the plant back to the ground and destroying the refuse. Don't mulch after the first year, and remove fading blossoms immediately to help control Botrytis fungus. Native from Bhutan to Tibet and China.

Paxistima canbyi

Paxistima canbyi
(pak-SIS-ti-ma CAN-bee-eye)

Canby Paxistima

ZONES 5B to 8

Broad-leafed evergreen

Canby paxistima is most popular in the gardens of the Northeast and Pacific Northwest as an excellent evergreen ground cover. It grows only 12 to 24 inches high and spreads slowly to 3 to 5 feet. Its lustrous, dark green

leaves change to an attractive bronze in the winter. Paxistima is a finely textured, neat, and compact shrub that is useful as a facer for taller shrubs, as an edging plant, or as a low hedge. The flowers and fruit are inconspicuous. Best bought in a container, it is easily transplanted into moist, well-drained, acid soil. Although found on rocky soil in the wild, under cultivation it seems to appreciate soils that are high in organic matter. Denser and more compact in full sun, it tolerates partial shade well. This is a shrub to leave alone once established—it rarely requires feeding or pruning, and has no severe pests. It is best grown in regions of high atmospheric moisture. Native to rocky woods and slopes in the mountains of West Virginia, Ohio, and Kentucky.

Philadelphus coronarius
(fil-a-DEL-fus cor-o-NAR-ee-us)

Sweet Mockorange

ZONES 5 to 8

Deciduous

While its white, late-May flowers are legendary for their powerful fragrance, and have been popular for ages, unfortunately, the sweet mockorange has little else to offer. Usually a coarse, leggy, and straggly shrub that grows rapidly to an upright and irregular 10 to 12 feet high and wide, even the smaller cultivars are irregular and unattractive when they are not in flower, which is about 50 weeks out of the year. It is easy to grow, not particular about soil, and will perform well in sun or partial shade. Free from serious pests, its wide-ranging root system is highly competitive and indicative of its tolerance to adverse conditions. It requires annual pruning to maintain a semblance of presentability. Do so right after it completes flowering by removing all older wood, or even cutting it to the ground. Use *Philadelphus* where its fragrance can be appreciated—in the border, near outdoor living areas, entryways, and windows. Be aware that many of the mockoranges offered by nurseries are not as fragrant as others. It is safest to select for fragrance only when the plants are in flower. Native to Europe and southwestern Asia.

Philadelphus × lemoinei (Zones 6 to 8). Among the cultivars of this hybrid are some of the best choices for fragrance, including 'Avalanche' (4 feet tall with single, white flowers), 'Girandole' (4 feet tall with double flowers), and 'Innocence' (8 feet tall with single flowers).

Philadelphus × virginalis also has many cultivars, which are generally less fragrant than *P. coronarius* or *P. × lemoinei,* but many of which are hardier (to Zone 4 or 5). 'Minnesota Snowflake' is a fragrant one, 6 feet high and hardy to Zone 4.

Philadelphus × 'Frosty Morn' is a new hybrid that is hardy to Zone 4, with double flowers that rival *P. × lemoinei* for fragrance.

Photinia × fraseri
(foh-TIN-ee-a FRAY-zer-eye)

ZONES 7B to 10

Broad-leafed evergreen

This evergreen shrub is best known for its bright, bronzy-red, new foliage in the spring that is showier than many flowers. It also produces attractive, ivory-colored flowers in many 4-inch clusters in late March and April. If left unpruned, it will grow at a moderate rate to a rounded 10-foot-tall and somewhat wider

Photinia × fraseri

shrub, but it is easily restrained. Use it as a screen, formal or informal hedge, or espalier, or train it into a single-stemmed small tree. Its lustrous, dark green foliage makes an excellent background. While not fruiting as profusely as other photinias, its red berries are quite attractive to birds. Plant photinias in well-drained soil that has been amply amended with organic matter. Even though they are heat resistant in the desert, they should be watered generously. Take care not to splash water onto the leaves since they are susceptible to fireblight. If fireblight occurs, the ends of branches will appear blackened, as if burned. Carefully prune them out, sterilizing the shears in alcohol or Clorox after each cut, and destroy or dispose of the refuse. Spray regularly for aphids and scale.

Photinia serrulata (Chinese Photinia; Zones 7B to 10). This is an extremely large shrub or small tree that grows 36 feet high. Its large, coarsely textured leaves make a good screen. The dull white flowers are profuse in the spring; they gradually change to a brownish-pink and are quite showy. These are followed by profuse red berries.

Picea abies 'Nidiformis'
(pye-SEE-a AY-beez ni-di-FORM-iss)
Bird's Nest Spruce
ZONES 2 to 4, and of increasingly limited use south of Zone 6B
Conifer

This is a popular dwarf spruce that makes a dense, low, flat-topped evergreen cushion, 3 to 6 feet high and 4 to 8 feet wide. It is useful as a specimen or curiosity in rock gardens, entryways, or other focal spots. Preferring well-drained, sandy, and moderately moist soil, it will tolerate others as long as there is sufficient moisture. The further south below Zone 5 that it is planted, the weaker it will become, since it prefers the moist climates of deep winter cold and summer coolness. It does not perform well in hot, dry, windy locations or with reflected heat from walks and pavements. Like all spruces it is best in full sun or light shade. This spruce is also a poor choice for polluted urban environments. Many other choice dwarf forms of the Norway spruce are available, from low- and wide-spreading to erect or pendulous, but this is the most common one. Native to northern and central Europe.

Picea glauca 'Conica' (Dwarf Alberta Spruce; Zones 2 to 7) is a stiffly conical and extremely slow-growing (about 1 to 2 inches per year) dwarf, often described as looking like an upside-down ice cream cone. It may eventually reach 6 to 8 feet in extreme old age. The finely textured, light green needles and unusual form make this an interesting, "cute" specimen or

oddity, which is probably best used in a focal grouping. Especially in hot, dry areas, it is very susceptible to red spider mites. A heavy shower with a strong stream of water will help to control this problem. For severe infestations, a miticide is necessary. Native to northern North America.

Pieris japonica

Pieris japonica
(pye-AIR-iss ja-PON-i-ka)
Japanese Pieris
ZONES 6 to 9
Broad-leafed evergreen

A beautiful, broad-leafed evergreen related to rhododendrons and kalmias, the Japanese pieris is grown for its delicate, whitish or pink-ish-white, pendulous panicles of flowers that bloom in early spring (mid- to late March) and which last for 2 to 3 weeks, and for its beautiful, deep green foliage with bronzy-red new growth in the spring. Growing slowly to a 9- to 12-foot height and 6- to 8-foot spread, with an upright, irregular, and rounded outline, use pieris as a specimen, in the shrub border, or in groups or masses. It is especially nice to combine with other acid-loving, broad-leafed evergreens, and integrates well into a foundation planting. Preferring moist, acid soil, it is not quite as particular as other members of the heath family. Protect it from wind and winter sun, especially in cold winter areas. When pruning is necessary, which is seldom, if ever, do so just after flowering. Leaf spots, a dieback fungus, lace bugs, scale, and mites can be severe problems. In the northern limits of its range and in exposed situations, the flower buds, which are naked all winter, are often killed. Several cultivars are available for more compact form, pink flowers, and unusual foliage color and texture. Native to Japan.

Pieris floribunda (Mountain Pieris; Zones 5 to 8). Hardier, lower, and bushier than *Pieris japonica* (growing 2 to 6 feet high with a similar spread), this pieris has upright panicles of fragrant white flowers that remain effective for the month of April. Additional plus points include greater resistance to lace bugs and tolerance of higher pH levels. Unfortunately, it is rarely available. Native to cool, damp mountain slopes from Virginia to Georgia.

Pieris forestii (Chinese Pieris; Zones 8B to 10). This shrub is more tender than *Pieris japonica,* with extremely showy scarlet foliage, larger leaves, and a denser, larger habit. Native to China.

Pinus mugo var. mugo

Pinus mugo var. mugo
(PYE-nus MYOO-go)
Dwarf Mugo Pine
ZONES 2 to 8, but not in the desert
Conifer

Often sold as a diminutive, cute little cushion that will only grow 2 to 4 feet high, many homeowners are surprised to find a 10-foot-tall, 15-foot-wide haystack monster on their doorsteps 15 or so years later. If a reliably small plant is desired, then it's probably worth your while to seek out the more hard-to-find cultivars, such as 'Compacta', 'Gnome', or 'Slavinii'. The mugo pine, however, can be pruned annually by removing approximately $2/3$ of each young, expanding candle in the spring, which will maintain a compact, dense form. Use the mugo pine for textural evergreen interest in a foundation planting, as low masses, or in groupings. Plant it in moist, deep loam in full sun or partial shade. Many other dwarf pines are becoming increasingly available, although they are less common than the mugo pine. Such dwarf pines include especially selected cultivars of *Pinus strobus* (white pine), and *Pinus sylvestris* (scotch pine). *Pinus mugo* is native to the mountains of Europe, from Spain to the Balkans.

Pittosporum tobira 'Variegata'

Pittosporum tobira
(pit-o-SPOR-um toe-BY-ra)
Tobira; Japanese Pittosporum
ZONES 8B to 10
Broad-leafed evergreen

Dark green, clean, leathery evergreen foliage; fragrant, early, creamy yellow, spring flowers with a scent like orange blossoms; and a broad, dense habit all have made this a popular plant in southern and western gardens for screens, massing, in the border, and foundation planting.

It is particularly effective in containers or trained as a small, crooked-stemmed tree. Smaller cultivars, some of which have variegated foliage, are available for facing plants and ground covers. However, another selection is suggested if a formal hedge is desired—this pittosporum does not respond well to hard pruning or shearing, although frequent light pinching can help to maintain a compact habit. Allowed to grow naturally, it reaches 6 to 15 feet in height and is usually slightly wider. Fairly drought resistant, it nevertheless appreciates adequate water and an annual light fertilization. Aphids and scale can be a problem. Full sun to partial shade is best, although it tolerates dense shade well.

Pittosporum crassifolium (Zones 9 to 10) is a large shrub that will grow up to 25 feet high, although it can easily be held to a 6-foot hedge. The finely textured, gray-green foliage responds well to shearing, and tolerates wind and coastal salts. 'Nana' is a 3-foot dwarf.

Pittosporum eugenoides (Zones 9 to 10) is an excellent and popular hedge plant, with wavy-edged, glossy, light green leaves that respond well to shearing. Yellow, fragrant flowers are produced on unpruned plants.

Pittosporum napaulense (Golden Fragrance Plant; Zones 9 to 10) is a 12-foot high, 8-foot wide, coarsely textured shrub. Grow this one for its excellent spring display of profuse, golden-yellow flowers and powerful fragrance.

Platycladus orientalis
(formerly *Thuja orientalis*)

(plat-i-CLAD-us ore-ee-en-TAL-iss)

Oriental Arbovitae

ZONES 7 to 10

Conifer

Like the American arbovitae, this species is a 50-foot tree from which many dwarf, shrublike cultivars have been developed. Northern gardeners should beware—it is frequently offered in bargain sales far north of its range of hardiness. Many of the dwarf cultivars are extremely popular in the South, especially the bright yellow- or blue-foliaged forms. 'Aurea Nana' is a popular, rounded yellow dwarf, while 'Blue Spire' is a pyramidal form with blue leaves. The Oriental arbovitae, besides being more tender, differs from the American arbovitae in the distinctly vertical, fan-shaped planes of its branches. While it is tolerant of drier soils and less atmospheric moisture, it still needs protection from harsh, dry winds. Native to northern China and Korea.

Potentilla fruticosa
(poh-ten-TIL-a froo-ti-KOH-sa)

Bush Cinquefoil

ZONES 2 to 8

Deciduous

Few shrubs earn as many plus points as the bush cinquefoil for suitability in a shrub border, as a foundation planting, for massing and edging, and as a low, informal hedge or facer plant. Its bright yellow, 1-inch flowers are steadily abundant from June until frost. Its dense, upright stems grow slowly to a neat, rounded plant, 1 to 4 feet high and 2 to 4 feet wide. Its dainty, finely textured, deciduous foliage is a handsome bright green. Bush cinquefoil will grow well in any soil, from wet to dry, heavy to light. It tolerates extreme cold and drought, is virtually free from pests (although occasionally susceptible to mites during dry spells), and requires no pruning. It will flower most abun-

Potentilla 'Abbotswood'

dantly in full sun, but tolerates partial shade nicely. In short, it is one of the most care-free plants around. Many cultivars are available in a range of flower colors (white, yellow, orange, or red), sizes, and foliage color (bright green to gray-green). Orange- and red-flowering varieties fade quickly in full sun, so they are best planted in partial shade. Native to meadows and bogs, northern and mountainous Asia, Europe, and North America.

Prunus laurocerasus
(PROO-nus lar-oh-sir-ASS-us)

English Laurel

ZONES 7 to 10

Broad-leafed evergreen

Grown for its large, dark, evergreen leaves, this large shrub (or small tree) is most commonly seen as a formal hedge, screen, or background plant in southern gardens. Give it partial shade (except on the coast) and protect it from scale and fungal leaf spots with regular spraying. It is not particular about soil. Left unpruned, in southern climates it has been known to grow 25 or 30 feet tall. In northern climates, 4 to 6 feet is more likely. Expect high maintenance as a clipped hedge, due to its extremely rapid growth rate. Shearing will mutilate the large leaves, so it is better to prune selectively. Beware of its greedy, far-reaching roots. Native to southeastern Europe and Asia Minor. *Prunus laurocerasus* var. *schipkaensis* is hardy to Zone 6, with protection. It has smaller leaves and only grows 9 feet tall. 'Otto Luyken' is another excellent, low-growing form, hardy to Zone 6B.

Prunus tomentosa

Prunus tomentosa
(PROO-nus toe-men-TOE-sa)

Nanking Cherry; Manchu Cherry

ZONES 2 to 8

Deciduous

One of the most handsome of the deciduous shrubby cherries, this is a broad shrub that

will eventually reach a picturesque, open 6- to 10-foot height and 15-foot spread. It accepts shearing well, making a beautiful, dense hedge, although the fruits are sacrificed. The handsome bark is a shiny, exfoliating, reddish-brown and a distinct attraction in the winter. But the chief beauty of this shrub lies in its pink buds that open into white, fragrant flowers in early to mid-April (March in mild climates), followed by scarlet fruits that are deliciously edible. Use this plant as a specimen, a hedge, in groups and masses, or in the shrub border. Native to northern and western China, Japan, and the Himalayas.

Prunus cistena (Purple-leafed Sand Cherry; Zones 2 to 7). Valuable for its extreme hardiness and intensely reddish-purple foliage that holds its color all summer long, the pinkish, fragrant May flowers and blackish fruits are of secondary importance. This is a small shrub that grows rapidly to an upright and irregular 8 to 10 feet.

Prunus maritima (Beach Plum; Zones 4 to 7) is a generally inferior, rounded, dense, 6-foot-high bush that is useful for its tolerance to the salt sprays and sandy soils of the seacoast. The fruits are deliciously edible, and follow white, early May flowers. Varieties have been selected for larger fruits.

Prunus glandulosa (Dwarf Flowering Almond; Zones 5 to 8). Distinctly offensive when not in flower, this is a straggly, 4-to 5-foot-high, upright, awkward shrub that is commonly grown due to its ease of propagation.

Prunus triloba (Flowering Almond; Zones 6 to 9) is a large, treelike shrub growing 12 to 15 feet high, that is chiefly attractive when in bloom. The flowers are small, pinkish, double, and roselike in late April (earlier in the South), and are borne in large quantities. Unfortunately, they are frequently killed just as they are opening by a late freeze.

Punica granatum

Punica granatum
(POON-i-ka gra-NAY-tum)

Pomegranate

ZONES 8 to 10

Deciduous

A deciduous shrub valuable for its showy, waxy orange or scarlet flowers in July and August and brilliant yellow autumn foliage, a few varieties will also produce delicious fruits. It is an excellent desert shrub, quite tolerant of heat and alkaline soils, that withstands considerable drought if the quality of the fruit is unimportant. *Punica granatum* will arch to a fountainlike height of 12 to 15 feet and form a dense, twiggy mass. Several cultivars are available for flower variation, from a single or double scarlet to white, yellow, and red. Selections are also available for fruit quality ('Wonderful' is the most popular form for fruit), and for size, ranging from 18-inch pot or edging plants to 15-foot border shrubs. Plant pomegranate in full sun for best blooms and fruit. The fruit quality is best when the shrub is watered regularly and deeply. Native from southeastern Europe across Asia to the Himalayas.

Pyracantha coccinea 'Mohave'

Pyracantha coccinea
(pye-ra-CAN-tha cok-SIN-ee-a)

Scarlet Firethorn

ZONES 6B to 10

Broad-leafed evergreen (semideciduous in the North)

Showy, white flowers in the spring, excellent evergreen or semievergreen foliage, and powerfully spectacular red or orange fruit in the fall and winter are features of this all-season shrub. The form can always be called irregular, although varieties range from upright to prostrate. And several dwarf forms are available. Growing at a medium to fast rate to 6 to 18 feet in height and spread, the vicious thorns on pyracantha make an excellent impenetrable barrier. Useful as a specimen, screen, or barrier hedge, it is an especially popular espalier against walls and along fences. Espaliering is easy to do as long as you keep up with it. Be sure to respect its ultimate size and thorniness by resisting the apparently common temptation to plant it next to doors, drives, walks, or patios, where it will eventually attack people, cars, bare feet, and so forth. A nasty plant to prune, give it plenty of room to grow. This is an easy plant to grow in full sun and well-drained soil but don't try to move it after it is established. Guard against standing water on its foliage at bloomtime, because fireblight is a serious problem. Scale, aphids, spider mites, apple scab, and lace bug can also be damaging. Many varieties are available, most of which are hardy only to Zone 7. 'Kasan', 'Lalandi', 'Thornless', 'Wyatti', and 'Chadwicki' are all hardy to Zone 6. 'Teton' is a new, strongly vertical (12 feet high by 4 feet wide) form, also hardy to Zone 6. 'Fiery Cascade' is the hardiest (Zone 6) red-fruiting form. 'Mohave' has beautiful, heavily borne fruits that are scab resistant. Native from Italy to western Asia.

Raphiolepis indica
(ra-fee-ALL-epp-iss IN-di-ca)

India Hawthorne

ZONES 8B to 10

Broad-leafed evergreen

Raphiolepis is one of those easy-to-care-for garden workhorses that is both spectacularly showy and extremely serviceable for a multitude of purposes. Its leathery, evergreen foliage and neat, dense, restrained habit, 3 to 5

Raphiolepis 'Springtime'

feet high and wide, make it an excellent low background, mass, informal hedge, or large-scale ground cover. Consider it as a foreground or facing plant in a shrub border, or as an excellent, trouble-free container plant. The flowers bloom in midwinter or spring, usually repeating in the fall, and vary from white to red, according to the cultivar. Dark-flowered cultivars are generally lighter the further south they are grown. India hawthorne prefers full sun, but tolerates partial shade well, in addition to a variety of soils. While reasonably tolerant of drought, it looks its best when frequently watered. Minimize splashing water onto foliage, since fireblight and leaf spots can be problems, and protect from aphids. Native to southern China.

Rhododendron species
(roe-doe-DEN-dron)

Rhododendrons and Azaleas

Hardiness varies according to the variety

Some evergreen, some deciduous species

Probably no other group of plants illicits as much devotional praise and obsessional frustration as the genus *Rhododendron*. Where they can be grown, few plants can match the bewildering variety of striking, often brilliant flowers borne in legendary profusion. Besides their famous flowers, rhododendrons and azaleas frequently offer outstanding form and foliage, along with more subtle qualities apparent on close inspection. Unfortunately, there are many areas in the United States where these plants do not adapt well—in the desert or the Plains States you will probably find rhododendrons difficult, if not impossible, to grow. Fortunately, the vigorous and diverse breeding efforts concerning this genus are expanding the range somewhat.

Rhododendron is an extremely complicated genus containing over 900 species, of which over 10,000 named varieties are listed in the International Register of Names. The genus is divided into several series, one of which is *Azalea*. Botanists are still arguing over exactly what anatomical characteristics separate *Azalea* from *Rhododendron*. While many azaleas are deciduous, and most rhododendrons are evergreen, there are important exceptions in each case. A common misconception is that azaleas are always smaller in form and leaf than rhododendrons, while in fact several rhododendrons are tiny, rock-garden dwarfs with leaves smaller than any azalea. And whether or not a plant is evergreen has little bearing on the matter—both azaleas *and* rhododendrons have deciduous and evergreen species. For most people it is enough to understand that while all azaleas are rhododendrons, not all rhododendrons are azaleas, and leave the

stamen counting to the botanists.

The finicky, frustrating reputation of rhododendrons is actually misleading. *If planted in a favorable location and given the proper growing conditions, azaleas and rhododendrons are easy, care-free, and long-living plants.* The trick is in having, creating, or finding those favorable growing conditions. Look for the following points:

■ *Acid soil (pH 4.5 to 6.5) that is well drained and retains moisture well.* If you are amending your soil to provide these conditions, we suggest a mixture of ¼ soil, ½ organic matter (peat, composted oak leaves, ground cedar, or composted pine chips are excellent for their acid reaction), and ¼ coarse sand. Volcanic sand, if available, is highly recommended, because it is porous and retains moisture well. Guard against using sand that has been mined from near the sea, as it is probably high in deadly salts. The addition of some slow-release fertilizer is also beneficial. For those of you with serious heavy-soil problems, raised beds may be the best answer. Even mounding the soil and planting high can improve drainage enough to mean the difference between death and survival for your rhododendrons. If you have neutral or alkaline soil, you may want to choose another plant besides a rhododendron. Realize that, while you can acidify your soil, it is a tricky operation, and you will have to keep it perpetually acidic. Rhododendrons will let you know when the soil has reverted to its alkaline state by declining in vigor and developing chlorosis (leaves turn yellow while the veins remain green)—actually an iron deficiency caused either by alkalinity, which makes the iron in the soil unusable, or by an actual lack of iron. Probably the best way to acidify the soil is with ferrous sulfate, although flowers of sulfur can be used. A soil test report will tell you exactly how much to apply. Some commercial growers have even used dilute sulfuric acid with great success. Ammonium sulfate can be used, but with great caution—its powerful, quick-acting nitrogen can burn tender roots.

■ *Protection from winter sun and wind and excessive summer heat.* This point is especially important for the evergreen varieties. Due to their shallow root systems, rhododendrons cannot reach below the frost line and transmit water to their leaves when the soil is frozen. Yet their evergreen leaves constantly transpire water, even in the coldest winter. Sun and wind at this vulnerable time can be deadly. Rapid freezing and thawing is also destructive, and can be lessened by protecting from the sun during the winter. A 3-inch organic mulch in the fall will moderate winter soil temperatures and add needed organic matter to the soil. Contrary to popular opinion, the evergreen leaves are much more tolerant of sun during the growing season. And most deciduous types can be grown in full sun if the summers are not too hot. The fact remains, however, that the optimum exposure for nearly all rhododendrons and azaleas is the filtered shade of high tree branches in both summer and winter. The eastern side of a sheltering structure is also a good planting location.

■ *Adequate atmospheric and soil moisture.* Realize that most rhododendrons in cultivation are native to the Northeast and Pacific Northwest of the United States, and eastern Asia and Japan, where rain is both plentiful and evenly distributed the year round. They will not tolerate drought for any length of time. Water them regularly during dry periods, but avoid keeping them soggy. Beware of water that is alkaline or high in salts. The very best water is rain water, and those interested in growing rhododendrons successfully would be well advised to capture rainwater to help them through the dry periods.

A mulch is very helpful to retain moisture and keep the roots cool. Organic matter that breaks down with an acid reaction is best, such as oak leaves, pine needles and bark, or cedar chips. Avoid peat as a mulch, since it forms a crust and actually repels water when dry; also avoid maple and elm leaves because of their heavy matting properties and alkaline reactions. Mulch to a settled depth of 2 to 3 inches, and no deeper. Where plants have problems with flower spot or petal blight, it will be necessary to replace the mulch each year.

■ *Benign neglect.* One of the most common mistakes with rhododendrons and azaleas is overfeeding. They are extremely sensitive to excessive levels of nitrogen around their fibrous roots. They do benefit, however, from infrequent light feeding with a fertilizer formulated for acid plants. In good garden soils, little fertilization should be necessary. If you are using organic mulches such as wood chips, sawdust, or shredded oak leaves, additional nitrogen will be needed. Avoid manure; it is usually high in salts, to which rhododendrons are extremely sensitive.

Never cultivate around the roots of rhododendrons and azaleas. Use mulch, or gentle pulling for weed control. Encourage adequate hardening off of any new growth before the onset of winter by ceasing any fertilization two months before the first frost. Anticipate weather condtions in the fall, and just prior to the first hard freeze, send your rhododendrons into winter with plenty of moisture by giving them a good, deep watering.

Pruning should seldom be necessary. Remember that most rhododendrons will naturally try to achieve an open, picturesque form. If greater density is desired, prune lightly back to the nearest growth bud early in the spring after flowering. Late pruning will remove next year's flower buds. Or prune more heavily to rejuvenate old plants, always leaving at least two visible growth buds. Not all rhododendrons break new buds on old wood like forsythia or privet. If you want to test your rhododendron's ability to sprout, cut back one or two inconspicuous branches in late winter. If they sprout, the rest of the plant can be cut back the following year. See page 46 for more pruning details.

The descriptions that follow do not attempt to be exhaustive for this complex genus. In general, to achieve dependable results, it is best to purchase named varieties. Plants grown from seed can be extremely variable

and often disappointing. For particular cultivars adapted to your area, consult with the staff at your local nursery. And for further information, refer to *Rhododendrons of the World* by David G. Leach (New York: Charles Schribner's Sons, 1961) and *Azaleas* by Fred C. Galle (Birmingham, AL: Oxmoor House, 1974).

Rhododendron arborescens (Sweet Azalea; Zones 5 to 7). Producing white flowers in early June and July with a delightful fragrance similar to heliotrope, this deciduous shrub will grow 8 to 20 feet high and wide. It is cloaked with bright green leaves in the summer that turn dark red in the fall. Native from New York to Georgia and Alabama, along mountain streams, and in cool mountain meadows.

Rhododendron calendulaceum (Flame Azalea; Zones 5 to 8). The long-lasting June blooms of this deciduous eastern native range from yellow through orange and scarlet. In the fall, the fiery colors are echoed in the foliage as it changes from yellow to bronze. This shrub is quite variable both in color and fragrance, so it is best to purchase it when it is in bloom. Most selections will reach 6 to 8 feet in height. Native from Pennsylvania through Georgia and west to Tennessee.

Rodododendron canadense

Rhododendron canadense (Rhodora; Zones 2 to 6). Found wild in bogs and in moist, very acid soils, this small, rounded, 3-to 4-foot, shrub has small, deciduous leaves and light purple flowers in mid-May. It is most useful in a low, wet spot in a garden with cool summers. Native from Newfoundland and Labrador to New York and Pennsylvania.

Rhododendron carolinianum (Carolina Rhododendron; Zones 5 to 8A). This restrained, 3- to 6-foot, rounded shrub bears white or pink flowers against dark, medium-sized, evergreen leaves. It is native to the Blue Ridge Mountains of Carolina and Tennessee.

Rhododendron catawbiense (Catawba Rhododendron; Zones 5 to 7). This is one of the hardiest large, evergreen rhododendrons, growing to an open 6- to 10-foot height and width in the garden, although it often reaches 15 to 20 feet in the wild. Reddish-purple trusses of flowers are borne in great quantities in mid- to late May, against the handsome, dark green leaves. Many beautiful cultivars are available, from bright red to purple or white, some of which are among the hardiest rhododendrons for harsh climates. Native to the Allegheny Mountains from West Virginia to Georgia and Alabama.

Rhododendron, Gable Hybrids (Gable Hybrid Azalea; Zones 6 to 8). Actually quite a variable group of hybrids, these were bred for supposedly increased hardiness, although they should not be considered for use north of Zone 6. Their evergreen foliage tends to redden and fall in the northern part of their range. The flowers are generously borne in May, and are predominantly in the red-to-purple hues, with some light violets, orange-reds, and pinks.

Rhododendron × gandavense (Ghent Hybrid Azaleas; Zones 5 to 7). Many of the cultivars of this deciduous shrub are hardy to −20°F, and some are being grown as far north as Zone 4 with apparent success. A diverse parentage has resulted in a proliferation of cultivars, from white and yellow flowers to pink, orange, and red, and they may be single or double. Usually growing 6 to 10 feet high with a comparable spread, the Ghent hybrids appear to perform best in light shade.

Rhododendron impeditum (Cloudland Rhododendron; Zones 5 to 8). The hardiness rating of this rhododendron is largely based on the availability of snow cover or similar protection during the winter (as is true with most other dwarf rhododendrons). Growing only 18 inches high and wide, with densely borne, tiny, gray-green leaves, it makes an attractive plant for a sheltered spot in a rock garden. It is one of the many garden plants with flowers usually listed as blue, although they are actually more of a mauve or lavender. This shrub is even more sensitive than most rhododendrons to hot, dry summers.

Rhododendron

Rhododendron, Indica Hybrids (Indian Hybrid Azalea; Zones 8 to 10). This group of tender, evergreen azaleas was originally developed for greenhouse forcing, but many cultivars have since been selected for outstanding landscape plants for mild climates, and are a common sight in gardens of the deep South and California. They generally fall into two groups: The Belgian Indica hybrids are the most tender and should not be grown where temperatures fall below 15°F. The southern Indica hybrids have been selected from the Belgian hybrids for greater sun tolerance and more vigorous growth. Most are hardy to 10°F, although damage to flower buds can occur below 15°F. Flower colors for both groups range from white through violet, pink, red, and salmon.

Rodododendron arborescens

Rhododendron catawbiense

Rhododendron kaempferi (Zones 6 to 8). This species and its hybrid forms are covered in May with flowers, ranging from white to rose to red-orange and salmon. The shrub can reach 5 to 6 feet high in five years or so, and may eventually grow 10 feet tall. The leaves are semievergreen in the North and evergreen in the South, and often turn red at the onset of cold weather. They should not be planted where winter temperatures drop below –10°F. In their native Japan, they are frequently found growing on sunny hillsides and by the sea, but their flower colors last longest when grown in light shade. It is one of the few deciduous azaleas that will flower well in the deepest shade.

A seedling Exbury Azalea

Rhododendron, Knapp Hill-Exbury Hybrids (Zones 6 to 8, although some newer cultivars are hardy to Zone 4). Spectacular, brilliant flowers literally cover these shrubs in late May and early June, and are available in hundreds of different shades of white, pink, rose, red, salmon, yellow, and orange. The flowers are large, borne in many huge trusses. The medium green, deciduous foliage turns into electric yellows, oranges, and reds in the fall. Like most of the deciduous azaleas, it is somewhat less finicky about soil acidity and winter shade than its evergreen cousins, but is relatively intolerant of hot summer conditions. It will generally reach 4 to 8 feet in height with a comparable spread.

Rhododendron keiskei

Rhododendron keiskei (Kiesk Rhododendron; Zones 6B to 8). This shrub is unusual for being one of the few evergreen rhododendrons to bear yellow flowers. Extremely variable in size, forms range from a 6-inch, rock-garden shrublet to an 8-foot, open, loose shrub. But all have small, finely textured leaves.
Rhododendron × kosterianum (Mollis Hybrid Azaleas; Zones 5B to 7). Quite similar to the Ghent hybrids, these deciduous azaleas are not quite as hardy or long living. Cultivars are available from yellow and gold flowers through salmon and orange-red. They bloom in late

May. Unfortunately, many nursery people offer "Mollis hybrids" that are actually *Rhododendron molle* grown from seed. Thus, it is always best to select plants when in bloom. Mollis hybrid azaleas will perform well in full sun and neutral soil, and grow to a restrained 3- to 8-foot rounded form.
Rhododendron lapponicum (Lapland Rhododendron; Zones 3 to 7). Grow this unusually hardy evergreen shrub in rock or alpine gardens where summers remain cool. Small, purple flowers appear in June on a low, 1½-foot, prostrate form against tiny, dark green leaves.
Rhododendron × 'Loderi' (Loderi Hybrid Rhododendrons; Zones 8 to 10). Famous for their powerful fragrance and showy flower clusters in shades of white to pink, this evergreen rhododendron should not be grown where winter temperatures fall below 0°F. Although the growth rate is slow, these shrubs are eventually too large for most gardens—they reach an open, loose, 8 feet or more in height and width.

Rhododendron maximum

Rhododendron maximum (Rosebay Rhododendron; Zones 4 to 8). This North American native is the tallest evergreen rhododendron hardy in the North. In the wild it can reach as tall as 30 feet, but a height of 4 to 15 feet is more likely in most northern gardens. Since the habit is loose and open, it is best to use this plant in large masses; it can make a splendid hedge. The flowers are pink in bud and open to white or rosy-purple. The flowers are borne late in the season, in June or July, but are unfortunately partially hidden by the large 4- to 8-inch leaves. This rhododendron must be grown in at least partial shade to thrive.

Rhododendron mucronulatum

Rhododendron mucronulatum (Korean Rhododendron; Zones 5 to 8). This deciduous shrub illustrates the contention that not all rhododendrons are evergreen. It is the first of all hardy rhododendrons and azaleas to flower—the bright, rosy-purple blossoms can appear as early as mid- to late March. For this rea-

son, it is extremely susceptible to premature warm spells and late freezes, which can kill the flower buds overnight. It is most important to plant this shrub where it is sheltered from southern or southwestern sun in February and March. The nice, early flowers and compact habit make them a good choice for planting near the house on the northeastern side, or in a sheltered shrub border. 'Cornell Pink' is a particularly beautiful pink form.

Rhododendron nudiflorum

Rhododendron nudiflorum (Pinxterbloom Azalea; Zones 4 to 9). A hardy, deciduous azalea with pinkish-white, fragrant flowers that bloom in late April or early May, this one features a low, neat habit, usually 4 to 6 feet wide and high. The foliage is bright green in the summer, turning to a dull, yellowish-brown in the fall. This shrub will perform beautifully in full sun and dry, sandy, rocky soils—a rare exception for the genus *Rhododendron*.

Rhododendron obtusum (background)

Rhododendron obtusum (Hiryu Azaleas; Zones 7 to 9). A few cultivars of this evergreen azalea are hardy to –10°F. Unfortunately, many of the more tender varieties are commonly sold as far north as Zone 5B, with disappointing results. In milder gardens where hardiness is not a problem, the Hiryu azalea has proven to be a reliable, spectacular, and popular shrub. Several of its brilliant red cultivars have become familiar sights in the landscape—'Hinodegiri', 'Hino-Crimson', and 'Hershey's Red', for example. The form is broad, low, and spreading, reaching 3 to 6 feet high and perhaps twice as wide at maturity. The small leaves give it a fine texture. The flowers appear in March and April in great quantities, and range from white to pink, to lavender, to scarlet.

Rhododendron, P.J.M. Hybrids (Zones 5 to 8). This group of evergreen rhododendrons grows 3 to 6 feet high into a rounded, relatively dense mass. The dark green foliage turns a deep purple in cold weather, and is some-

Rhododendron carolinianum

times deciduous in the northern extremes of its range. It is, however, one of the most cold hardy of the small-leaved rhododendrons. The flowers vary in the intensity of their bright, lavender-pink color, so it is best to buy this plant when it is in bloom.

Rhododendron schlippenbachii

Rhododendron schlippenbachii (Royal Azalea; Zone 5). The royal azalea is a deciduous, upright, rounded shrub, growing 6 to 8 feet high and wide. In the summer the foliage is a dark green; in the fall it presents an electric kaleidoscope of color, in yellows, oranges, and brilliant reds. The fragrant, pale pink to white flowers are borne in early to mid-May, but vary in intensity when grown from seed, so buy this plant when it is in bloom. Unlike most other rhododendrons and azaleas, this one does not require acid soil, being comfortable with a pH range of 6.5 to 7.

Rhododendron vaseyi (Pinkshell Azalea; Zones 5 to 9). The deciduous foliage of this hardy North American azalea is a medium green in summer, which changes to a light red in the fall. The delightfully fragrant flowers are a clear, pale pink, and are borne in early to mid-May. The graceful, delicate effect of this shrub is enhanced by its pleasantly irregular habit, growing 5 to 10 feet high, usually with slightly less width.

Rhododendron viscosum

Rhododendron viscosum (Swamp Azalea; Zones 4 to 8). Unlike nearly all rhododendrons and azaleas, this shrub actually thrives in damp, soggy soil, and is a perfect answer to that problem wet spot in the acid garden. In addition, it features small, white or pink blossoms that have a powerful, clovelike fragrance. The habit is loose and open, ranging from 3 to 8 feet high and 3 to 8 feet wide. Consequently, this shrub does best in masses where an informal, naturalized look is desired.

Rhus copallina (fall color)

Rhus copallina
(ROOS koh-pa-LINE-a)

Flameleaf Sumac; Shining Sumac

ZONES 5 to 8

Deciduous

For some strange reason, nurseries seldom offer this plant, preferring its larger, weedier, and shorter-lived cousin, the staghorn sumac. Yet it is the best sumac for ornamental use. While occasionally reaching 30 feet in the wild, this open, picturesque shrub rarely exceeds 8 feet in cultivation. It will spread into clumps through suckering, but in a much more restrained and controllable manner than the staghorn sumac. Its shiny green foliage is darker than any other sumac, and the compound, large, almost tropical leaves turn a brilliant red-orange in the fall. Unlike other sumacs, the flameleaf sumac is an excellent subject for containers. It is easily transplanted and adaptable to many soils, but prefers well-drained ones and is intolerant of standing water. A relatively long-living plant, use it as a specimen for fall color and interesting silhouettes. It is also beautiful when naturalized in large groups and masses.

Rhus typhina (Staghorn Sumac; Zones 4 to 8). While individual plants live for a short time, the profuse suckers with which this large 25-foot shrub forms massive colonies are hard to suppress, and weedy. A beautiful, picturesque shrub with finely textured foliage and downy stems and fruit, it also has the gorgeous fall color and structural interest that the flameleaf sumac has. The temptation to use it as a focal specimen is common, usually with disastrous results, since it dies after a few years and moves on through its suckers. It is best to reserve this shrub for massing and naturalizing in large waste areas.

Rosa species
(RO-za)

Rose

Hardiness varies according to the species

Mostly deciduous, some evergreen species

Volumes have been written extolling the virtues of this most venerable, popular, and com-plex genus. The hybrid teas, floribundas, grandifloras, and climbers are represented by an incredible profusion of cultivars that have placed the rose at the pinnacle of horticultural breeding. While they are usually grown for the beauty of their individual flowers, to call them hobby roses would be to diminish their popularity and significance. Words like passion or obsession are closer to fact. For a complete discussion of these beauties, consult Ortho's book, *All About Roses.*

Perhaps not as well known, but infinitely more useful to the landscape gardener, are some of the species roses whose descriptions follow. Unlike the hobby roses mentioned above, these are generally much easier to grow, relatively pest free, and require little special attention to pruning or feeding. Most display more seasonal and short-lived (but effective) flowers, excellent foliage qualities, larger size, increased hardiness, and occasionally attractive fall fruit and foliage color.

Rosa banksiae (Banks Rose; Zones 8 to 10). This tender, large, semievergreen or evergreen shrub will climb on trellises and fences as high as 18 feet. Grown without support, it will form a sprawling, rambling mass 6 to 8 feet high and nearly twice as wide. The flowers are yellow fading to white and are borne in unbelievable profusion. White and double-flowered forms are available. Native to China.

Rosa foetida (Austrian Briar; Zones 4 to 9). The single, deep yellow flowers of this 10-foot-high and -wide shrub have been popular for centuries. 'Bicolor' is a form with coppery-red flowers tinged with yellow. 'Persiana' has smaller, double yellow flowers. Native to western Asia.

Rosa Hugonis

Rosa hugonis (Father Hugo Rose; Zones 5 to 10). This is one of the best and most popular of the yellow-blooming species roses. The single, canary yellow blossoms appear in May, along with the late tulips, and are thought by many to be the most exquisitely beautiful rose blossom in bud. The plant grows rapidly to 6 to 8 feet high and often wider, with an upright, arching, twiggy habit. The finely cut foliage is nice, but this plant tends toward raggedness when not in bloom. Prune the oldest wood to the ground each year after blooming to encourage more flowering and to keep the plant neater. Use Father Hugo rose as a screen or informal hedge, in the shrub border, or espaliered on a trellis. Native to central China.

Rosa rubrifolia (Redleaf Rose; Zones 2 to 8). Especially valuable in the harsh, northern prairie states, this rose features clean, reddish-tinged foliage. The single, pink flowers in the spring are not particularly overwhelming. Native to central Europe.

Rosa rugosa flowers

Rosa rugosa Rose hips

Rosa rugosa (Rugosa Rose, Saltspray Rose; Zones 2 to 10). Especially well adapted to the sandy soils and saline environment of coastal gardens, the rugosa rose is probably the easiest rose to grow. The flowers range from rose-purple to white, single or double, according to the cultivar selected. After a heavy late-spring bloom, they continue to bloom lightly all summer. Forming a dense, brambly mat 4 to 6 feet high and wide, the stout, upright, and prickly canes withstand pruning well and make an effective barrier hedge. The leaves are an outstanding deep, lustrous green that changes to yellow in the fall. They make an effective backdrop for the brick-red hips. This is an excellent choice for difficult, rocky or sandy soils. Native to northern China, Korea, and Japan.

Rosa spinosissima 'Altaica'

Rosa spinosissima (Scotch Rose; Zones 4 to 10). The free-spreading, suckering habit of this 3- to 4-foot-high shrub makes it a useful, rapidly growing bank or ground cover, especially where erosion is a problem. It is available in a variety of flower colors, from pink to white to yellow, single or double. The blossoms are generally fragrant, and appear in late May and early June in prodigious quantities. The low habit, profuse blooms, variety of cultivars,

and ease of culture have all contributed to its popularity. Native to Europe, Western Asia, and now naturalized in the northeastern United States. This is the only rose native to Ireland.

Rosa virginiana (Virginia Rose; Zones 4 to 10). This is another rose that is excellent by the sea, but is extremely easy to grow anywhere in well-drained soil. In addition, it is our most beautiful native rose, attractive in all seasons. The flowers are single, pink, and open in June. The foliage is a crisp, glossy dark green and unusually free from pests. In the fall it develops brilliant foliage coloration, starting with purple, then changing to orange, red, crimson, and finally yellow. The hips are bright red, borne in great quantities, and are effective into the winter. The canes add to the winter interest because of their reddish hue. This rose can grow 6 feet high and spread indefinitely by underground stems, but is easily restrained into a 3-foot hedge. Where its vigorous habit spreads a bit too far, simply cut the whole shrub back to the ground. It will rapidly recover into excellent form. Native from Newfoundland to Virginia, Alabama, and Missouri.

Rosa wichuraiana (Memorial Rose; Zones 6 to 10). Especially in milder climates where its foliage is semievergreen or evergreen, this trailing rose makes an excellent ground cover. Spreading 8 to 16 feet or more, and achieving a maximum of 1½ feet, it forms a dense mat of glossy, deep green foliage that few weeds can penetrate. The small, white, fragrant flowers appear in late June through July, making it one of the last rose species to bloom. Native to China, Korea, and Japan.

Rosmarinus officinalis 'Collingwood Ingram'

Rosmarinus officinalis
(Rose-MARE-i-nus oh-fish-i-NAL-is)
Rosemary

ZONES 7 to 10

Narrow-leafed evergreen

Best in mild, Mediterranean climates with dry summers and wet winters, this is the rosemary familiar to good cooks. Its evergreen, fragrant foliage clips and shears well. Trailing forms are excellent cascading over walls with their grayish-green, fine texture. Use larger types as a clipped hedge or in the dry shrub border. Lower types make excellent, erosion-controlling bank or ground covers, spilling over rocks and walls. Size varies according to variety, from 2 to 6 feet high and often twice as wide. The showy flowers are light blue and appear in late winter or very early spring. Certain cultivars, such as 'Collingwood Ingram' and 'Lockwood de Forest', have been selected for bright blue flowers. The shrub is attractive to birds and bees. Rosemary must have sharp drainage; overwatering and overfertilizing will result in rank, stretchy growth. It tolerates heat, sun, infertile soil, and drought. Set ground cover vari-

eties 2 feet apart for a quick cover. Native to southern Europe and Asia Minor.

Salix gracilistyla

Salix gracilistyla
(SAY-liks gra-sil-i-STYLE-a)
Rosegold Pussy Willow

ZONES 5 to 10

Deciduous

If you are determined to grow pussy willows, this one is distinctly the best. Its rapid growth to a 6-to 10-foot height and width is quite restrained and neat compared to other willows. And its catkins are the largest, earliest (March), and most beautiful. The stamens on male catkins are a shimmering gold, while underneath there is a distinctly rosy fuzziness. Use this willow to naturalize in damp or wet, difficult soil, or possibly as an accent in the shrub border for its bluish-gray foliage. The branches are wonderful to cut and force indoors in earliest spring. Preferring moist, even water-logged soil, the rosegold pussy willow will also tolerate dry soils. Like all willows, it is plagued by many pests and is a weak-wooded, somewhat messy, and short-lived plant. Prune heavily to keep it vigorous and healthy. Native to Japan, Korea, and Manchuria.

Salix caprea (Goat Willow; Zones 5 to 10). Often sold as a cute little pussy willow, this will quickly become a messy, awkward giant, which grows 25 to 30 feet tall and spreads 15 to 20 feet. Avoid this plant.

Salix discolor (Pussy Willow; Zones 4 to 10). Grown for its fuzzy gray catkins in poor, wet soils, this is a wild, unruly, and huge shrub, growing 20 feet high and as wide, and forming a mass of upright stems. It is a messy plant, constantly dropping twigs, leaves, and branches. Native from Labrador to South Dakota and south to Missouri.

Spiraea species
(spy-REE-a)
Spirea

ZONES 5 to 10

Deciduous

To most, the word spirea means bridlewreath or Vanhoutte spirea, two old-fashioned favorites that seem to be as awkward, large, and cumbersome as they are popular. While many superior, more dwarfed varieties are available to the diligent searcher, the unfortunate fact remains that no spirea is particularly inspiring when it is out of bloom. Easily transplanted, rapid growing, and low in maintenance, spireas are not particular about soil. While they are subject to many pests, including fireblight, leaf spot, powdery mildew, and a host of insects, none appears to be fatally serious if the plant is placed in a location with full sun and good air circulation. Spireas differ as to when they should be pruned: summer-flowering types should be pruned in late winter or early spring, since they bloom on the current year's wood; spring-flowering types should be pruned directly after blooming. Older, leggy plants of either type can be renewed by cutting them to the ground in early spring. Use spireas in a shrub border as an inexpensive, rapidly growing, and easy-to-care-for filler, where their dull, non-blooming appearance can be masked. The lower-growing types make passable, coarse ground covers.

Spiraea albiflora (Japanese White Spirea) is a low (1½ feet), rounded, dense shrub with white flowers that produce on the current year's growth in late June and July. The relatively neat, compact habit of this plant makes it superior to many other spireas. Native to Japan.

Spirea × bumalda 'Anthony Waterer'

Spiraea × bumalda (Bumalda Spirea) is a low, spreading shrub growing 2 to 3 feet high and 3 to 5 feet wide, with white to deep pink flowers blooming from mid-June to August on the current year's growth. Native to Japan. 'Anthony Waterer' is an extremely popular deep rose cultivar, but several other superior cultivars are available. They include 'Crispa' (growing 2 feet high with twisted leaves), 'Gold Flame' (low growing with brightly colored red, copper, and orange foliage in early spring and fall), and 'Nyeswood' (especially dense and compact with good, pink flowers).

Spirea japonica (Japanese Spirea) is similar to *Spirea × bumalda*, except for a larger, coarser habit that grows 4 to 5 feet high. 'Atrosanguinea' is a superior, deep rose-red cultivar that grows from 2½ to 4 feet high, and is hardier (Zone 4B). The Japanese spirea blooms on new wood from early June through July. Native to Japan.

Spirea nipponica 'Snowmound' (Snowmound Spirea) is a delightful, dwarfish, white-blooming spirea that grows 3 to 5 feet high and as wide. It is a superior choice to the Vanhoutte spirea because of its denser, neater, more compact form. Native to Japan.

Spiraea prunifolia (Bridalwreath Spirea) is a rangy, coarse, open shrub, growing 4 to 9 feet tall and 6 to 8 feet wide. The dull white flowers appear in April on old wood. Native to Korea, China, and Formosa.

Spiraea × vanhouttei (Vanhoutte Spirea) grows rapidly to become an 8- to 10-foot-high, arching, fountainlike shrub, spreading 10 to

12 feet. This is an extremely tough shrub that is popularly used in the border and for massing. Its size definitely limits it to large gardens. The white flowers are effective from early April to May and appear on old wood.

Symplocos paniculata

Symplocos paniculata
(Sim-PLOE-kos pan-i-ku-LAY-ta)

Sapphireberry; Asiatic Sweetleaf

ZONES 5 to 8

Deciduous

Brilliant, unusual blue fruits practically cover this shrub in the fall and are often described as turquoise or azure blue. They are the truest blue of any so-called blue-fruited shrubs available, and are a tremendous eye-catcher in the garden. Unfortunately, they are frequently as attractive to birds as they are to people. The profuse, powder-puff, creamy white flowers that bloom in May and June are actually more showy than many old-time favorites, such as deutzia, honeysuckle, and Mockorange. Curiously, this beautiful shrub is seldom offered by nurseries. It is large, growing 10 to 20 feet tall and wide, and fruit production seems to vary from plant to plant. For more dependable fruit production, plant two or more of these shrubs together for crossfertilization. Sapphireberry transplants easily into any well-drained soil. Full sun is best for optimum fruit production. Long living and pest free, it is a dependable bloomer whose flower buds are hardy to –25°F. Native to rocky slopes, edges of woods, and forest glades in full sun, from the Himalayas to Japan.

Syringa vulgaris

Syringa vulgaris
(sir-ING-a vul-GAYR-is)

Common Lilac

ZONES 3B to 7, somewhat successful further south

Deciduous

Beloved by gardeners since time immemorial

for its mid- to late-May, powerfully fragrant flowers, the common lilac is a wonderful plant for the rear of a shrub border or any out-of-the-way place where its delightful scent can be appreciated. Resist the temptation to plant it as a specimen or in highly visible spots; it has little to offer when not in flower, which is about 50 weeks out of the year. A large, upright, often irregular shrub growing 20 feet in height and 12 to 15 feet in spread, the leaves are gray to dark green or bluish-green, and are often covered with powdery mildew by midsummer. An incredible profusion of cultivars is available for flower color: pinks, blues, violets and purples, white.

The plants live a long time, and seem to survive the most adverse calamities. However, lilacs are not easy to keep looking attractive. They normally produce good flowers only every other year. Plant them in full sun in neutral, rich soil that is high in organic matter. While they respond well to light, annual fertilization, too much will decrease flowering. Remove spent flower blossoms immediately to increase next year's bloom, and prune out 50 to 75 percent of the basal suckers each year. Old plants can be renewed by cutting them back severely, almost to the ground. Lilacs are plagued by many irritating, although usually not fatal, diseases and insects. Most lilacs do not perform well in mild climates. Exceptions are cultivars selected for this purpose, including 'Lavender Lady', 'Blue Boy', Chiffon', 'Mrs. Forrest K. Smith', and 'Sylvan Beauty'. Native to southern Europe.

Tamarix hispida

Tamarix hispida
(TAM-a riks HISS-pi-da)

Kashgar Tamarix

ZONES 5 to 10

Deciduous

For a bright pink, August to September display under the harshest seashore conditions, try this slender, wispy, 4- to 6-foot shrub. Like every tamarix, its winter appearance is impossible and needs to be well hidden in the shrub border. This is, however, the neatest and most restrained of the tamarixes for the small garden. The foliage is needlelike, similar to junipers, but deciduous, creating a feathery, light green effect. Tamarix must have well-drained soil and is touchy about transplanting, so always purchase young, container-grown plants. However, it is extremely tolerant of salty, sandy soil, harsh, dry winds, and considerable drought. While it makes an excellent choice for desert gardens, it will need periodic watering. If the soil is too fertile it will become quite leggy and rangy. All tamarix plants grow very rapidly. Prune when dormant in early spring. Native to the region of the Caspian Sea.

Tamarix ramosissima, (also called *T. pentandra* and *T. chinensis* (Five-stamen Tamarix; Zones 2 to 10). This is the hardiest tamarix of all—larger, leggier, and more awkward than *T. hispida*—growing 10 to 15 feet high, 20 to 30 feet in mild climates. Since it flowers on new growth, it is best to cut this plant back hard or even to level it to the ground each year after the leaves drop in the fall. Its root system can become quite invasive. It performs beautifully in coastal gardens and the arid Southwest. In mild areas it readily naturalizes, often becoming difficult to handle. Native from southeastern Europe to central Asia.

Tamarix parviflora (Small-flowered Tamarix; Zones 5 to 10). Similar in form and flower to *T. ramosissima,* this one flowers on old wood, so prune it hard each year just after flowering. Native to southeastern Europe.

Taxus × media 'Hicksii'

Taxus species
(TAX-us)

Yew

ZONES 5 and 6B to 8

Conifer

While the species are large, 40- to 50-foot-high trees, the many cultivars available are among the most useful coniferous evergreen shrubs for the landscape. Hardy and trouble free, with handsome dark green foliage and a wide variety of dense, refined forms, about the only drawback they have is overuse. Like junipers, yews are often planted without consideration for their ultimate size. Your nursery will help you to select the appropriate variety, but be sure to ask how big it will grow. Yews accept formal pruning well and are often clipped into hedges or other shapes. Consider them also for massing, as an evergreen touch to the shrub border, and as a foundation plant. When allowed to develop their natural forms, the effect is usually graceful and appealing. Give yews soil with excellent drainage and they will prove to be generally easy to grow and pest free, in sun or shade. In heavy, wet soils they will be stunted and sickly, if they survive at all. Give them adequate moisture and protect them from sweeping wind. In hot, dry climates, give them a northern exposure and hose the foliage frequently during the driest periods. Beware of their colorful, red fruits, the inner portions of which are poisonous.

Taxus baccata (English Yew; Zones 6B to 10). This least hardy yew has several cultivars that are excellent for southern gardens. Native throughout Europe.

Taxus cuspidata (Japanese Yew; Zones 5 to 10). Many excellent cultivars of this species are available, ranging from a low, 1-foot-high and 3-feet-wide form with yellow new growth ('Aurescens') to a 40- to 50-foot pyramidal form ('Capitata'). Native to Japan and Korea.

Taxus × media (Anglojap Yew; Zones 5 to 10). A hybrid between the above two species, this yew has an extremely wide variety of cultivars, from low, spreading types to tall, narrow ones.

Thuja occidentalis 'Globosa'

Thuja occidentalis
(THOO-ya awk-si-den-TAL-is)

American Arbovitae

ZONES 2 to 10

Conifer

While this is actually a large, upright, coniferous tree growing 40 to 60 feet tall, many slow-growing cultivars have been selected that are often used in foundation plantings, as hedges, or as screens. Varieties range from inches-high, rock-garden plants to 20-foot, columnar small trees that are useful as screens. Most cultivars turn an ugly yellow-brown in cold weather— 'Nigra' and 'Techny' are two that retain good, dark green foliage all winter long. Plant arbovitae in well-drained moist soil in full sun. It is tolerant of highly alkaline soils, and will perform best in areas of high atmospheric moisture. The branches and foliage are quite susceptible to damage from winter winds, snow, and ice. While many pests are listed as potential problems, these plants are generally easy to care for and trouble free. Native from Nova Scotia and Manitoba south to the Carolinas and Tennessee.

Tsuga canadensis 'Pendula'
(TSOO-ga can-a-DEN-sis PEN-dyu-la)

Sargent's Weeping Hemlock

ZONES 4 to 8B

Conifer

This is the most commonly grown dwarf hemlock. It displays a graceful, pendulous habit and refined, evergreen foliage. While it can reach 5 to 6 feet in height and two or three times that in spread in extreme old age, a more reasonable size to expect in one lifetime is 3 to 4 feet high by 8 to 9 feet wide. This plant makes an outstanding focal specimen in a border, by an entryway, in a raised bed, and in a container. Plant it in well-drained, moist, acid soil. Unlike most conifers it tolerates shade well, in fact, preferring partial shade. If drainage is good, the soil is moist, and if there are no drying winds it will tolerate full sun. Hemlock will not tolerate wind, drought, or waterlogged soils, and in areas where summer tem-

peratures exceed 95°F, it is likely to develop leaf scorch. This is not a plant for heavily polluted areas. If the location is right, hemlock is usually a trouble-free and long-living plant. Native from Nova Scotia to Minnesota, and south along the mountains to Alabama and Georgia.

Vaccinium corymbosum (fall color)

Vaccinium corymbosum
(vak-SIN-ee-um core-em-BOE-sum)

Highbush Blueberry

ZONES 4 to 8A

Deciduous

While primarily grown for its delicious fruit, both in home and commercial gardens, the highbush blueberry makes an outstanding ornamental plant when it is given the right growing conditions. It is a fairly large shrub, often reaching 6 to 12 feet high and 8 to 12 feet wide, but grows slowly and is easily restrained. Its dark, almost blue-green, lustrous foliage consistently turns into bright yellow, bronze, orange, or red combinations in the fall, which densely covers a rounded, compact form. Just as the leaves emerge in May, small white flowers are borne in great quantities, followed by the popular fruits that ripen in late July through August. Even without a spraying program, a single bush will usually provide enough berries for a few pies, some jam, and the birds.

If given moist, acid (pH 4.5 to 5.5), well-drained soil that is high in organic matter, blueberries are generally an easy plant to grow. While they are native to swampy soils, they perform best in sandy, acid ones in the garden. Mulch them well to promote a cool, moist root run, give them full sun to partial shade, and regular, adequate moisture. When grown commercially for fruit, a regular spraying program and protection from birds is usually necessary. Grown in the landscape for ornamental purposes, the fruit yield is generally sufficient without any elaborate precautions. Use highbush blueberries as a tasty and attractive addition to a shrub border, in a foundation planting, or massed naturally in large areas. Check with your local extension agent for the cultivars that grow best in your region. Native from Maine to Minnesota and south to Florida and Louisiana.

Viburnum species
(vye-BUR-num)

Hardiness varies according to the species

Some evergreen, some deciduous species

Viburnum is a particularly diverse genus that contains a wide range of valuable shrubs for the garden. Some are grown for their moderately attractive and powerfully fragrant blossoms; others display extremely showy combinations of flower, fruit, and fall color. Most perform best in a moist, well-drained soil that is slightly acid, although they are generally quite adaptable to other soils. Many insects and diseases can attract viburnums, although these shrubs are usually untroubled if kept vigorous.

Viburnum × burkwoodii (Burkwood Viburnum; Zones 6 to 10) is an upright, somewhat straggly shrub, 8 to 10 feet high and 5 to 7 feet wide. It is grown primarily for its powerfully fragrant blossoms that are pink opening to white and appear in early to late April before the leaves appear. This is a fine plant for a shrub border, where its fragrance will perfume an entire garden. In southern gardens the foliage is evergreen.

Viburnum × carlcephalum

Viburnum × carlcephalum (Fragrant Snowball Viburnum; Zones 6 to 9) is another delightfully fragrant shrub that produces white flowers in late April or May. Its loose, open growth, 6 to 10 feet high and wide, blends well into the shrub border.

Viburnum carlesii (Koreanspice Viburnum; Zones 5 to 8) is a popular fragrance shrub for northern gardens, producing pinkish-white flowers in late April to early May that have a spicy, sweet scent. It will grow to a rounded, dense, 4 to 5 feet high and 4 to 8 feet wide, occasionally reaching a height of 8 feet. Native to Korea.

Viburnum davidii (David Viburnum; Zones 8 to 10) is a small (1 to 3 feet high and 3 to 4 feet wide), dense, large-leafed, evergreen shrub that does well in southern gardens. The dark, metallic-blue fruits on this shrub are especially appealing. Native to China.

Viburnum dilatatum

Viburnum dilatatum (Linden Viburnum; Zones 5B to 8) is an upright, open shrub that grows 8 to 10 feet high and 5 to 8 feet wide. The white flowers in May and June are a welcome attrac-

tion, but this shrub's most outstanding season is in September and October when the fruits ripen. The bright red fruits are profusely borne and often remain effective well into December. This shrub is most effectively used in a shrub border, where its tendency to become leggy can be minimized. Be sure to plant several together—crossfertilization improves fruiting. Native to eastern Asia.

Viburnum × juddii (Judd Viburnum; Zones 5 to 10) is a relatively new hybrid similar to *Viburnum carlesii*, except that it is more reliably hardy in northern Zone 5.

Viburnum macrocephalum (Chinese Snowball Viburnum; Zones 7 to 10) bears white, round balls of sterile flowers in late May to early June that are the largest flower clusters of any viburnum, often 8 inches in diameter. In the northern part of its range it needs protection from winter winds, and it is one viburnum that must have well-drained soil. It is a dense, rounded shrub, 6 to 10 feet high and wide, and in southern areas it is semievergreen.

Viburnum opulus (European Cranberry Bush; Zones 4 to 10) is a popular and very effective shrub because of its delicate, pin-wheel, white flowers that put on a beautiful show in mid-May. The sterile showy flowers are on the outside of the cluster, while the fertile, less conspicuous flowers are on the inside of the cluster. Bright red, berrylike fruits are effective from September to November, and are usually accompanied by good fall foliage color. This is a large shrub, growing 8 to 12 feet high (possibly 15 feet), and spreading 10 to 15 feet. It is best used in large gardens—in a border, as a screen, or for massing. Unfortunately, it is terrifically susceptible to aphids (especially 'Rosea'), which disfigures young leaves. For this reason, *Viburnum trilobum*, a nearly identical American native, is recommended as a substitute. 'Compactum' is an excellent, dense, dwarf variety that is about half the size of the species. 'Nanum' is another dwarf that bears no flowers or fruits.

Viburnum plicatum var. tomentosum

Viburnum plicatum var. tomentosum (Doublefile Viburnum; Zones 5 to 9). Many experts consider this the most beautiful of all flowering deciduous shrubs. The profuse but lacy, pin-wheel, pure white flowers that bloom in May are gracefully arranged along the horizontally tiered, stratified branches. In the summer the foliage is a good, dark green, and in the fall it displays possibly the best autumn color of any viburnum, in tints of rust-red to purplish-red. It is one of the earliest viburnums to show good fruit color—the bright red fruits ripen in July and August, and are attractive to birds. Growing 8 to 10 feet high and slightly wider, this shrub makes an excellent focal specimen, and is a perfect horizontal complement to the

usually upright-oriented shrub border. It combines well with broad-leafed evergreens, and is particularly stunning against dark red brick backgrounds or with red-blooming flowers, such as some azaleas. Foundation plantings, masses, and screens are also good uses for this shrub. Doublefile viburnum will not tolerate heavy wet soils. Planted in fertile, well-drained but moist soil, it is generally an easily maintained, trouble-free plant. Native to China and Japan. Many superior cultivars have been selected for their form, flowers, and fruits, such as 'Mariesii' (largest flowers and best fruits), and 'Pink Beauty' (smaller flowers and leaves with outstanding deep pink blooms).

Viburnum × rhytidophylloides

Viburnum × rhytidophylloides (Lantanaphyllum Viburnum; Zones 6 to 10) is best known for the selection 'Willowwood'. This is a large shrub, 8 to 10 feet tall and wide, with large, coarse, leathery leaves that remain a dark green throughout the winter. It is slightly hardier than its parent, *V. rhytidophyllum*, performing well under harsh midwestern prairie conditions. The coarse texture of the foliage is accentuated in the winter when the leaves hang limply on the stems. Flowers and fruits are largely unimportant.

Viburnum tinus (Laurustinus; Zones 8 to 10) is an evergreen, 6-to 12-foot-high, upright shrub that is grown in southern and western gardens for its dark green foliage, pink-turning-to-white flowers, and bright, metallic-blue fruit. Its clean, dense foliage hugs the ground, making it an excellent choice for screens and hedges; and it responds well to formal pruning. While well adapted to shade, it will flower more profusely in full sun. Native to the Mediterranean region of Europe.

Viburnum trilobum, flower

Viburnum trilobum, fruit

coarse, usually rangy shrub that requires considerable pruning to keep it even halfway presentable. In bloom it is spectacular. In late May to early June it is heavily laden with clouds of rosy-pink bloom. Use weigela in the shrub border, in masses, and in groupings, where its awkward form and coarse texture can be hidden when not in bloom. Many cultivars and hybrids are available, from white to deep red flowers. While it prefers well-drained soil and a sunny location, weigela is nevertheless quite adaptable and pest free. Expect considerable dieback each year; prune after flowering to clean up the shrub's appearance. Variety *venusta* is the hardiest weigela (Zone 4), with finely textured leaves and rosy-pink flowers. Native to northern China and Korea.

Xylosma congestum

Xylosma congestum
(zye-LOZ-ma con-JEST-um)

Shiny Xylosma

ZONES 8 to 10

Broad-leafed evergreen

Valued for its clean, shiny, yellow-green foliage in all seasons, shiny xylosma will slowly grow to be an 8- to 10-foot-high and -wide, rounded, loose shrub or small tree. Some forms are spiny and make useful barriers. It responds well to pruning and can easily be trained into an espalier. Also use xylosma in a shrub border or foundation planting, as a container plant, as a formal or informal hedge, or for a high bank or ground cover. Plant it in any soil. It will tolerate heat and drought, but looks best when it has adequate water. Native to southern China.

Viburnum trilobum (American Cranberrybush Viburnum; Zones 3 to 9) is quite similar in all respects to *Viburnum opulus*. Since it is hardier and much more resistant to aphids, it makes an excellent substitute. 'Compactum' is a fine dwarf form, about half the size of the species, which produces excellent flowers and fruits. Unlike *V. opulus*, the fruits of *V. trilobum* make excellent jams and jellies. Native from New Brunswick to British Columbia, south to New York and Oregon.

Weigela florida
(wye-GEE-la FLO-ri-da)

Old-fashioned Weigela

ZONES 5 to 8

Deciduous

Out of bloom, the old-fashioned weigela is a

Weigela florida

Index to Plants

Italicized page numbers indicate illustrations or photographs.